Dana Kaminsky
June 1990

TEST YOURSELF: ARE YOU RAISING A TOO PRECIOUS CHILD?

All parents wish to provide for their children's needs. Yet, some parents want it all — including the "perfect" family. They race to provide their infants with intellectual stimulation, their toddlers with "meaningful" learning experiences, and their gifted adolescents with everything they need to make these young people *and their parents* feel successful.

If you can answer "yes" to any of the following questions, you may be saying "yes" too often for your child's well-being.

- **As a parent, have you vowed never to let your child lack for anything?**
- Did you have your first child at or beyond the age of thirty?
- Were there obstacles to conceiving your child?
- Was your child adopted? Premature?
- Does it bother you when your child is bored? Messy? Less than an A student?
- Is your child too precious to his or her grandparents?
- Are you a single parent?
- Is your child artistically, athletically, or intellectually gifted?
- Do you always put your children's needs first? Before your mate's? Before your own?

THE **TOO** PRECIOUS CHILD

W9-BBD-835

THE TOO PRECIOUS CHILD

The Perils of Being a Super-Parent and How to Avoid Them

Lynne H. Williams, M.D.
Henry S. Berman, M.D.
Louisa Rose

WARNER BOOKS

A Warner Communications Company

Author's Note

The case histories discussed in *The Too Precious Child* are composite portraits drawn from years of experience with our patients. No real names are used, and no actual individual is portrayed.

Warner Books Edition

Copyright © 1987 by Lynne H. Williams, M.D., Henry S. Berman, M.D. and Louisa Rose
All rights reserved.

This Warner Books edition is published by arrangement with Atheneum Publishers, a division of Macmillan Publishing Company, 866 Third Avenue, New York, NY 10022.

Warner Books, Inc., 666 Fifth Avenue, New York, NY 10103

W A Warner Communications Company

Printed in the United States of America
First Warner Books Printing: September 1989
10 9 8 7 6 5 4 3 2 1

Library of Congress Cataloging-in-Publication Data

Williams, Lynne H.
　The too precious child.

　Bibliography: p.
　1. Parenting.　2. Child rearing.　I. Berman, Henry S.
II. Rose, Louisa.　III. Title.
HQ755.8.W534　1987　649'.1　86-47949
ISBN 0-446-38935-8 (pbk.) (U.S.A.)
　　　0-446-38936-6 (pbk.) (Can.)

Cover photograph by Sherman Hines/Masterfile
Cover design by Harold Nolan

To our very precious children
Tavis and Shepherd
Julia and Alissa

Contents

Introduction

We upwardly mobile Americans want it all; we strive for important, fulfilling careers, but we yearn as well to create close families. Child-rearing in our rapidly changing society is a challenge, and we appreciate from our own experience just how difficult a task it can be. Harmonizing career and family seems at times to be an almost impossible task. To add to the difficulty, some of us have fallen into the trap of trying to do it all perfectly. We want to be perfect parents of perfect children.

The experts on child development have played a part in this scenario, filling the bookshelves, magazines, and airwaves with exhortations and warnings. The concept of a "head start," popularized a generation ago, has today taken on new—and pernicious—meaning. See that your newborns receive enough intellectual stimulation. Push early learning. Be available with the "right" kind of attention.

Our anxious concern to provide all the right opportunities begins in early childhood and continues through adolescence (and sometimes beyond). How can we make sure that Sean gets a really good nursery school education? Should three-year-old Lisa have a computer? Will she lose out in the race to graduate school if she can't compute? What about five-year-old Jason, who is not even vaguely interested in learning how to read? Yes, the pediatrician says he's normal, but maybe Jason needs testing —maybe he even needs a tutor. If Timmy hasn't earned outstanding high school grades, does he have a future? Nowadays, freshmen college students identify themselves as being "premed" and "prelaw." There isn't time for them to explore the life of the mind.

With the trend toward smaller families born to older parents, there is an even tighter focus on fewer and fewer children. While we believe that such parental attention springs from loving, well-intentioned impulses, we have seen significant problems created by the pressures at home and in school for children either to perform perfectly or to be perfectly happy.

Take Karen, a mother for the first time at thirty-five. She's on an extended leave of absence from her job so that she can be with her son, Nicky. Home now day after day with her little one, she can't find any time for herself, not a moment while her child is awake. She reads to him, plays games, sings, but no matter how much attention she pays to him, he wants more. She admits she's going crazy, but she doesn't see any solution. She wants Nicky to have every advantage; she wants him to have a perfect mother.

Why not put the little boy in a playpen to amuse himself for a while each day? "No way," she says. "He would cry. He wouldn't tolerate it. He needs too much attention." She goes on to mention a study that indicted the playpen as the killing ground of incentive and curiosity, a place where IQ points may be lost.

She and her husband have definite plans for their son's childhood. Only healthful food, no war toys, exposure only to good music. She knows the books she wants him to read, the movies she wants him to see, the museums she will take him to when he's a bit older. What's going to happen, though, when he mopes his way through museums, despises whole-grain bread, and covers his ears to the opening strains of *Peter and the Wolf*?

How is Nicky going to find out who he is and what he wants for himself if his parents won't let him experiment, make mistakes, enjoy some of the "wrong things" like comic books and pop music? How will he learn what he really feels if his parents deny the expression, even the experience, of boredom, anger, and sorrow because those feelings threaten their image of family perfection?

This book is about the predicament of families in which a child is the focus of too much attention. It is about the plight of the child who can't be messy or miserable or bored without a storm of parental concern and guilt, who must be perpetually "on," whose performance in every area is scrutinized and weighed, and whose job it is to make his or her parents feel successful.

Our title, *The Too Precious Child*, is the diagnostic phrase we use to describe a syndrome that we see occurring more and more frequently. The "Too Precious Child" is too important, too special, too much the center of parental attention. This is a child who is not free to follow his or her own bent, not free to be messy or ordinary, not free to be fully a child, not free to ever really be an adult, either.

To give you, the reader, some sort of yardstick by which to measure your expectations, we have devoted significant sections of our book to child development and have shared with you more of the important research than is available in most popular books on child-rearing. We've included this theoretical material because we believe it will offer you a valuable context in which to make decisions. It certainly has helped us, both with our patients and with our own children, who, like yours, force us to struggle with the usual questions: When can she give up the pacifier? How much allowance? Shouldn't he be more responsible about his homework? What do I do when they don't want to go to school?

In the chapters that follow, we'll offer some historical perspective, take a long look at the scope of the problem, and offer examples and anecdotes about children who aren't allowed to develop normally. We'll give examples of parents locked in repetitive battles and parents who've figured a way out. We'll introduce you to parents who push too hard or hold on too tightly as well as to parents who have learned how to support their children's growth. We'll talk about types of temperament and styles of parenting. We'll take you from birth (and even before) through adolescence and to the very threshold of adulthood. We think this book will be meaningful no matter what the age of your children, and hope that, in addition, it will be useful to teachers, school counselors, therapists, pediatricians, specialists in adolescent medicine, family physicians, and other professionals who work with children and families.

Our task is difficult: to convince some of the most dedicated and concerned parents in the world that they may be doing *too much*, that parental overinvolvement is not good for children, not when they're young, not when they're teenagers, and not when they become adults. Our hope is that by exploring new perspectives and new responses, parents can help take the heat off today's over-pressured children. We have tried to make this book positive and useful, and we hope it will help parents and children relax and enjoy each other more.

THE TOO PRECIOUS CHILD

Ask Yourself: Could I Be or Become an Overinvolved Parent?

Here's a checklist of characteristics and situations that might lead parents to overprotect—or to create unrealistic expectations for—their child. "Yes" answers don't necessarily mean a parent is overinvolved; they merely show that the potential exists.

1. Is your child more wanted than you know you were at your birth?

2. Are you and/or your spouse going to have your first child in your thirties?

3. Were there obstacles to conceiving a child?

4. Is your child adopted or were you adopted?

5. Were you or your spouse overvalued or undervalued as a child?

6. Was your baby premature or otherwise too small to go home with you from the hospital?

7. Was it a difficult or disappointing delivery?

8. Was there an injury or congenital defect, or serious illness at birth?

9. Before conception was there a known genetic risk?

10. Has your child suffered from a serious medical illness or an injury with serious consequences?

11. Were you or your spouse raised in a culture that puts an emphasis on firstborn sons?

12. Does this child have extraordinary meaning to a grandparent?

13. Has either you or your spouse suffered from a life-threatening illness? Has your spouse died?

14. Was the child conceived to hold a marriage together or have some other powerful function for the marriage?

15. Was your child born to fulfill some special parental agenda (religious, academic, artistic, or athletic)?

16. Are you a survivor of a disaster—either natural or political—or do you have parents who were survivors?

17. Was/is this a difficult baby?

18. Do you have many very specific and strong opinions about children and childhood? Are you a professional working with families or children?

19. If you are divorced, have you been involved in any custody disputes?

20. Are you a single father or mother who has never married?

21. Has there been a previous death of a child?

22. Is your child exceptionally bright or does he or she show extraordinary talent?

If you've answered yes to any of these questions, or know a child or family in any of these situations, we hope you'll read on.

CHAPTER ONE
The "Too Precious" Epidemic

In nineteenth-century Russia, an anxious couple carefully wrapped their new baby daughter, Sarah, in warm blankets and went to consult the rabbi. "What can we do to protect this child?" they asked him. "Three babies have been taken from us, and we can't bear the pain of losing another." The rabbi pondered the situation, then offered his advice. "God is jealous," he told them, "so don't display too much love or act in any way that shows you think she is special."

One hundred and fifteen years later, a pair of equally protective parents, the Blooms, are interviewed by a *New York* magazine reporter.

"We *want* to devote ourselves to the baby," Donna explains. "The whole point in having her was to experience her. And if we hadn't been prepared to give up a few years of our lives to her, there would have been no sense in having her."

Here are dramatic extremes from dramatically different times. The Blooms will never sit helplessly by a cradle watching their beloved baby lose a battle with diphtheria or whooping cough or typhoid. Because they feel so completely in control of their decision to have a child and so confident of that child's survival, they can freely imagine her future. They see her learning to ride a bicycle, going to college, falling in love, pursuing a career, raising a family—and they want to make sure that what they do as parents will enable her to live a full and happy life.

> The Blooms did extensive research, reading such treatises as *Magical Child* and *The Family Bed*. They decided that they would not employ any outside help for their baby but would share the labors, with Donna taking a primary role. And to this day, though their baby, Ariane, is twelve months old, they have never left her in the care of any housekeeper, baby-sitter, or relative, with the exception of a few hours last summer when a local teenager pushed the child on a couple of walks.

Sarah was special, but her parents didn't let her know she was. They tiptoed around trying to fool God, praying that their child would survive. (She did and lived into her nineties.) Ariane is special, and her parents are giving her the message loud and clear: we are devoting our lives to you.

> Ariane has no crib. She sleeps in Donna's bed. And she takes all her meals with her parents, frequently accompanying them to restaurants and dinner parties.[1]

The Blooms exemplify a new breed of parents who have decided to go all out for parenthood, to be perfect parents, to create a perfect childhood for their perfect child. Often these parents are educated professional people, who bring extraordinary energy and concern to raising their children.

Susannah, a San Francisco lawyer, is another good example. She's unusually articulate and self-aware; and she makes no bones about what she's doing and why she's doing it.

> *"I'm not going to have another baby. I'm thirty-eight. I had to have a C-section, and I don't think I'm up to going through the recovery again. So everything is going into Pete. Besides, if I had a second child, I don't know if I would be as thrilled with every little nuance. A second child would be like having a job; there wouldn't be the same sense of wonderment."*

Susannah returned to work on a part-time basis only, and when she was home, she set herself the explicit goal of giving her son her complete attention. She remembers with some remorse a day when Pete was two years old.

> *"I had to do some paperwork, so I put him in front of the TV set, but I was overridden with guilt—all those violent cartoons. I had turned on the TV for my benefit, not his. I didn't do housework or very much cooking. I wanted to be available when Pete wanted me to play with him."*

Susannah and her husband, Bill, agreed to put their needs for privacy and shared time as a couple on hold for the early years. Until he was three, Pete nursed on demand.

> *"He slept in our bed, and I would wake up two or three times a night to nurse him. I was tired a lot of the time because I didn't get a full night's sleep. I breast-fed for those three years because I think there are a lot of benefits. There's a wonderful closeness. He never cried for more than a minute. (I can't stand to hear him cry.)*

But breast-feeding did take energy, and it interrupted my sleep."

What lies ahead for the Arianes and Petes who, by the hundreds of thousands, learn (fast) that they are the be-all and end-all of their parents' lives? Certainly, we're not advocating that their parents listen to that nineteenth-century rabbi's advice and withhold their love. We believe that children are precious and wonderful, that they deserve our attention and caring and concern. But our message in this book is that there are necessary boundaries that help children define themselves—that are not respected when parents sign up for total devotion.

What worries us is an overinvolved style of child-rearing that is becoming increasingly prevalent, which we call the "Too Precious Child Syndrome." Here are none of the horrors of child neglect and abuse, no child welfare workers, no courts of law putting parents on trial. Instead, there is a very different problem, a *surfeit* of parental attachment and concern that may lead to suffocation of a child's individuality and to the stunting of his or her emotional growth.

Parents who feel too guilty to enjoy themselves away from their children, who sacrifice all their adult interests to what they perceive to be their children's needs, who tuck the little ones into the "family bed" at the expense of their adult sex lives, may sooner or later demand a sacrifice of those very children to whom they sacrificed their adult lives. "Abandon your efforts to grow up, to become your own self, and instead live out *our* dream."

There is no question that the intense absorption of a mother and father with their new baby is a normal and necessary part of becoming parents. By the second year, however, a toddler's demands for separation convince most parents that a little more space and a few more boundaries are a good idea.

Yet, some parents have great difficulty in letting their child take the necessary first steps toward independence; they prefer the closeness, the enmeshment. They're afraid of what's waiting out there, the dangers lurking in the great world beyond the home, and so they discourage signs of individuality. What happens if they succeed in their efforts to bind their children to them?

Doctors Benjamin Spock and Michael Rothenberg take note of the trend we're talking about, this new concept of parenthood that causes many parents to

> feel inside that they are called on to give up all their freedom and all their former pleasures, not as a matter of practicality, but almost as a matter of principle. Others just get obsessed. They forget their hobbies and interests. Even if they do sneak off when a good chance comes, they feel too guilty to get full enjoyment. They come to bore their friends and each other. In the long run, they chafe at the imprisonment. They can't help resenting the baby unconsciously.[2]

What a sad and unnecessary price both parent and child will pay if that resentment is allowed to simmer beneath the surface of all that apparent devotion. And this unhappy dynamic is not the exclusive province of stay-at-home parents. Recent studies of working mothers reveal that some women overcompensate for the guilt they feel about being away from their children by immersing themselves in their children's lives and catering to them.[3]

A QUICK LOOK BACKWARD: THE GOLDEN AGE
THAT NEVER WAS

Many of us who see ourselves caught in the rush and tumble of a society of overextended adults and stressed children bemoan the loss of an idyllic past, a nostalgic age of innocence, when children lived simple and unpressured lives, occupied with wholesome and appropriate tasks like shucking corn and shooing chickens rather than mastering the intricacies of Simplex puzzles and Questron Electronic Books.

Yet, historians of family life have now shown us that until quite recently, children were as likely to be considered a burden as a cause for celebration. They were unpreventable and often unwanted. Family planning meant abstaining from sex. Exhausted by frequent pregnancies and the demands of too many children, many mothers had little to give to their young ones.

Bonding, the process of attachment between parent and infant, presented difficulties in earlier times. As was illustrated by the story of Sarah's parents at the beginning of this chapter, children often died young, and parents learned not to hazard the emotional dangers of becoming too attached to their offspring. In seventeenth-century Europe, babies often were sent to a wet nurse for the first year of life. If they survived, they would be returned to their families. If not, then the family wouldn't have risked much.

Those children who survived the dangerous diseases of childhood often were put out to work at an early age. Childhood was not viewed as a special and protected time. A walk through a Rhode Island textile mill in 1820 would have revealed over half of the workers to be children. In 1904, there were no playgrounds for the children who grew up in New York City's cramped tenements. When automobiles began to crowd the only outdoor play space available to these children, a *New York Times* editorial righteously observed that modern life "cannot be retarded to enable heedless children to get out of the way."[4]

When did our historical view of childhood begin to change? Viviana Zelzer, a Columbia University sociologist, identifies a "profound transformation in the economic and sentimental value of children—fourteen years of age or younger—between the 1870s and 1930s."[5] There is tangible evidence for this transformation: the growing and continuing interest in child welfare that first blossomed in the work of social reformers like Lillian Wald and Jane Addams; the creation of organizations providing services for children and families; and the passage of protective legislation.

As child health improved, as women asserted their rights, and as couples began to enjoy a greater control of reproduction, childhood began to be seen as a more important and valuable period; and scholars and researchers such as the distinguished psychologist G. Stanley Hall started to take an interest in child development.

FROM PROJECTION TO EMPATHY

Perhaps the new trend toward overinvolvement that we've been observing is a natural accompaniment to our relatively recent interest in children's needs. Like any new thing, it arrives with passion and enthusiasm—and imbalance. But what we'll be calling for in this book *is* balance. And so the question arises: Can one ever know how involved a good parent should be or how much caring is enough?

What seems to us a useful way to frame our present concerns is to turn to the work of the fascinating and controversial historian Lloyd deMause. In his essay "The Evolution of Childhood," he observes:

> Because psychic structure must always be passed from generation to generation through the narrow funnel of childhood, a society's child-rearing practices are not just one item in a list of cultural traits. They are the very condition for the transmission and development of all other cultural elements, and place definite limits on what can be achieved in all other spheres of history.

DeMause then asks us to consider

> those moments which most affect the psyche of the next generation: primarily...what happens when an adult is face to face with a child who needs something. The adult has, I believe, three major reactions available: (1) He can use the child as a vehicle for projection of the contents of his own unconscious (projective reaction); (2) he can see the child as a substitute for an adult figure important in his own childhood (reversal reaction); or (3) he can empathize with the child's needs and act to satisfy them (empathic reaction).

(By "empathic," deMause means "the adult's ability to regress to the level of a child's need and correctly identify it without an admixture of the adult's own projections. The adult must then be able to maintain enough distance from the need to be able to satisfy it.")[6]

Seen in this way, overinvolvement is as much a failure of empathy as is neglect. Parents who characteristically respond to their children with indulgence or an attempt to "perfect" them are unable either to understand their children's true needs or to consider objectively what would be the best way to satisfy them.

So, in a sense, we can look at Too Precious Parenting as a conceptual and emotional advance, a sign of progress along the way, and still a failure to reach what we would identify as the goal: "empathic" parenting. This book is both an attempt to evoke empathy and to get at the root cause of the contemporary hurrying and pushing of children to achieve more and more (faster and faster) that we read about in books like David Elkind's ground-breaking *The Hurried Child.*

The drive for early learning, the provisioning of the child with all sorts of material goods and advantages, the compulsion to be perfect parents making perfect decisions, we believe, are symptoms of a failure of empathy and objectivity. These qualities admittedly are difficult to come by in the heat of those intense and memorable moments of child-rearing when your three-year-old is screaming bloody murder and pounding his fists on the floor in full and disapproving view of the other shoppers at the supermarket or when your twelve-year-old who was forbidden to pierce her ears defiantly seats herself at the dinner table with *four* earring holes punched through her lobes.

What we advocate in this book isn't always, or maybe ever, easy. If you make the attempt to combine empathy for your child's feelings with an objective assessment of his or her needs, you'll find you have to ask yourself a lot of questions. We don't offer—or prescribe—a simple formula for successful child-rearing.

THE DIFFERENCE BETWEEN PRECIOUS AND TOO PRECIOUS

Certainly, we're all for love and caring, for preciousness as opposed to Too Preciousness. Where do we draw the line? Too Precious Children have parents who are constantly shaping, molding, worrying, or indulging them. They can do very little, if anything, without parental interference and attention. Precious children have parents who spend time with them (and some time away from them), who enjoy them (and also enjoy time without them), who care about their education (but don't insist on competitive performance), and who help them discover their unique abilities (without insisting that they be stars). They have empathic parents who are attuned to their children's needs and love them for what they are.

And with empathic parenting, perhaps we will be able to discover a truer sense of the importance of all children. As Mairead Corrigan Maguire, winner of a Nobel Peace Prize in 1976, has written, "And if I feel this passionate love for you and your life, and for my other children—Mark, Joanne, Marie Louise and John, I also feel passionately for the lives of the little children who are mine also: children who today die of starvation in Ethiopia. And the little children in Moscow and the little children in New York, who are told they must be enemies..."[7]

How can we value all children if we overvalue our own, if in our attempts to help them be successful, we make them pawns in a competitive struggle that bears no relation to reality? Writes Eda LeShan, the well-known family counselor, "It is one of the strange ironies of modern life that during an era in which we find ourselves so concerned about the psychological needs of our own children we seem to be failing in our collective responsibility for meeting the human needs of all our children."[8]

Too Precious Children have parents who are more than just "concerned" about their psychological needs; these parents are possessed by a vision, often a very competitive one, of doing everything perfectly, following an ideal sequence of steps that will lead to a "successful" child.

This formulation is nowhere promoted with more vengeance than at Glenn Doman's Better Baby Institute in Philadelphia. Parents who attend his early-learning seminars are instructed in his "Eighty-nine Cardinal Facts for Making Any Baby into a Superb Human Being." This translates into teaching infants and very young children to read flash cards with words or dots. Early learning, according to this approach, will produce human excellence. Children trained in this way can at a young age read words, do math problems, and recite facts. Will they become "superb human beings"? Maybe.

The hyped-up craziness that may accompany the Too Precious Parents' battle for success is apparent in a popular magazine's report from one of the principal war zones: Manhattan.

> Roberta Schoenfield, whose children are fourteen,
> ten, and five, recently received a telephone call from a
> less experienced mother, a lawyer, looking for advice on

the city's private-school situation. "She was so agitated," Schoenfield says, "it was hard to imagine her conducting important legal negotiations. Her two-year-old had been rejected by the 92nd Street Y's toddler program. 'Now she'll never get into their nursery school,' this woman kept wailing. 'She'll never get into Dalton. And she'll never go to Harvard.'"⁹

And Susan Reed, writing in *People* magazine, chronicled a new development: the Too Precious not-yet-existent Child.

> Recently a woman called one of the tonier private schools in Chicago requesting a kindergarten application. When asked the child's age, she replied, "Oh, I don't have any kids yet. But I'm thinking of getting pregnant." Says Edward Zigler, director of the Bush Center in Child Development and Social Policy at Yale University: "As parents get older and have fewer children each one becomes a precious object. Almost too much—or the wrong kind—of energy is expended on the child."¹⁰

A Too Precious Child is overvalued. If he can sing on key, he's headed toward musical stardom. If she learns how to read, she's probably born to be a scholar. Overprotective parents are often blind to their children's faults and problems in a way that may inhibit their development.

"Nothing is too good for my child," is the slogan of overindulgent parents, and so all sorts of gifts are lavished without any *quid pro quo*. Perhaps these are the parents who grew up with the good life, or perhaps they achieved it for themselves. They're used to the best of everything, and they want to pass it along.

How much to give is a real question for newly affluent parents. They remember wanting things, and now
they can create the sense of having them by giving them
to their children. The mother who always wanted a fancy
dollhouse buys an elaborate model for her little girl, then
watches in dismay as the child dismantles it. Or the father
who longed for a good baseball glove when he was young
equips his unathletic son with the finest equipment in the
store and then berates the boy because it sits in the closet
gathering dust.

Sometimes, for competitive parents, the child for
whom nothing is too good isn't good enough to be "my
child," and so he or she must be equipped with the
proper attributes. "*My* child" must be better than your
child, smarter, more athletic, more talented, better
dressed, better educated.

People magazine, in describing the children for
whom nothing is too good, calls them the "gourmet children":

> Their parents are usually in their 30s, affluent
> and mesmerized by that vague Valhalla called "The
> Top." With fierce determination they feel that nothing
> is too good for their young, and the ordinary not nearly
> good enough. When the kids are small, every gurgle
> gets lavish attention, and when they have lurched on to
> 3 or 4, it is time to face a challenge that—as these par-
> ents see it—can decide their entire future: kindergar-
> ten.

As we discuss Too Precious Children, one of the big
issues is this question of push.

> "Parents should be concerned about 3-year-olds
> enjoying themselves, not about getting into Harvard,"

says Joan Lutton, principal of the Cushman School (tuition $1350) in Miami. "We shouldn't lay these things on children when they're little. Then they become unhappy people." Psychologist Zigler agrees that many high-pressure kindergarten curricula are reflections of exaggerated and often harmful parental expectations. "I pay for my young son to take clarinet lessons now," he says pointedly. "But I don't do it thinking that he's going to play in Carnegie Hall as a direct result." Zigler's moral: For too many parents and their kids today the fundamental pleasures and rewards of learning are getting lost in the competitive shuffle.

If the "competitive shuffle" were a new dance, those stereotypical Yuppies (creatures we all hotly deny any relation to) probably invented it. They seem prepared to go to the most extraordinary lengths to get the best. They want to drive the Best Car, listen to the Best Stereo, eat at the Best Restaurants—and when they produce offspring, they're going to have the Best Child, at the Best School. In the same article in *People*, we learn of the admissions director at a prestigious private school in Chicago who received a letter requesting admission to the following year's kindergarten from the parents of a three-year-old. Attached to the request was documentation:

A four-page resume that listed the child's accomplishments, from word games to hanging on chin-up bars, and detailed 11 programs she attended during the "structured" part of her day—tennis, gymnastics and French lessons among others. In addition, boasted the parents, she had picked up Spanish from her babysitter, plus Mandarin and German from other members of the household staff. The child was rejected because the admissions committee felt she simply didn't know how to play.[11]

What's your reaction to the story? Ours was that the school ought to have admitted the little girl and given her a sorely needed opportunity to play. But far more common than a school that values play is a school that puts an ever-greater burden on young children to achieve in ways that can be demonstrated and tested and recorded. We talked with a friend in New York City who had taken her four-year-old daughter, Felicia, to a private school interview. "Where are her records?" asked the admissions director. Felicia's mother was puzzled. After all, what kinds of records would a four-year-old have? She'd been in a preschool program, but so far, to her mother's knowledge, Felicia hadn't acquired a transcript. The admissions director was insistent. She had to have the records.

Felicia is lucky. Her mother, whose peers are lining up at all the exclusive urban gateways to early education, concluded that too much push was wrong and decided to let her daughter have a year of kindergarten in an unpressured neighborhood school.

Some kids aren't so lucky, as *Harper's* magazine reveals:

> Nancy Godreau, who directs the St. Thomas More Playgroup, recalls a mother asking her a typical father's question: "Where does my child stand?" The little girl was a favorite, and so Godreau started in with "Caroline is such a friendly child, and she's so sensitive to the feelings of the other children." She went on in that vein until the mother broke in: "I don't know where she got *that* from! What I want to know is where she stands in terms of her *leadership* abilities.[12]

What happens to "gourmet children"? According to some child-development experts, they get "hothoused," a word used to describe what happens when infants and toddlers receive a heavy dose of early educational stimulation. Researchers have described the negative effects of inappropriate formal instruction on babies and have emphasized the value of unstructured play for children.[13]

The little girl in Chicago with the four-page résumé may learn Mandarin and gymnastics, but many experts feel that the intense effort committed to these formal pursuits may interfere with her normal development. As Dr. Edward Zigler has observed, "Children learn for the same reason that birds fly. They're programmed to learn, and they do it beautifully. You can't stop children from learning—and you certainly don't have to push them to."[14]

GOURMET BABIES: AM I AT RISK?

The more you care about your children and the more you may worry about their lives and futures, the greater may be your temptation to overprotect or to push them into too early acquisition of skills. In the next chapter, as we consider the kinds of parents and the life situations that can produce a Too Precious Child, remember that when we talk about risk, we are talking about *potential*, not actuality.

If you are perceptive enough to realize that you are overinvolved with your child or that you may become so, first congratulate yourself. Most people think that their next-door neighbor or their sister-in-law is terribly overinvolved, but that they themselves are only doing for their child what ought to be done. Once you identify yourself as a candidate for overinvolvement, you can take steps to understand and correct the situation. Painful as the necessary changes may be, you will be doing yourself and your child an enormous favor. We believe you stand to reap immediate rewards in a happier home situation, and permanent rewards in a better lifelong relationship with your child.

CHAPTER TWO
The Children Who Mean Too Much

Who *are* the children we're talking about? Probably you've met at least one. Some of them are whiny and demanding, some fearful and clinging—the kinds of kids the other kids won't play with. Still others are everybody's idea of the "perfect" child. They get all A's. They preside over half the clubs at school. They clean their rooms. They're obedient to parents and teachers and are eager to fulfill adult expectations. But whether they're overindulged, overprotected, or overpushed, these children share common difficulties in discovering true autonomy. It is extraordinarily difficult for them to find out where they leave off and their parents begin, to know what they really want as opposed to what their parents want for them.

Who or what creates a Too Precious Child? Parents? Fate? Life in our times? There is no single answer. We believe that the causes are what health professionals term "multifactorial," a nice bit of jargon that pays homage to the incredible complexity of human personality. Each human being starts life with inherent talents, traits, susceptibilities, and strengths. These latent characteristics then intersect with the birth experience. (If Einstein had been deprived of oxygen for a few minutes during delivery, his future would have been irrevocably altered.) Once born, the new human being must deal with a particular physical and psychological environment, a given moment in history, a certain type of society—and a special set of life experiences.

The following tale spanning three generations illustrates what we mean by "multifactorial."

Felix was born in turn-of-the-century Cleveland, the youngest of five children, of whom only two lived. His mother and older sister fussed and fretted and worried over him from the moment he was born. Male children, said his mother, were fragile and needed extra care if they were to survive. Felix grew up, married, and had an only child, Anne, who quickly became the object of excessive family attention and concern. Everything she wore or touched or ate was scrupulously clean, and as a young child she was often discouraged from crawling and exploring because it was too dirty or dangerous. Anne wanted to learn how to ride a horse, but her father didn't think it was safe. Meanwhile, Aunt Harriet loved telling stories about how well she had cared for Felix, how delicate his health had been as a boy, how devotedly she had nursed him through a series of dreadful diseases—and how sad it was that Anne's uncles had died in infancy.

Let's stop our story for a moment to speculate on the outcome. Must Anne, who has received so many messages about how dangerous the world is, necessarily grow up to become an overinvolved and overprotective mother? On the one hand, she's an only child, brought up in a fearful and overconcerned atmosphere, the focus of too much attention. On the other hand, she's young and intelligent. If she marries a man who is a confident and involved father, if she gives birth after a normal pregnancy to a perfectly healthy child, she may side with that part of herself that didn't like all the cautiousness and allow her own child more range and freedom than she had.

> *Anne married a career navy man and insisted she wanted several children, though her husband would be away from the family for long periods of time. Her first pregnancy ended in a miscarriage. It would have been a boy. When she finally did have a son, she couldn't overcome her superstitious fear that her aunt and grandmother were right. Boys were delicate. George had to be walked to school until he was in the fifth grade. If he had the slightest sniffle, he wasn't allowed outside. When he begged to go with his friends and their father on an overnight bicycle trip, Anne said no.*

Anne, who had been an overprotected child herself, was *at risk* for producing one. But it took a combination of background (those family themes of male fragility) and circumstance (a miscarriage) to turn that risk into a reality. Anne never thought about her behavior; her fears seemed quite natural to her, and her husband, who might have counteracted her influence, was away most of the time. Eventually, their likable and obedient son decided to make a bid for independence, and at age twenty-two, much to his mother's anxious dismay, he signed up for the Peace Corps and went off to Africa for three years.

As we begin to explore the parental needs and fears, the special characteristics of the child and the difficult situations that contribute to Too Preciousness, we want to emphasize that *no one factor taken by itself is decisive.* For example, a Nervous Nellie who gives birth to a healthy and irrepressibly cheerful child may learn to relax and let go, but if that child then develops diabetes, all those dormant parental fears may surface in overwhelming abundance.

For purposes of discussion, we've grouped the kinds of risks that may lead to Too Preciousness under three headings: (1) risks associated with parental needs and fears and expectations that predate the actual child, (2) risks associated with the special needs of the child, and (3) risks arising from particularly difficult situations.

PARENT-CENTERED RISK

Here, overinvolvement has its roots in the needs of one or both parents, and Too Preciousness arises not as the result of issues with a particular child but with the "generic" child, the concept of the child. Parents in this category may harbor special agendas for their children even before they are born.

What leads to parent-centered risk? Perhaps, like Anne, one of the parents is an only child, with complex feelings about being one, who then through force of circumstance is able to have only one child. Perhaps parents have an unusual investment in the parental role. They may expect to enjoy a powerful "birth experience," and place extraordinary value on parenting activities. In some cases, parents who have survived a difficult childhood—a distant and unloving father, a cold, critical mother, an unhealthy pressure to succeed, a bitter parental divorce—determine to undo or ease their own sorrow by seeing to it that their children enjoy a perfect, untroubled, and un-fettered youth ("You will be a happy child so that I can feel better"). Quite an agenda.

CHILD-CENTERED RISK

Some children become Too Precious because of their own special difficulties or abilities. Something about the child elicits an overwhelming response from the parent. Some of these children start life too little or too early or too sick. Children with chronic illness fall into this cate-gory. Often there is an attribution of specialness to the child's strength, resistance, "fighting nature," and so on. Sometimes, parents realize that not all the dangers arise from physical problems.

> *Robin, at eight, has had major surgery twice to cor-rect a congenital heart defect. Now as her family sits around a friend's swimming pool, she's pestering her mother, Jean, to let her go swimming with the other kids. The day is cool and windy, and Jean has a momentary twinge of fear. Part of her wishes Robin would sit in a chair, wrapped in warm blankets. She pauses for a mini-second. "Go ahead," she says cheerfully. "You can swim for ten minutes." Robin runs off, elated.*

Jean tells her friends that helping Robin to have a normal childhood has become a paramount concern. She had wanted to protect her child from any sort of stress or exertion until she realized that all the danger didn't re-side in Robin's physical condition. The surgeons said Robin's heart problem was correctable and that she would grow up to be a normal, healthy adult. But how would she do that if all she heard was "Watch out. You can't do that. Be careful. You're fragile."

Children with unique abilities—the musical genius, the athletic wonder, the young intellectual giant—are also part of this second group. Even though parents contribute to the risk by focusing on the child's differentness and specialness, clearly the impetus toward overinvolvement comes from some attribute of the child.

Pamela was amazed—and gratified—by her seven-year-old daughter's precocity. Sybil had taught herself to read at the age of three and was now devouring books on ancient history and mythology. This child was clearly going to be an intellectual star. When Pamela found adventure comic books in her daughter's room, she was horrified. "I'm throwing these out," she told a tearful Sybil. "These are junk and I don't ever want to find you reading them."

Pamela, like many parents of intellectually gifted children, was amazed and gratified by her daughter's unusual mind. She enjoyed telling Sybil about other members of their family with high IQs and began to plan a glorious future for the little girl, a future uncontaminated by any form of intellectual trash.

In her zeal to protect her daughter's intellect, Pamela forgot that her child was obviously capable of choosing challenging books to read and didn't want or need her mother to take over her mind. In addition to support and encouragement for their abilities, gifted children like Sybil need a chance to be ordinary and enjoy the things that everyone else does.

RISKY SITUATIONS

There is a third group of children at risk for over-involvement, whose difficulties do not arise from their own attributes or from their parents' prior agendas. The problem resides primarily in the difficulty of the situation.

For example, a child labeled "impossibly difficult" by unsure first-time parents might pose no particular problem for experienced and even-tempered parents. Quite possibly the innate personality of the child and that of the parent just don't mesh. An active and sociable mother may become exasperated with a quiet introspective daughter. Mother wants her child to run and bike and swim, invite her friends for sleep-overs. Daughter wants to sit under a tree and look at the leaves or read a book. There's nothing unhealthy here, no crisis situation, no grave deficits or enormous talents. What needs to be investigated is the interaction.

This sort of troubled interaction may be compounded. Take a child who is struggling with the painful realities of divorce and a parent who more than anything else needs to have a happy child, and you can probably predict the results. Unless, of course, that parent is able and willing to examine the interaction and change.

When Janet and Spencer divorced, Alexa was only three. They agreed with perfect unanimity on only one thing: that they were not the kind of people who would allow their differences to interfere with their daughter's happiness. When Alexa would become tearful as she prepared to leave her mother to go to her dad's house, Janet would feel angry. She'd done everything she could to make this a Good Divorce and Alexa was supposed to be a happy child. Spencer had the same reaction to his daughter's tears. Neither adult could tolerate the little girl's normal reaction to separation because they saw her tears as a sign of their marital and parental failure.

AWARENESS IS THE KEY

By being alert to potential risks, parents can work to add space and freedom to what might otherwise become a constricting family atmosphere. Of course, not all families who fit our risk categories will have problems. And, sometimes, simply by being aware of the possibility of overinvolvement, parents are able to work toward a more balanced vision of who their children are and what they really need.

We all recognize that in certain loaded situations such as divorce, chronic illness, or death, parents may have to work especially hard to provide a normal "bread-and-butter" childhood. A good clue to the existence of such situations is the strong impulse not so much to return to "normal" but rather to "make up" for some loss or failure or disappointment.

It's not always the incredibly wanted child who is Too Precious. Sometimes, the loss or failure the parents want to compensate for is their own negative reaction to the idea of having a child. Perhaps, having experienced an unhappy pregnancy or contemplated (and then rejected) the idea of abortion, the parents vow to make it up to their baby.

Some of the scenarios we present are recognizably dramatic: a child born of a rape, a child conceived during a brief marital reconciliation, a child whose paternity is a family secret. In addition to these obviously loaded situations, there are other, perhaps more subtle, setups for overinvolvement. Though not uncommon, they may prove uncommonly difficult for both the parents and children involved.

PARENT-CENTERED RISK

Parents Who Wait

We are witnessing today a surge in the numbers of older first-time parents, especially among the affluent educated professionals for whom the demands of career and the excitement of living life as a single person or as a childless couple had once taken priority. For many professional women, the desire to have children may first blossom in the early thirties, possibly stimulated by the knowledge that conception and pregnancy become more difficult as one grows older. There are certain undeniable advantages to waiting. Older parents tend to be significantly more settled, less in need of adventure and new experience. They've established careers, worked on their relationships, stabilized their finances, and have usually carefully considered their decision to bring a new life into the world. For many couples who wait to have children, there is a mutual commitment to the many tasks involved in child-rearing and family life. Older fathers may have much more time to spend with their infants and children, whereas younger fathers in their peak career-building years may be simply too work-oriented to be very available.

Nevertheless, there are not only potential physical problems with waiting to start a family, there are also emotional risks. Having waited so long, these older parents may have too many expectations of how wonderful having a child will be. Now that they've finally made the decision to be parents, they may feel they must devote themselves 150 percent to it. Indeed, as one writer has put it, the child who is born late into his parents lives is *so* wanted, has been so waited for, that "too much is riding on him. Older parents are often overprotective parents. And sometimes, they raise kids who think they're the center of the universe, which is not a very good thing for anyone to think about themselves."[1]

The Achievers Become "Professional" Parents

We've touched briefly on the fact that parents who wait are often those who have given their energies and devotion to building strong and successful careers. These are people who have set high standards for themselves, who have a deep commitment to their work, high expectations of what they can accomplish and what they can expect to enjoy. What happens when these achievers become parents? What happens when the reality of one's career comes into conflict with the ideal of parental devotion?

Ted and Paula are neonatologists, sharing responsibility for developing the newborn service at their hospital and for raising their two children, ages two and three. Even though Paula has Ted and her own parents to help out, she still feels tired all the time, increasingly guilty, and torn between work and home. She knows how impor-

*tant it is to be available and active with her children and
she tries, but when she comes home she just feels used up.
Recently, she's noticed that her older child doesn't run to
the door to greet her. He just continues what he's doing
and wanders over when he's finished. Paula is sure he's
angry at her for being away. The thought is unbearable.
Should she quit her job?*

Part of the problem may lie in unrealistic expectations about children and child-rearing. Parents who are
high-powered professionals are accustomed to demanding and finding the best. They look for quality in every
detail of their lives—the best vacation spot, the best car,
the best chocolate, the best breed of dog. Now, they are
determined to have the best child—to whom they expect
to be the best parents. They are educated people; they
have money and high standards and a deep interest in
this new adventure. The only thing they don't have is
time.

There is a popular notion that time has two dimen-
sions: quantity and quality. Well-meaning experts tell us,
"It doesn't matter how *much* time you spend with the children, it's the *quality* of time that matters." So these parents
decide they will make a virtue out of the necessary com-
partmentalization of their lives and provide the best possible time to their youngsters. There's quantity time at
work, quality time at home—and shattered nerves on the
sidelines.

Women are most commonly afflicted by this type of
pressure. When both parents work, the mothers seem to
shoulder most of the burden of caring for the children
when they are ill, taking them to dentist and doctor appointments, and leaving work when necessary to respond

to any of the other problems that invariably come up: a sick baby-sitter, a school vacation. In two-career families that might manage quite comfortably on one income, mothers may often experience intense conflict over their desire to continue building their careers—after all, they could stay home if they really *cared*, couldn't they? If their children are sick or unhappy or having personal difficulties, many women are apt to blame themselves because they have chosen to work.

Some people go to great lengths to be flawless parents. Writer Linda Wolfe, a keen observer of the urban middle class, notes:

> With New York motherhood becoming a technocratic specialty, there is now a surge of instruction in that subject: classes that teach mothers how to exercise their babies, how to do arts and crafts with their toddlers, even how to sing lullabies and recite nursery rhymes. "It's as if no one had any mothering instincts anymore," says Nancy Pike, who recently came across a group of mothers in Central Park who were taking a class in how to roll rubber balls toward their babies. "Or at least, they no longer trust the instincts they have."[2]

Less benign are the efforts of some superconcerned parents to create an emotionally perfect child by adding preventive child-psychiatry appointments to their crowded calendars. Troubled by the possibility of making mistakes in the crucial early years, they hope to insure their child's emotional future by taking action *before* any problem arises. All of this adds up to more pressure and expectation for the child.

The Too Precious Pregnancy
THE SPECTER OF INFERTILITY

Many of those who want to start a family suddenly find themselves struggling with the fears and problems of infertility. Couples who have confidently expected that they would choose the right time to have a child become uneasy when pregnancy does not occur within the first four to six months. According to *The Harvard Medical School Health Letter Book*, 10 to 25 percent of American couples are unable either to have any children at all or to have as many as they would wish.[3]

For these people, the pregnancy they have so carefully avoided for so many years becomes the elusive thing they now so desperately want. Barbara Eck Menning, a nurse-specialist in maternal-child health, has written about the deep feelings evoked by the inability to conceive—surprise, denial, isolation, guilt and unworthiness, anger, depression, and grief. And when these couples, who have embarked on the expensive, painful, and frequently embarrassing search for reproductive success do manage to conceive, imagine the expectations these parents have of the child they have struggled so long and valiantly to produce.

Menning observes some of the effects on parenting of the long and arduous attempt to procreate.

> Not only do they have to do everything just right, they often feel they cannot use child-care or baby-sitting to get a little relief now and then. If the woman has had a career, she often has guilt feelings when yearnings for the stimulation of adult minds and challenges creep into her consciousness. If the child is, in fact, the

only child they conceive, they share a lot of the feelings of second-child infertility about *overprotection* of the child and pressuring it to succeed and be all things to them. In a sense, the child conceived under these circumstances is a little set up for life problems too.[4]

But, after all, how understandable it is that one would have a complex emotional reaction to the birth and rearing of a child who took four years and $24,000 to conceive. How could this *not* be a miracle baby? In these circumstances, parents may have a hard time separating from their children; they have great difficulty letting their toddlers move away, take a little risk, learn to swim, pet the neighbor's dog. How incredibly difficult it must be for those parents who know that this precious child is truly irreplaceable.

Sometimes, too, these very same parents are shocked to find themselves feeling let down. The long-awaited child seems something of an anticlimax.

Polly and Donald finally conceived after several years of trying. They'd spent many thousands of dollars on tests and treatments, subjected their relationship to profound stress, struggled with the idea of adoption, and tried to keep both sets of in-laws at bay throughout the process. Finally, Emily was born. She was pink and perfect and ALIVE! Secretly, though, both Polly and Donald felt an uneasy disappointment they would never express. Was this it? They began to focus on all that Emily would become, what wonderful opportunities they would give her. Their financial and emotional sacrifices would be justified by the extraordinary child they would create.

RISKY AND DIFFICULT PREGNANCIES

Another group of parents who may experience the feelings and reactions of the Too Precious Pregnancy are those who have encountered difficulties during pregnancy. Perhaps there have been problems—bleeding or the threat of a miscarriage—that cause a giant question mark to hover over and cloud the remainder of the pregnancy.

> *Not only was Kate ill throughout most of her pregnancy, but there were also a few tense weeks when she was spotting. Kate knew the spotting meant she might miscarry, an outcome she dreaded. She also knew it might indicate that something was wrong with the baby. Her doctor ordered strict bed rest, and Kate complied, wondering through the long, weary days and sleepless nights whether her child would be normal. All she and her husband could do was wait and watch and pray. "If this baby makes it, we'll know he's special," they told each other.*

A baby born after a difficult pregnancy may be considered an extraordinary achievement, and, as a consequence, the parents may find themselves treating their healthy, active child with kid gloves.

Some pregnancies begin under a cloud of painful uncertainty. Those who are carriers of a genetic disorder, who know that debilitating and life-threatening disease such as muscular dystrophy, Tay-Sachs, cystic fibrosis, or hemophilia run in their families, may feel that each pregnancy is like a game of roulette with incredibly high stakes: the life and health of their child. They must make the difficult decision about whether to try to have children or whether to abort a fetus with a serious genetic abnormality.

When they do have a normal baby, they are understandably inclined to be indulgent and extremely protective.

> *Ed and Marion know that they have sickle-cell trait and that the child Marion is carrying has a chance of being born with sickle-cell disease. When Caroline is born and a normal hemoglobin pattern is confirmed, the family has a great celebration. Gifts pour in. Toys abound. Caroline spends her early years with enough stuffed animals to stock F.A.O. Schwarz.*

Some of these healthy babies grow up to develop a sense of guilt that they were able to survive in health when another sibling has been affected or died. They may carry the burden of being extra-valued not for *who* they are but for the fact that they exist.

Ghosts in the Nursery

Parents who have lost a child may have trouble believing in the sturdiness and health of a subsequent child. So, to begin with, a surviving or succeeding child must cope with intense parental anxiety. Often, too, they must contend with what Selma Fraiberg, the late famed child analyst, termed a "ghost in the nursery."

> *Brian died at the age of five from a rare form of cancer. His parents weren't sure they wanted another child or could ever love another child as much as they*

had loved Brian. When Nicholas was born, with wisps of dark hair and a dimple in his chin, their joy was clouded by the renewal of their grief for Brian. He looked like Brian. Sorrowful and guilt-ridden, they wondered how they could help Nicholas grow up to be himself, free of the shadow of the older brother he had never known.

Sometimes, the parents unconsciously decide that the task of the new child is to help them forget the one they lost. What must it be like to inherit the legacy of preciousness for oneself as well as the child who has gone before? What extra burden of expectations and fears weigh upon the new child who hears about her sister who died at the age of three, an "angel" at birth and in death? Who could live up to such a legacy?

On the carved mantelpiece in the living room of Diana's house is a picture framed in silver. It is her older sister, Kelly, who died in a car accident at the age of four. On Kelly's birthday and on the major family holidays, they all go to visit Kelly's grave. Her mother cries, and Diana feels helpless. She knows she has to be wonderful and good, so that Mom and Dad won't be so unhappy. Sometimes at night she lies awake and wonders what it would have been like to have an older sister. Sometimes, she thinks she hates Kelly.

There may be many ghosts that inhabit a nursery, memories of parents, grandparents, aunts and uncles, teachers, special friends. Some of them may be friendly and their presence a blessing. Others, as Selma Fraiberg cautioned, threaten to intrude on the parent-child relationship.

In every nursery there are ghosts. They are the visitors from the unremembered past of the parents, the uninvited guests at the christening. Under favorable circumstances, these unfriendly and unbidden spirits are banished from the nursery and return to their subterranean dwelling place. The baby makes his own imperative claim upon parental love and, in strict analogy with the fairy tales, the bonds of love protect the child and his parents against the intruders, the malevolent ghosts.[5]

In some families, the departed may have undue influence—"Your grandpa always hoped you'd grow up to be a doctor" or "You're a troublemaker, just like your Aunt Lydia"—and parents need to make sure their young impressionable child has a chance to become his or her own person.

Children will do best when they know about all the family members who are important and who may affect them. If a much loved relative has died, the child needs to know how the parent feels. Example: "Sarah, you remind me so much of my sister Sarah and you're named after her. Sometimes my memories are happy and sometimes when I think about her I feel sad because I loved her very much. But even though you sometimes remind me of my sister, you are really *you*. You are my special girl."

Magical Themes

The influence of the dead may sometimes take on a magical quality, especially when a birth or conception date seems to coincide with the death or birthday of an important family member.

February 3 was the anniversary of his father's death. Rick was stunned when he realized that this same date was the one the doctor had given as his baby's due date. Could it be that this child represented some special link, some incarnation of his father?

Sometimes, the magical significance is related to a special place.

India was a special child, conceived during her parents' visit to the East. They knew she would be a peaceful, spiritual person and told her so from the moment she was born. They frowned on normal displays of anger or excitement and shuddered when she wanted to run and shout.

Names, too, may have a special importance, and they may place a burden of expectation on their recipients. Parents may name a child for a living parent, a deceased family member, for a culture hero or a president. What agendas are attached to such names? During the sixties and seventies, parents gave their children names like Che and Krishna and Moon Unit. Names for a free new age. But, on reflection, is a name like "Che" any less oppressive to its tiny recipient than "Hollister Edward Bancroft IV"?

The Cluttered Agenda

Mental-health experts are fond of using the word *agenda*, borrowed from the world of affairs, as a kind of shorthand—a useful bit of jargon that signals the presence of prior expectations. We're familiar with formal agendas for certain kinds of situations, but while the order of business for a public meeting is explicit and is written down on a piece of paper, our personal agendas may be only faintly perceived. Sometimes, they are completely unexamined.

When Too Preciousness emanates from parental needs, we may find that parents bring a long and often unrealistic "to do" and "to be" list to the creation and nurture of a new human life. New parents might want to reflect on the kinds of expectations they bring to parenthood and ask themselves some questions.

What kind of parent do I want to be?
What kind of child do I want to have?
What kind of parent do I *not* want to be?
What kind of child do I *not* want to have?

By answering these four questions, one can begin to get at some of the unconscious agendas a parent might have. For example, I want to be the kind of parent who laughs with my children. The reason I want a child is so I can have a cuddly little baby. I can't stand children who talk back. I want to be the kind of father who is there for my kids—not like my dad.

Agendas aren't necessarily bad, but they are prior decisions that may need to be adjusted to reality. You may not be able to laugh as much as you'd like if your child has a serious health problem. When your cuddly little baby hits the terrible twos, you may be in for a nasty shock. You may decide to be a more involved father than your own and then feel resentful when your child runs off to watch a favorite TV program instead of spending time with you.

Children often pay a high price for their parents' prior needs and unrealistic expectations. They may be forced to live without the security of limits because their parents had too many. They may be expected to bring home all A's on their report card because it bolsters their parents' self-esteem. They may be expected to provide parents with constant entertainment or constant adoration.

Children may be consciously unaware that these agendas exist and yet feel them as shadowy unvoiced presences, or they may know exactly what their parents expect, even though something about that expectation doesn't feel quite right. But whether subtle or overt, the problem with agendas is that they really have very little to do with the real and actual child who is called on to fulfill them.

CHILD-CENTERED RISK

Not all parents become overinvolved because of their own prior needs or expectations. Sometimes, there is something special about the child—Sarah has cystic fibrosis or Stephen has an IQ of 185 or Greg is a budding violin virtuoso—and that specialness creates intense parental focus.

Children may be brilliant and talented or afflicted with a chronic illness or born with a genetic defect. But whether the news is good or bad, the questions should always be the same. Will my child have a normal childhood and what can I do to foster it? How far should I go to protect my child and to recognize his or her specialness? The answers vary according to the specifics of the child—and to the ability of the parents to create as close an approximation of a normal childhood as suits the circumstance.

Too Little and Too Soon

Most parents-to-be assume that on or around their "due date" they will greet the arrival of a nice round pink healthy baby—and mostly that is what happens. But when a baby is born prematurely, certain problems are apt to occur. In the past, when babies were born much too soon, most did not survive. Now, babies even smaller than two pounds can and do. They are delicate, unfinished little beings whose physical immaturity places them at risk for all sorts of biomedical problems.

No matter how progressive the hospital staff in welcoming mothers and fathers—and even siblings—into the neonatal intensive-care unit, parents of preemies still have a tough time. The room is filled with the sound of warning beeps and whooshing ventilators—but not with the lusty cries of full-term hungry infants. These babies look fragile and different. They startle and twitch in their sleep (the result of immature nervous systems). They are hooked up to monitors and fed through tubes. In the hot and brightly lighted nursery, the babies look like tiny Lone Rangers, with their protective black eye patches.

It's hard to celebrate the birth of a baby when you aren't certain the baby is going to be normal, or even to live. Should you laugh or cry, pass out cigars or wait to see if the baby makes it? This psychological dilemma was succinctly expressed by John Kennell and Marshall Klaus, two pediatricians who are authorities on maternal-infant bonding: "For some adults it is difficult simultaneously to go through the processes of attachment and detachment."[6]

As medical technology improves, new emotional difficulties emerge. An article in a leading psychiatric journal delineated the psychological tasks that parents of premature infants must undertake.[7] Mothers, in particular, may blame themselves for failing to produce a full-term baby. Both parents must deal with a push-pull reaction; they must stay involved with the baby's care while it is still in the hospital and must prepare themselves to accept its special needs. If their child survives these critical early weeks with no abnormalities, they must then give up their intense concern and accept the baby as "regular."

> *Jeff and Corinne remember the weeks of ICU visits, the sick feeling of fear the time they heard their daughter's heart monitor go off and the whole nursery staff came running over to her incubator. They were grateful to the nurses who devotedly cared for their tiny three-pound daughter, Caitlin. They were also jealous. The nurses knew more, could do more for her. Even though Caitlin is now a healthy sixth-grader, they still experience tremendous remorse when they remember a day they failed to visit her at the hospital. They've been reluctant to allow her to sleep over at her friends' houses, and they either take their daughter with them to restaurants and parties or stay home.*

There is an obvious and critical need for these babies and their parents to survive the newborn period with their connection to one another intact. Our concern here is that many of the preconditions for *overattachment* are being set during this period as well.

Troubles at Birth

The pregnancy has gone splendidly. The parents-to-be have graduated *summa cum laude* from their Lamaze class. And now comes the moment we've all been waiting for, the crystallization of months of planning and preparation, the true test, THE BIRTH.

The long-awaited period around the time of birth is the most intense phase of the entire pregnancy. It is fraught with pressure, expectation, potential crisis, and hard work (labor is, after all, aptly named). Compared with the rest of the pregnancy, this period is as dangerous as all preceding nine months put together.

In their formative work on the relationship of parents to their newborn babies, pediatricians Marshall Klaus and John Kennell made an important observation:

> Some early events have long-lasting effects. Anxiety about the well-being of a baby with a temporary disorder in the first day may cast long shadows and adversely shape the development of the child.[8]

For new parents, worried about their ability to care for this new and possibly fragile being, any evidence that their baby is less strong or competent than other babies may be devastating.

Nine years later, Mark and Lisa vividly recall the day when Brendan, their first child, was born. The labor had been long and difficult, and there was a brief moment of fetal distress. Although subsequently all went well, the doctor recommended that Brendan be kept overnight in the neonatal intensive care unit, "just to be sure." In the morning, he was returned to his parents, pronounced "A-OK" by the neonatologist, the family physician, and the ICU head nurse. But Mark and Lisa remained wary and worried for months. They slept poorly, running in frequently during the night to check on Brendan's breathing. At the least sign of fussiness, they took his temperature. Even now that Brendan was nine, was rarely sick, and could run with the best of them, his parents remained protective and nervous about his health.

Endless versions of this story could be told—maybe it's a low one-minute Apgar score (the system used at delivery to record the condition of the baby), or a slightly elevated bilirubin (showing mild jaundice), or a brief cyanotic (blue) spell, or an abnormal lab test. There is probably no time in life when the phrase "We'd better check this out" can have more far-reaching consequences than at or around the time of birth.

The experience of having one's new baby taken away and put in an intensive care unit, just at the time parents want to begin being parents and hold and feed and care for their baby, is confusing, sad, and frightening. Few of us would want our babies put in medical jeopardy so that we could feel better as parents. However, physicians and hospitals need to know that there may be long-term negative consequences of medical policies and attitudes that fail to recognize the vulnerability and importance of the baby-parent alliance in those first crucial hours and days.

Faith had her baby in a well-regarded hospital in New York City. The birth was normal, and although Marianna was small, she was doing fine. The next day, though, when Faith went to get her from the nursery, she noticed her baby looked blue. She gestured desperately to the nurses, who were busy elsewhere. There was sudden frantic activity, and then the baby was swept up and taken to the newborn ICU. "What's wrong with my baby?" asked the distraught mother. "We can't tell you anything," answered the nurses. "You'll have to talk to your pediatrician." The pediatrician, it turned out, was on vacation. The house staff doctor who was caring for the baby was not authorized to discuss the problem with Faith. Marianna remained in an isolette. Faith was unable to hold or touch her. Two days later, when the pediatrician returned, she told Faith that everything was normal. "What happened, then?" she asked. "What went wrong?" "She's fine," said the pediatrician, dismissively. But not to Faith. The baby who had seemed strong and healthy was now potentially fragile. Anything could go wrong.

What happens next in cases like this? Often, parents will take their child to the doctor far more frequently than average, and they'll tend to worry more about health and safety. The child begins to get the message: you are not strong or competent or safe. Unless I worry about you all the time, you might stop breathing.

Parents who experience these early difficulties can take steps to reassure themselves by asking their pediatrician some carefully phrased questions beginning with "Is my child fully recovered?" If the answer is "No," ask for more information. If the answer is "Yes," then ask, "Does the fact that my child has had this problem mean that he or she is in any way worse off than a normal baby?" If the answer is "No," you can go home and try to get as much sleep as your healthy newborn will let you. If the doctor says there is a greater risk, then ask what you can do to reduce it, what signs or symptoms to watch for, how long your baby will have this greater risk, and what information you need in order to cope with future difficulties.

Sick Babies

Parents may *fear* that something is wrong, learn that all is fine, and yet remain unable to accept the normality of their child. For example, physiological jaundice in newborns is a condition that is fairly common. The baby's immature liver is unable to clear its system of a bilirubin, a waste product produced by the breakdown of red blood cells. Treatment is actually quite simple. The baby is placed under ultraviolet light, the jaundice disappears, the liver starts functioning effectively—and the baby is fine. Yet parents whose babies are successfully treated with "bili-lites" may remain anxious.

Why don't they just relax and forget about the whole thing? It seems that parents often find it difficult, once their protective pumps have been primed, to erase the image of a child as sick or vulnerable. For years afterward, they may act as though their child is in need of extra protection.

If it's difficult to let go, to treat a child as completely well, even when his or her initial difficulties were temporary and have no future significance, then how very much more difficult letting go must be for parents with babies who have very real and serious illnesses or handicaps. The child may have contracted a life-threatening infection, suffered from heart failure, or developed severe breathing problems requiring a respirator. The parents are caught in the bind of "anticipatory grief," of getting ready to mourn the lost one—who may very well survive.

Let's say that everything goes fairly well, and the parents can at last take their baby home. Still, their worries are far from over.

While "normal" infants go to the pediatrician for "well baby" checkups, graduates of the neonatal intensive care unit attend "high risk clinics," where the long-term effects of prematurity are followed up. From one visit to the next, parents may hold their breath, waiting to learn what kinds of problems their "high risk" children will face. Will they be all right, or will they have problems with physical, intellectual, or emotional development? This "high risk" label extends the period of anxiety and interferes with the parents' ability to accept the child as normal and regular.

Doctors Morris Green and Albert J. Solnit are pediatricians who have studied disturbances in the psychosocial development of sick children and have described what happens when parents expect that their child will die. Such parents typically are afraid to leave the child with a baby-sitter and are "overprotective, overly indulgent, and oversolicitous." The child, meanwhile, may have "pathological separation difficulties," and is commonly "overly dependent, disobedient, irritable, argumentative, and uncooperative." This is also a child who usually has frequent minor medical complaints and may have trouble learning in school.[9]

It is striking how often parents who consult mental-health experts for help with their child will mention a serious illness in the newborn or infancy period:

"We almost lost Adam when he was only three months old," Bill says, reaching for his wife's hand. "It was the hardest day of our lives. When the doctor told us

*that he had meningitis and would have to be watched
closely and treated in the ICU for several days, we were
devastated. He never got really sick, and he didn't need
to be in the hospital as long as we feared. But for months
afterwards, whenever Judy would be holding him and
looking at him, her face would get so sad. She'd cry a lot.
Things are fine now, but you know it's still hard to yell at
that boy."*

So hard, that Bill and Judy fear they've created a
monster. Adam is whiny and demanding. He can't take
no for an answer. Actually, he's almost never had to. Bill
and Judy hate to say it, fearing that his behavior is caused
by emotional or developmental problems as a result of his
early illness.

Stages of Grief

If the long and anxious wait for the good news isn't
easy, how much more difficult to find out that the news is
bad, to know that your child will suffer permanent effects
from early sickness or prematurity-associated brain damage, or to learn that he or she has been born with a congenital problem. Parents in this situation who experience
and resolve their grief will be far more successful in coping with the reality of their child's problems than those
who are unable to move through the necessary stages.
Sorrow has a pattern, and the grief process described by
Dr. Elisabeth Kübler-Ross in her book *On Death and Dying*
applies to this as to any important loss.[10]

The first response is *denial*, which may take one of
two forms. It may be intellectual denial (e.g., "This isn't
really happening").

Evan was so cute his mother found it hard to be-
lieve what her pediatrician had just told her. How could
he have Down's syndrome? That was something that
happened with older mothers, and she was only twenty-
four. He looked fine. Maybe his ears were a little small,
but he'd be okay. Maybe the doctor didn't know what he
was talking about. Maybe she ought to get another opin-
ion.

Or, it may be affective denial (e.g., "It doesn't bother me").

When Phil learned that his newborn son, Todd,
might die, all he said was "Well, I've got to get back to
work."

After denial comes *anger*. Some parents never move beyond it, remaining bitter forever that "this has happened to us" or seeking to place the blame on others. Many a lawsuit for medical malpractice originates in this second stage of grieving. Children growing up in this atmosphere may have difficulty understanding why their parents are angry and may feel guilty because they believe they are at fault.

Mickey was in and out of the hospital with surgeries
and procedures and treatments related to his spina bi-
fida. The nurses trembled when they heard he was being
admitted, not because of Mickey but because of his
mother, who made everything so difficult. She was mad
all the time and took out a lot of the anger on the staff.

Moving beyond anger, many parents enter the stage of *bargaining*. It is during this stage that Too Preciousness takes root. Parents begin to make supernatural deals and promises.

> *To his parents, David was a miracle. At four, he had survived two cardiac surgeries and was doing well. To everyone else, David was a bit much. He constantly interrupted when others were talking, was rude, and could manipulate his parents for anything. Why not be firmer, give more structure, teach limits? "We vowed if our son was spared we would treat him as a special gift from God," said David's mom and dad.*

After the denial and anger and bargaining—as the reality begins to sink in—many parents experience *depression*.

> *In the beginning, when four-year-old Michelle's leukemia was diagnosed and she went into remission, her parents had been so positive. They had done all the right things, read the right books, even started a parent support group. As the days and weeks wore on, and Michelle suffered a relapse, they began to get quieter, less energetic, stopped talking much to each other, and felt very little hope for the future. They constantly bought Michelle presents, responded sadly to her every request, and were unable to take pleasure in time spent with her.*

Finally, if parents are able to grapple successfully with the fact that there is something wrong with their child, they come to the stage called *acceptance*. For many parents, this process of coming to terms with a child's disability takes a long and circuitous route, with many side trips back through denial and anger and bargaining.

"You know," says Glynis, "my first response to learning that my child had cerebral palsy was to pretend that everything was going to be just fine, no problem. I was just going to cope. But I vacillated between saying it was all okay and getting mad or trying to work out a deal with God. Now I watch Vanessa trying so hard to do everything the other kids do, and I help her do as much as she can. If I get impatient or cross sometimes—well, I'm entitled. Vanessa isn't perfect just because she has a handicap—and after all, it's normal for mothers to lose their tempers sometimes."

When Older Children Develop a Serious Problem

There are a number of special situations that can transform an average, regular, unsuspecting youngster into a Too Precious Child practically overnight. A serious accident, a life-threatening illness, or a debilitating chronic disease may cause the transformation.

The call came at work: Donny had been in an accident. As she drove to the hospital, Bev, a single parent, prayed and promised. If God would let her child be okay, she would give him everything he wanted. She would stop going to night school and stay home. She would never make him eat anything he didn't want. She would take him with her on all her vacations.

Serious illness seems an especially bitter blow when it strikes teenagers. Here they are, poised on the brink of life's great adventures, ready to explore the world, fall in love, find out who and what they will become—and suddenly they're cast back into the role of dependent child.

There is a difference, though, between the adolescent and the child, an advantage the adolescent has acquired by virtue of age. In most cases, these older children have spent most of their life being "regular" people; they've experienced a normal give-and-take in their families. While it may be possible to project a myth of specialness or to idealize seriously ill small children, it's harder to create such a fiction about an adolescent. Open the door to their hospital rooms and you'll find them listening to Van Halen and drinking smuggled-in Budweisers.

Other Bad Things

Parents frequently have a list of things they pray won't happen to their child. The bad things typically include—in addition to serious illness and injury—having a child get lost, kidnapped, or sexually molested. When parental nightmares become real, if only for a brief time, they can contribute powerfully to the development of Too Preciousness, not only because they are shattering events in themselves but also because they give reality to the "twilight zone" of parental fear.

"It was awful," said Claire. "We went shopping and Danny was right there next to me. I was looking for mattress pads, and then all of a sudden he was gone. I was frantic. All that went through my mind was what had happened to that little boy in Florida who disappeared and never was found. I ran up and down the aisles calling, 'Danny, Danny.' People were staring, but nobody helped. And then I found him riding a Big Wheel from the toy department right down the aisle from me. I

didn't know whether to scream at him or cry. I just knew in a flash that God had given him back to me for a special purpose. That sounds funny, but I know it's true. Daniel is very special."

Gifted and Talented Children

We've been talking about the worst situations, children who may become too special because of something bad that has happened to them or their bodies or minds. You might wonder why this next group we're going to discuss, the gifted and talented, is any problem at all. Wouldn't any parent be ecstatic to have a child who is endowed with some wonderful quality such as an extraordinary intellect, or an outstanding artistic talent or athletic skill? (We're talking here about kids who are truly unusual, not just perceived to be so by overly proud parents.)

Having too much may be a more desirable problem than having too little, but it may be just as difficult for these children to enjoy a regular childhood. In terms of the development of the Too Precious Syndrome, the same preconditions exist; there is something special or different that may lure the parent into overprotection ("You can't play baseball. You'll ruin your hands for the violin"). How much more reasonable to say, "Rickey, baseball and playing the violin may not mix. If you want to get really good on the violin, you may have to give up Little League."

Parents of precociously gifted children must perform a tricky balancing act if they are to support and foster their children's unusual abilities, and at the same time let them be children.

Missy had a natural gift for dance. She zipped through all the ballet classes that the Y offered. Her teacher suggested she try out for the school affiliated with the city's well-respected resident ballet company, but Missy's parents couldn't decide what to do. Images of monomaniacal young dancers, driven and anorexic, mingled with those of their own Missy, poised and beautiful, dancing with a famous ballet company.

It was eleven-year-old Missy who resolved their conflict. She enlisted her teacher's help, and together they convinced her parents to let her attend the ballet school. Missy agreed that she'd keep up with her schoolwork, take care of the cats, and maintain her friendships.

Missy's parents couldn't exactly identify what they feared, but author of *The Hurried Child*, David Elkind, the child psychologist, recounts what can happen when youngsters like Missy forgo a normal childhood. He describes a pseudonymous college student, Diana, who since the age of four had spent all of her spare time playing tennis. She was very, very good—so good, in fact, that she attended a top college on a tennis scholarship.

In the process of becoming a tennis whiz, she had focused so single-mindedly on her athletic skills that she'd missed out on many of the important experiences that help children develop and mature. Elkind describes college-age Diana, a student assistant in a nursery school, "constantly engaged in trying to re-create the childhood she had never had. When the toddlers did finger-painting, she wanted to do finger-painting with them. On her birthday, she wanted a birthday party just like the one the children got."

He concludes, "She's like many teenagers who've

been pushed too early. Whether they were pushed into sports or music or academics, we see these adolescents mourning for a lost childhood. They imagine all the things they might have done if they weren't practicing the piano all the time, or skating.... Kids who have been trained to be tennis stars, skating stars or pianists, and who haven't been allowed to express other parts of themselves may feel empty in adolescence."[11]

Overinvolvement with a talented child may stem from a parent's own wishes, disappointments, fantasies. (The stage mother is a classic example.) Ivan Lendl, the tennis star, was raised by a mother who wanted so fiercely to be the number-one woman player in Czechoslovakia that, according to an account in *Sports Illustrated*, she would tie young Ivan up to a fence to keep him from toddling off, while she practiced for hours on end. Later, she transferred her drive for perfection onto her athletically gifted son.[12]

Guiding the intellectually gifted is a tricky business. Athletes in our culture enjoy a good deal of support and approval, and far more money is spent in our schools for talented athletes than for talented thinkers. Children who are superbright may attract more resentment than praise from fellow students and teachers, and may, in fact, feel more normal and ordinary in a group of their intellectual peers than they do in regular classes. In many school systems, though, parents will be hard-pressed to find anything except lip service paid to programs for the gifted.

In these situations, parents may have to consider having the child skip a grade or sending him or her to a special school or program outside of their regular school district. In reaching your decision, it may be helpful to ask yourself the following three questions:

What do your child's teacher and school
        recommend?
What does your child want to do?
How is your child doing in the present situation?

If your child is bored in the classroom, spends most of the time daydreaming, and is unable to make friends, then a change to a special gifted program may be the right choice, even though the school is unenthusiastic. If he or she is happy in school and has made friends there, a change may be less desirable.

> *Amy's parents began to discuss private school as their daughter approached ninth grade. The large public high school that their daughter would attend offered very little to the academically gifted and did not foster the kind of real intellectual interests she had developed. Nevertheless, when it came time to make a choice, Amy voted for public high. All her friends were going. Amy's parents supported her choice, but during her ninth and tenth grade summers, they encouraged her to attend special enrichment programs at a nearby college.*

If a child does exhibit a special ability, that talent should be allowed to bloom and flourish. A "regular" childhood for a gifted child includes encouragement to develop special gifts. If Jeff has musical talent and wants to pursue it, he needs a good teacher and the opportunity to practice his instrument. If Denise has a real enthusiasm and gift for art, she needs materials and enough free time to use them. (Too many of these youngsters are given no support, no materials, no encouragement from their schools or their homes.) The gifted and talented child becomes Too Precious when parents seek to exploit his or her ability, dragging the musical child to auditions, or pushing the brilliant young scholar who wants to stay with friends to skip grades.

How do you foster normal development in a gifted or talented child? By remembering that this human being, no matter how unusual, needs to learn how to share, how to communicate his or her wants and needs, and how to participate in the life of the community at large. Even though a child is a figure-skating champion, he or she can still help with the dishes and set the table. Teenage prodigies can take time out from their training and development to go to a movie with friends or to a basketball game. In other words, every moment of a special child's life need not be special.

Twins, Triplets, and Beyond

People are endlessly fascinated with multiple births; twins or triplets, not to mention the larger broods, seem special and miraculous. In fact, parents of multiples soon learn that their offspring are an instant conversation piece. People stop in the street to stare and ask questions. At school, heads turn when they enter the classroom. The children soon learn that they are special and interesting —but they get attention as part of a pair or group, not for themselves as individuals.

For these children, the task of establishing an individual identity is complicated. Not only do they have to establish boundaries between themselves and their parents—they've got to find out where they leave off and their sibling begins. How easy can it be to gain a sense of your own identity, when your twin sister Laura shares it?

RISKY SITUATIONS

We've looked first at the kind of parental impulses that create too intense attachment and then at some of the "too special" children who may elicit it. Sometimes, though, intensity emanates neither from parent nor child but instead from a "loaded" situation that creates the pre-conditions for Too Preciousness. Sometimes, people who might otherwise manage to find a reasonable balance between closeness and distance have to contend with circumstances difficult enough to tip the scales toward overconcern. There are endless twists and turns of fate that may tie a family up in knots; the examples we offer next merely begin to convey the range of possibilities.

Only Children

In large families, there are many outlets for parental ambition, many shoulders upon which family obligations come to rest. If one child wants to run away and join the Hare Krishnas, there's another one who might actually prefer to stay home and join the family business. Growing up as the sole repository of parental expectations may create enormous pressure. "You're the youngest, the middle, and the oldest all rolled into one" is the way one only child expressed her feelings of pressure.

> *Wendy is an only child who wants to drop out of college and travel for a year. Her mother's response was to call a psychiatrist. "I don't know what Wendy thinks she's doing," said the mother. "We've made it very clear what we expect from her. We've given her everything."*

The burden of being an only child who must live up to a parental agenda may make it difficult to become a truly autonomous adult.

> *"I never wanted to stay in Indiana," said forty-seven-year-old Bob, "but I knew how much my parents counted on me. I was their only child. Even though I didn't want to go into the family dry-cleaning business, I knew if I didn't, it would kill them. I do what they need me to, but I dread getting up in the morning."*

In addition, only children may have difficulty staying in the child role. There's a tendency to have the child join the parents as a kind of pseudo-adult. Parents may recognize the pitfalls of this kind of interaction and counteract them by providing frequent opportunities for their child to be with other children. Only children need to experience conflict with their peers. That's how they learn to control the bossy, critical streak that they share with first-born children. They don't belong in the midst of parental conflict. Often, if there are only three people in the family, parents find it temptingly easy to draw the only child into discussions and dramas that are really adult business. An important distinction for parents to keep in mind is that their child is part of the sibling subsystem in the family, even though there is only one member of that subsystem.

Adoption

Parents who have searched for a child to love and raise as their own know what a lengthy, expensive, emotionally difficult process adoption is. While their friends produce child after child with apparent ease, adoptive parents, sometimes after years of struggling with infertility, are screened and rescreened. They are required to complete exhaustive paperwork, submit themselves to endless scrutiny, and spend anywhere from $3,000 to $15,000 in legal fees. To some, it doesn't seem fair.

What is expected of a child whose parents had to jump through so many hoops, spend so much money, and wait so long? Often, far too much. To add to their difficulties, families who adopt may have trouble acknowledging, let alone discussing, their negative feelings. Adoptive parents may feel they've gone through so much self-justification, they just want to be left alone. And so, except for the Big Question—When do we tell Tommy he's adopted?—some parents just don't want to have to deal with the unpleasant emotions the situation may churn up: for example, resentment of this child who has drained the family bankbook before he's even arrived on their doorstep.

Adopted children shoulder big agendas. They must fill the role of the "longed-for child," even though they may harbor a secret suspicion that life might have been better if "my real mother had wanted me." Their parents may want to prove they are as good as, or even better than, the natural parents could have been. ("I am a better parent; I wanted you and am raising you, and she didn't —or couldn't.")

Survivors

There is one special group of children who grow up with enormous obligations, not to the living but to the dead. These are the children who have survived terrible tragedies: the children of the Holocaust and their children are vivid examples of this category, as are survivors of wars, floods, fires and revolutions.

In all these cases, there is a great deal of visibility. Survivors' stories are known—part of the public record, part of history. Parents, society, peers, all have tremendous expectations: "You will succeed in spite of what happened—or on behalf of everyone else who died." Sometimes, these children have a violent reaction to having to be so especially good.

Divorce and the Great Custody Wars

Twenty or thirty years ago, children whose parents were divorced came from "broken homes," and the common wisdom was that they were anything but precious. Most likely—the scenario went—they would become juvenile delinquents. Now that divorce is a common phenomenon, however, we don't see so many references to "broken homes." And, although custody is still usually awarded to the mother, we are seeing more and more fathers who want to remain active participants in their children's lives. This is all to the good. Their children are apt to be healthier and happier, and will have an easier time adjusting to their new family situation and getting on with their lives.

What happens, though, when parents who separate begin to divide up their child's time?

Amanda was a beautiful baby, and when her parents divorced, they agreed that they would share equally in her upbringing. Amanda grew up splitting each week between mother and father. It seemed that her little suitcase was always being packed and unpacked. Both of her parents remarried, and now there were four sets of grandparents. She always was dressing up and showing off her ballet steps. She had lots of hugging and kissing and attention. What she didn't have was time to be alone.

Parents may feel reluctant to insist on the usual rules; after all, the kids are suffering because of the divorce, so why make them more miserable? Or they may fear they will lose the child.

Rick lived with his mom and spent weekends and one weeknight with his dad. Neither parent expected Rick to do chores or to spend much time on his homework. They took him to movies and let him watch TV whenever he wanted to. If either Mom or Dad suggested that Rick help in the kitchen or work on his spelling, Rick just said he wanted to go live with the other parent—and the demands stopped.

Custody battles breed Too Preciousness. Here are troubled parents caught in the midst of divorce, trying to woo and win and impress their children. They can't really function as parents; they're more like contestants. If each parent is trying to win custody, one of them is going to feel disappointed by the outcome and probably wronged.

Jeff was convinced he was the better parent, and although Celia had custody, he made regular threats to go back to court. When Tony and Beth came back to Celia after their weekends with Dad, Celia knew she was in for a rough time. They were tired, grimy, stuffed with cake and ice cream and candy, loaded down with presents. Celia had to get them unpacked, find out if they'd done their homework (they never had), then get them bathed and into bed and back to the real world. They were always tired and grumpy when they came home, and there was usually a battle. "It's a great deal," said Celia to her friends. "Jeff gets to spoil them and play with them, and I have to make them take baths and ground them."

From Celia's point of view, it was a no-lose situation for him and a no-win situation for her. Daddy is fun; Mommy's always nagging about something. But, in truth, Jeff doesn't have much motivation to turn disciplinarian in his limited time with the children.

Recently, there has been a trend for couples who divorce to arrange for joint custody. This is a laudable resolution of the parents' differences, with both mother and father recognized as equally important, but it is not a panacea.

Alan splits his week between his parents, who have chosen to live in the same school district, so that they can pursue this arrangement. His mother shares a duplex with his grandparents, so he gets a lot of attention when he's with Mom—and lots of attention when he's with Dad, who's always planning special things to do. Alan has two bedrooms, each fit for a crown prince, each fully stocked with clothes and toys. But a lot of the time he's irritable and listless. He doesn't seem to get enough rest.

Alan is the victim of excess, of a great social experiment that may result in overstimulation and overfocus on the child. In truth, the legal child-care arrangements parents make at the time of divorce must be tempered by concern for each child's particular needs. There is no one final formula for success here, and flexibility is all. We do know that children do best when their parents are able to cooperate and to be responsive to a child's changing developmental needs—and to realize that those needs change from year to year; for example, a teenager may suddenly announce he or she wants to live with the parent who has been less available.

> *Susie, a bright, attractive, and energetic fifteen-year-old, with dark-gray nails and four earrings, is a typical teenager: she can't stand her mother ("She won't let me do anything"). When Susie announces she wants to go live with her father, though, all hell breaks loose. Her mother, who has been the custodial parent, is loath to send her six hundred miles away to a father who's been only casually involved with his daughter's upbringing. Susie does go, and she's back in a few months. Life with Dad and her stepmother wasn't quite the liberated paradise she imagined.*

Susie's mother managed somehow, through veils of resentment, to glimpse what her daughter needed to do. Alan's parents, on the other hand, were so concerned with being involved and participating in their son's upbringing that they forgot to stay attuned to what he really needed at that time: a calmer atmosphere, less performing for adults, a real home base.

FOUR PRECEPTS FOR DIVORCED PARENTS
(really for all parents)

Avoid overstimulation.
Provide clear structure and limits.
Avoid putting the entire family focus
    on the child.

Be comfortable with allowing your child to
be "bored" on occasion.

The Pitfalls of Single Parenthood

As a parent in a two-parent home, you may know little about child-rearing, but at least you have someone with whom to share the blame if things go wrong. As a single parent (whether by divorce, death, or choice), all you've got is you, and that knowledge may at times feel overwhelming. Carl Whitaker, the famous family therapist, has said that if he were a single parent, he would marry anyone.[13]

Single-parent families can function quite effectively. The children may flourish, and the "single parentness" may be just something that the family learns to deal with. In fact, some families function better with single parents than they did with two enemies living in a state of war beneath one roof.

Nevertheless, parents who go it alone must cope with special problems. In a subgroup of single parents, at especially high risk for overinvolvement, is the single parent who adopts or the single woman who hasn't found a compatible mate and decides to have a baby on her own. These people may have vast reserves of love and energy to invest in a child and may also feel an especially strong need to prove to the world that they are wonderful parents, setting the stage for the appearance of a Too Precious Child.

Many divorced and single parents crave their children's good opinion. They have taken a vow that goes something like this:

"I will make it up to you for

(a) the divorce;

(b) the death of your other parent;

(c) any guilt you may feel for the divorce or for the death;

(d) any difficulties you may experience because I chose to have you without providing you with a father."

Much of this "making it up" backfires and leads to difficulties. The youngster who is the object of such attention may feel more depressed ("Why is everyone always trying to be so nice to me? Is there something wrong with me?") or more entitled ("Mom will get me anything I want").

In addition to overcompensation, there is a tendency, especially for single parents of only children, to make a child into a pseudo-adult. David Elkind talks about the inappropriate roles parents may be tempted to assign their children, expecting them to be the voice of conscience, decision-maker, partner, surrogate, status symbol, and therapist.[14] For a lonely and overburdened adult, there is a strong temptation to share problems with the person who is closest; but if that person is a child, it is a temptation that needs to be resisted.

TOWARD "A BREAD-AND-BUTTER CHILDHOOD"

If you've read this chapter and found yourself in one or more of the categories of risk we've been describing, you've actually taken the first step toward reducing that risk: recognition. Our goal for the rest of this book is to help you create a more normal and unpressured child-hood for your child. Children need closeness and parental involvement, *and* they need space and encouragement to be self-reliant. How do you do that?

The question is as old as the ages. At the turn of the century, children's book author Kate Douglas Wiggin wrote:

> There is no substitute for a genuine, free, serene, healthy, bread-and-butter childhood. A fine manhood or womanhood can be built on no other foundation; and yet, our American homes are so often followed with hurry and worry, our manner of living is so keyed to concert pitch, our plan of existence so complicated that we drag our babies along in our wake, and force them to our artificial standards, forgetting that "sweet flowers are slow and weeds make haste."[15]

These words were written at a time we now imagine as the lost golden age of childhood innocence, a kind of *Saturday Evening Post* front-porch fantasy of family life. In all the years since her book appeared, our lives have become even more fragmented and frantic, and her vision of childhood serenity harder than ever to achieve.

As we begin our exploration of certain key points in childhood development, pointing out the places where closeness promotes growth and where it interferes, we'll hold on to that vision of children who don't have to fulfill parental visions of perfection or brilliance or total intimacy but who are free to be their own authentic selves.

CHAPTER THREE
The Perils of Being Too Special

Most of us would like to shelter our children from every sort of threat and danger, both those we know about and those we vividly imagine. Our wish is to spare them physical or emotional pain as we guide them safely and surely along the path we know will lead to health and happiness. But even while we try to create as unpressured and serene an atmosphere as we possibly can, we need to be alert to the consequences of too much sheltering. If children are prevented from struggling with child-sized problems, how will they gain the experience and confidence they need in order to deal with the world beyond the home? Psychiatrists' couches are filled each day with Too Precious Children; the very immunity their parents tried to provide has instead created a sense of weakness, defeat, or anxiety. The annals of psychiatric literature are replete with case studies of adults whose childhoods sound idyllic but were, in fact, filled with parental overprotection and overadoration.

> Gretchen knew she was "special," and most of the time she didn't mind, even though it meant she had to be a lot more careful than the other kids because she was "sickly." After all, her mother was always nice to her and

protected her and dressed her in warm clothes so she wouldn't get colds. Gretchen learned that you could get colds from things that sounded like fun—like playing outdoors in the snow or staying overnight with your best friend or riding your bicycle more than just in front of the house. It wasn't until years later that she began to understand why she felt so endangered by normal activities and friendships—and to understand as well just how worried her mother had been about her "special" daughter, born three months too early and not expected to survive.

Parents who have had to deal with a fragile newborn, a seriously sick baby, or a child with a handicap or a chronic disease can easily identify with Gretchen's mother in her fearful attempts to protect her child's well-being. The irony of this loving desire to protect and guide is that it may lead to less safety and more emotional problems as parents cross the boundary from protection to overprotection, from guidance to intrusion.

When Michael was born with a deformed hand, his parents vowed that he would never be made to feel bad about it nor would he be stopped from anything he wanted to do. They never mentioned that anything was wrong with his hand and simply treated the one hand like the other. In order to prevent him from comparing himself unfavorably with other children, they kept him out of nursery school. Michael was a happy and confident child. When he first went to elementary school, however, he was teased about his deformity, especially by the older kids in the upper grades. He came home sobbing. He didn't know how to handle their taunting remarks.

Michael's parents had both succeeded and failed: succeeded wonderfully well in making him confident and failed in inoculating him against the rudeness of others. They had tried to protect Michael by keeping him out of nursery school, but when the time came for him to go forth into the larger world, he was unprepared for what he found there. The Too Precious Child is protected from the slings and arrows of life, but that very protection may become one of the arrows.

The Greeks offer us the legend of the mother who wanted to ensure that her Too Precious Child would grow up to be an invincible warrior by having him dipped into a magical river. Unfortunately, her son, Achilles, then went out of his way to show off his invulnerability and was killed by a poisoned arrow that penetrated his heel, the only part of him that had never been immersed in the river.

There *is* no magic river. Gretchen, whose mother did everything to protect her, grew up to be an adult who fears the very experiences and relationships that could nurture and sustain her. Michael couldn't stay home forever. His parents learned, fortunately at an early stage, that to give Michael lasting protection they had to help him to deal with the real world, not shelter him from it completely.

Of course, in the beginning of life, children do need complete protection, and infants, especially, seem cleverly designed to elicit it. They are adorable and therefore adored. Parents become hyperattuned to their baby's every sigh and gurgle, so that you might almost imagine the new family as a *syncytium*, a multicellular organism without clear cell walls.

The rightness of closeness during infancy is parallel

to the rightness of separation as children grow up. When we see "syncytium" behavior at later stages, we regard it as either silly or bizarre. It may also be quite damaging.

> *Heather sat and glared at her sixteen-year-old daughter. All she'd said to Barbara was "I'm feeling awfully chilly, dear. You'd better put on a sweater." Why was that so funny? Of course, Barbara didn't always think her mother was funny. Sometimes, the reassurance her mother needed in order to believe that her daughter was still alive—the constant telephone calls to "let Mom know you're okay"—made Barbara worry, too. Lately, she'd been thinking that she wouldn't go away to college. It might be better to live at home.*

What's in store for children who are trying to grow up without the right balance between support and freedom? To explore the difficulties they face, we've assembled a list of "perils," and we've posted them along the developmental pathway like hazard lights, flashing a warning. We hope that our flashing lights will help parents slow down, look around, and possibly rethink the route they're taking.

The Too Precious Child must always be "on."

One striking characteristic of many Too Precious Children is that they seem always to occupy center stage. They have a seemingly endless need to have others be entertained by them, watch them, and listen to them, and an incredible capacity for demanding that others entertain them.

Six-year-old Jared exhausts his grandparents—
and they love him dearly—with his incessant chatter and
prattle and demand that they "look" and "watch me" and
"listen to me." They recall their children and their other
grandchildren. All the kids had wanted to be the center of
attention at times, but they were nothing like Jared. He
wants to be the center all the time, and his weary
grandpa and grandma have concluded that they can't
have him for a very long vacation. Two days with Jared
is like two weeks with any of the other grandchildren.

If Jared exhausts his own grandparents by his incessant
demand for center stage, then what must he do to friends
and schoolmates and teachers? Often, adults dismiss these
children as "spoiled" or "selfish," but the labels don't
offer much help in understanding what the problem is or
how to solve it.

It is entirely appropriate for a young child to be self-
centered. There is no purpose in being thoughtful of
others when one is eighteen months of age (though many
parents of toddlers wish their offspring would be a bit
more considerate). The infant and small child has dependency needs that must be met by a willing and loving
caretaker. "I want a drink of water" is a request that will
be met, usually without a second thought. As children
grow up, parents begin to expect them to plan ahead and
get a drink before bedtime. By the time they are ready to
leave home, we hope they will be able to handle their own
thirst needs so well we don't even think about them. (The
complaint of eighteen-year-old "Miss Sophisticate" as she
peers into the depths of a fully stocked refrigerator that
"there is nothing to eat in the house" harks back to a

much earlier time—and reminds us that human development is not always linear.)

As children grow, we expect them to learn to share, wait their turn, and be considerate. These are all behaviors that teach the child about *community*, about others, about that group of people who exist in addition to and beyond the self. The Too Precious Ones have been taught to remain center stage, and they have not been taught to attend to others. At first, those "others" will be family members, neighbors, classmates. Ultimately, the concept of "others" will extend even farther—into the community, the country, and the world.

As children grow older, they learn how to be part of the whole; the child who is always "on" has been taught that he or she *is* the whole. Like many Too Precious Children, this child may be an only child or from a small family, may have parents who want the child to be "special" and "unique," or may be in a situation (such as divorce) in which the youngster is overly special in several environments.

To illustrate what we mean by being part of a whole, imagine a group of adult friends as they socialize: one tells a story, the others ask questions, frequently everyone laughs. The social rules dictate that there be some turn-taking and that the spotlight be rotated.

> *The women's group met once a month. Every so often, they would decide to get serious and select an important issue to discuss, but for the most part they just enjoyed one another's company. Trish would share her experiences and thoughts about being pregnant with twins, and then Martha and Rachel would offer the wis-*

dom accrued from their recent pregnancies, and finally the rest of the group would chime in with their support and excitement. Elaine might change the topic to her worries about her middle son, and then someone would recount her recent experiences howling with the wolves at Wolfhaven, a sanctuary for abandoned wolves. All the members took turns giving and receiving attention and support. No one was "on" all the time, and no one was off or out at any time either.

As we watch this group of adults interact, we see that there is both a foreground and background, and that both planes are important and real. Children need to learn that they can occupy both. It is not reasonable to insist that just because they are young, children must always be background—seen but not heard—nor is it reasonable to demand that they always be foreground ("Read us several more of your poems, David") or to allow them to preempt the foreground ("Mom, don't talk to Dad. Look at me!").

Young children live in a very rich and colorful but socially two-dimensional world. As they grow older, they begin to develop a sense of foreground and background, of self and context. The child who is always "on" has difficulty appreciating the meaning of context.

Angela sat at the table with the adults and talked animatedly about her school and her summer vacation. When the adults turned to another conversational topic, Angela launched into a story about the zoo in her hometown. At this point, her mother gently said, "Angela, that story doesn't fit into the conversation we're having now, so I want you to save it for another time."

Angela's mother is teaching her seven-year-old daughter about *context*, about distinguishing what fits and what doesn't in a given situation—in this case, a dinner table where there were mostly adults.

When lessons about "context" and "fitting in" and "other people's needs" begin, children may lack the cognitive capacity to grasp them. Preschoolers do not understand the concept of empathy.

> *"How would you feel if Billy bit you?"* asks the *nursery school teacher when she finds Timmy sinking his teeth into Billy's leg. Timmy regards her with a blank stare. As far as he is concerned, who knows and who cares? He's angry, and Billy's leg was in his way.*

By high school, empathy is a possibility.

> *Julia's parents had become resigned to collecting used dishes and glasses from all over the house. What a surprise when after returning from a session at camp as a counselor-in-training, she brought her dishes to the kitchen and proceeded to wash them. "We all pitched in at camp," she explained. "I knew if I didn't do it, someone else would have to."*

Children mature in their capacity to feel what the other person feels, but in the meantime, they can learn the rules: that they must share the spotlight with others, and that there is a time to speak up and a time to be quiet and listen. By the time they are in their adolescence, children will be expected to defer to the common needs of the family and (rather than venting their teenaged contempt for adults) to show at least a rudimentary respect for their parents. By this time, they will be expected to understand the concept that others have feelings and opinions and rights. With maturity comes a growing social depth of field and a broadening artistic range to their picture of human relationships. There are times to be in sharp focus, to be the center of the composition, and other times to remain off to the side.

Children who are always "on" never learn these things. Their parents have fostered their sense of "specialness" at the expense of important human skills. They may have great difficulty in distinguishing what is foreground (under the spotlight) from background (the context, or environment). For some of these children, only the foreground exists in all contexts; their social existence is a flat one.

> *Even though she felt devastated, the diagnosis of anorexia nervosa was no big surprise to Donna. Her fourteen-year-old daughter, Elizabeth, had been losing weight for months because "everyone can see how fat I look" and was now a bag of bones. The girl berated her mother constantly for "never paying enough attention to me." Donna was stunned. "I can't believe she really thinks that," she exclaimed. "I gave Elizabeth every ounce of my energy, spent every night over homework with her, went to every ballet class with her, not just every recital, every class. I think I've only told her I was too busy to pay attention three times in her life."*

Such children may pay a high price for their belief that the eyes of the world are always watching.

In many families, normal parental fatigue ensures that children are at times relegated to the background.

However, some circumstances interfere with the child's opportunities to learn the difference between background and foreground. A dramatic example of this type of situation occurs with the kind of custodial arrangements in which the child divides time between parents, with doting grandparents waiting in the wings to shower the child with even more attention.

> *"I don't have to and you can't make me," Ryan screamed at his mother. She knew he was right. Ryan split his week between her and his father—and in twenty minutes Ron was due to pick up his son. There was no way she could get Ryan to clean his room in that amount of time, and she couldn't tell him he had to stay home if he didn't finish. She always seemed to be giving in to Ryan's demands. Whether he wanted videotapes or toys or parental attention, he got it all—in both his mother's and his father's house. Both parents had trouble saying no because they knew he'd be leaving soon and because they feared he'd report back to the other parent, providing ammunition for a future court action for full custody, which both parents wanted.*

Ryan is in the foreground all the time, wherever he goes. He is never given the experience of dropping into the background and looking at the "context" of himself, his family, and his behavior. Responsibility and accountability are concepts that Ryan is going to have great difficulty understanding under the present arrangements.

The narcissism of the parent may collide with that of the Too Precious Child.

What prevents us from making a cool-headed appraisal of our children's behavior? Why is it so difficult to be loving and yet objective? We're adults, so why when our toddlers are misbehaving don't we just smile fondly at their antics, tell them to shape up, and make sure that we have enough time off to go to the movies or get together with friends?

Sometimes it's just not that simple. If you are a parent who has just gotten used to the extraordinary dependency and confinement and protection required by parenthood, you see the reward of your efforts in this gorgeous little being who gazes with fascination on your face. It's more intoxicating than simply staring at your own reflection. Here is the ultimate manifestation of self —but going beyond self.

Now come the "terrible twos." Your gorgeous Jason has little interest in you. What a blow! His main occupation is a tireless, relentless testing of the limits. Here is a true double whammy that goes to the very core of your self-esteem as a parent. You miss all the adoration, and your precious child isn't being precious!

This transition is a jolt, but only overly narcissistic parents withdraw their availability and support. Healthy parents recognize that their child's narcissism is simply developmental, not a terrible and permanent character flaw; and they know when to let go and when to stand firm.

Terry had a natural aptitude for music, and had been dazzling his teacher and his parents with the rapid progress he'd made after only four months of piano lessons. Terry's father, an accomplished violinist, basked in a vision of his son playing concertos with the local symphony. Terry, however, had a very different image in mind. He wanted to be cool and tough and devote himself to learning to play electric guitar. Piano was boring. His dad was disappointed and disturbed. Was he being unreasonable, imposing his own taste and goals on his son? On the other hand, the boy had only been studying for a few months. Should he be allowed to drop things so easily? After considering the situation, Terry's father made a counterproposal: "If you complete a year of piano and your teacher tells me you've made good progress, you may change to guitar."

Brittany's parents were remnants of the activist sixties. They, like most parents, had hopes and dreams for their daughter. Maybe she would be a social activist, possibly a writer for an important publication, possibly even a civil liberties lawyer. Brittany at eight had no interest in these dreams. What did she want to be? A CHEERLEADER! Her parents switched gears and took great delight in her enthusiasm.

Here, with Terry and Brittany, we have the stories of two precious children but not of Too Precious Children. The parents were alert to their own agendas and supportive of their youngsters' growing and individuating.

By contrast:

Meadow and Krishna went to the mountains of North Carolina to escape the confines of contemporary

*culture. There, in the tipi they built, Meadow gave birth
to her first child, a daughter named The Dawn, who was
carefully raised by her parents to wear her clothing inside
out and backward so she would never feel confined by the
rigid, up-tight right-side-out and frontward culture.
What did the child decide she wanted to be? A teacher.
Watching her eight-year-old daughter neatly line up her
"pupils" (other children of the local counterculture)
drove Meadow wild—they hadn't spent all these years
living in a tipi so that her daughter would be corrupted
by mainstream culture. The Dawn was forbidden to play
school or to attend a small educational play group with
the other children.*

We get into fairly predictable developmental crises
with our children when some need of theirs conflicts with
some need of ours. A healthy parent has the capacity to
postpone gratification and show empathy, and doesn't need
to come up "winners" all the time. "Special children"—children with special agendas tacked on to them—have addi-
tional self-esteem issues and obligations, and they stir up
extra issues in us. Although conflict is both healthy and
inevitable in family life, we sometimes fail to appreciate
conflict as a signal that there is some discrepancy between
our notion of the child and his or her notion of self. Too
Precious Children too often have to carry a burden not only
of their own self-esteem but also that of their parents.

Some parents communicate a sense of despair that
they have "missed it," somehow missed their chance at
greatness, brilliance, or happiness. Their children become
the New Destiny. Children are sensitive to such an intense
obligation and begin to realize that no matter how wonderful they are, they are never going to be able to make
the parental dream come true.

Gillian was special at birth. Her parents, both teachers in a Rhode Island community college, had wanted a baby for a long time; and her arrival was slated to be the fulfillment of their every dream. They had long ago abandoned any hope of making it in the academic major leagues, and instead decided to put their energies into seeing to it that their daughter had every educational opportunity. Gillian, as she was growing up, had dreams too—recurrent ones. "I would be up in the sky, and there were clouds everywhere and I would find a ladder and climb up through one of the clouds and into the clear sky. But when I climbed through and looked up, there above me would be a thousand more clouds with ladders."

Too Precious Children are incubated in an anxious atmosphere. Their parents suffer an unusual amount of pressure to "do it right" and transmit that pressure to their children.

The Too Precious Child Syndrome frequently begins before birth with a would-be mother and father who devote themselves even before they *are* parents—sometimes even before conception—to the *concept* of their child. Currently, there is a tremendous amount of cultural pressure connected with pregnancy and childbirth. There are scores of books, thousands of articles, telling us what to eat and drink—as well as the best way to think, feel, and prepare for the great event to come.

A lot of planning goes on in the home of the Too Precious Embryo. The couple may consult appointment books and five-year-planners to coordinate birth with work schedules and vacations. They may decide that a certain season would be most suitable or try to target a special date, a birthday or anniversary. There are even couples who consult astrological charts in order to produce a child at a favorable conjunction of celestial bodies.

Overinvolved parents-to-be typically begin preparing themselves early. Usually, their research focuses first on pregnancy and childbirth, but they also may start stocking their bookshelves with all the latest books on early enrichment. They may have chosen their "birth style" before conception, and commit themselves to this choice during the months of pregnancy with what amounts to quasi-religious intensity. Lamaze families become quite involved with one another; Bradley parents talk shop in their corner; and those who want pain medication find their own soulmates to hang out with.

A couple's involvement with pregnancy and childbirth gives us something to support and celebrate—we've been there ourselves—but we want to look at some of the traps that await those excited parents who've constructed too precise a dream of how it's all going to be.

Sometimes, alas, the process of childbirth isn't the euphoric family-centered experience the couple had imagined. Instead, the flawlessly prepared mother-to-be labors for hours, requests pain relief, then feels like a failure. Sometimes, the long-imagined all-natural childbirth is replaced—by medical necessity—with the technology of the cesarean section.

> *Rich and Cheryl, both divorced, met and married with the stated purpose of having a child. How delighted they were when Cheryl found herself pregnant a month after the wedding. Throughout the pregnancy, Cheryl ate, slept, exercised, meditated, and prepared herself or*

the Blessed Event. She avoided bad foods and bad situations. She and Rich read Leboyer and Lamaze and Grantly Dick-Read and The Birth Book *again and again. They considered a home birth but decided to seek the safety of a family-centered hospital birth. The moment arrived. Labor started and progressed for twelve hours. The couple calmly drove to the hospital. There they listened to cassettes of George Winston's gentle piano music, and Rich lit a candle he had brought for this wondrous occasion.*

But, labor went on and on and on for twenty-eight hours, then stopped progressing. There were signs of fetal distress, and finally, despite the nine months of preparation and meditation, the soothing music and the supportive hospital staff, a cesarean section had to be performed and a healthy baby girl was born. Four years later, Cheryl and Rich remained disappointed but seldom spoke of the disappointment. After all, who was to blame? Cheryl (for "failing to progress") or Rich (after all, he was the coach) or Susannah, their baby? They frequently shared with others how "special" Susannah's arrival had been, but they rarely mentioned the birth and would become quiet when their friends chattered about their "birthing moments." They decided not to have another child but instead to give their all to Susannah.

Usually, parents are able to carry the burden of a disappointing birth experience, and children are spared any blame. But, still, for children like Susannah, there may be a kind of "emotional fallout." Parents who begin with feelings of failure may attempt to overcome their guilt by showering their children with too much attention or by expecting them to perform so brilliantly that they erase any parental shortcomings. Here, indeed, is a breeding ground for Too Preciousness.

**Parents of a Too Precious Child may have difficulty respect-
ing their child's growing need for separation.**

This first venture from the womb to the world outside is only the beginning of a journey that will proceed
with many stops and starts and detours. Like the famous
Homeric traveler Odysseus, a child voyages from birth to
adulthood in a series of adventures and transitions.

One insightful guide to this journey is Joseph Chilton Pearce, an author, teacher, and developmental maver-
ick. In his book *Magical Child*, Pearce urges us to respect
our children's inner timetable and points out that development is no more amenable to parental scheduling than
the arrival of teeth. He suggests that parents can learn a
lot about how their child is developing by paying attention to what he calls "matrix shifts," points of transition
from one developmental phase to the next (for example,
being born, going to preschool or elementary school, en-
tering adolescence).[1]

Too Precious Children often have difficulties with
these matrix shifts. They may be underprepared or over-
prepared. The parent may push for a transition too early
or may hold the child back in an effort to postpone this
inborn timetable. Typically, parents who cannot tolerate
separation react either angrily or anxiously when it comes
time for their baby to reach out to the world and begin to
venture forth.

*Courtney's mother, Hollis, felt a real sadness when
Courtney began to lose interest in nursing and became
more interested in playing with her mom's earrings and*

trying to eat the dog food and opening the door to the stereo cabinet. Mom wanted to hold and feed her, but soon Courtney would want to get down and explore. Annoyed, her mother would set the child down, get up, and walk out of the room. Then Courtney would cry to be picked up again. "How irritating," thought her mother. "Why doesn't she make up her mind?"

Hollis didn't really understand that her child's new adventurousness marked an important transition point; instead, she felt rejected and angrily left the room, thereby withdrawing the protection her child needed in order to explore.

While some parents withdraw, others may simply refuse to allow separation and instead follow the young adventurer around, ready to wipe a runny nose or serve as guide and protector. This sort of parental behavior prevents the child from making the necessary transition to greater independence.

Adonis was the third child, but a first and greatly longed-for son, in his Greek-American family. His parents worried constantly about his appetite, and although he was measured above the seventy-fifth percentile in weight, both of them delighted in sneaking up on him as he crawled about the living room and popping a cookie in his mouth when he looked up in surprise.

The problem during this phase is one of distance, of allowing enough but not too much. Adonis has too little space and is having difficulty moving into the phase that's appropriate for his age. Courtney has too much, and is being pushed ahead prematurely, out of developmental sequence.

Pitfalls in this transition zone are many. Confrontations, battles, power struggles, all get their start here. They're normal, and if your baby is developing well, they are to be expected. The great dance of separation at this stage is one of many missteps, miscues, and stepping on one another's toes. If all goes well, the dance will begin to feel more rhythmic and musical over time.

The baby's task here is to move out into the world and announce his or her separateness. The parent's job is to understand this drive, be patient and confident, allowing the separation while remaining in the background for protection and comfort.

Too Precious Children and their families prefer the stage of fusion and closeness; they dislike and avoid the stage of separation and individuation.

After the passage from the womb to the world, the next big matrix shift is from the arms of the mother to mother earth, that greater world that lies beyond encircling parental arms. As our magical children travel on, they want to shed protection as they increase their abilities to move and communicate.

Now comes a critical time in the life of the Too Precious Child—and the Too Precious Parent. Some parents start out being overprotective and learn from the child's great desire to "do it myself" how important autonomy is. They see how eight-month-old Christopher delights in his newfound ability to pull himself up and cruise around the coffee table. They hear how nine-month-old Nancy amuses herself when she wakes up from her nap by babbling merrily to herself, "dadadadada" and "mmm-m-mmmamama." They learn how quickly eighteen-month-old Deirdre scurries away when her mother comes to pick her up, how actively she protests and kicks when her diapers are changed. Doing it yourself, entertaining yourself, doing what you want when you want, are all wonderful new possibilities, all normal and necessary parts of development.

But Too Precious Parents don't want Christopher cruising around the coffee table. They rush to pick him up. (He might get hurt!) When Nancy gurgles, they immediately go to her, short-circuiting her newfound ability to entertain herself. (She might be lonely!) When Deirdre scurries away, they scurry after her and insist she hold still. (She might grow up to be rebellious if she doesn't learn to obey now!)

Too Precious Children are burdened with big agendas.

Sometimes, the birth itself is fine, but the real baby isn't quite consonant with the dream baby, nor the dream child with the one who's been lying on the rug screaming and kicking for the past five minutes. How do parents who fantasized about a tiny, curly-headed girl with a cheerful, easygoing temperament reconcile themselves to the reality of a wispy-haired, colicky boy who really needs his parents to be patient with him?

Benny's parents were both psychologists. They often dealt with parenting issues. Then Benny was born—and was a difficult baby from the start. He was difficult to soothe, to hold, to awaken, to change, to bathe. His parents spent months working on Benny, shaping and conditioning him to their theoretical base. They were determined to make him "their son." They not only wanted him to be good-natured but also planned for him to study art and music at an early age. Benny seemed to have other ideas.

Lizzie was a plump baby and a plump child. Her mother, herself always ten pounds heavier than she wanted to be, had dreamed of having a daughter who would be petite and graceful, with a natural talent for dance. Every time Lizzie would eat enthusiastically and ask for more, her mother would go into a silent fury. Lizzie didn't understand anything except that mealtimes were tense times.

The Too Precious Child has trouble enjoying a magical childhood.

Too Precious Parents may have difficulty in allowing children the space for the fantasy play that is so important a tool in helping them learn to master their drives and begin to explore their universe. They tend to distrust unstructured play as impractical and time-wasting. After all, the kids could be learning computer programming.

Jonathan's parents bought him books and science kits and building sets but refused to invest in any toys that didn't seem useful. They didn't allow him much unsupervised play with neighbor kids, saying it was "just a waste of time." They wanted five-year-old Jonathan to spend his time more productively and asked his kindergarten teacher to assign some homework.

Is Friedrich Froebel, the inventor of kindergarten, turning over in his grave? In 1837, this German educator began what he called a "children's garden" because he prized play as the highest childhood activity—a point of view that is shared by many of today's experts. Brian Sutton-Smith, a developmental psychologist at the University of Pennsylvania and an expert on children's play, feels that "early play has a lot to do with vitality and zest for life." He advises parents to "forget about teaching the children about numbers and colors and the like, and just *play* with them."[2]

Some parents may swing too far in the opposite direction. They don't just give their children the freedom to play. They want to get in on the fun. This fascination with their child's fantasy life may lead them to intrude on their child's private world.

> *Melissa's mother, Gwen, had wanted to be a Montessori teacher. Instead, she had Melissa, who was a very dear, creative, imaginative child. No matter what Gwen was doing, when Melissa wanted Mom to play or wanted to show Mom something, Gwen would stop and go to Melissa. Gwen so enjoyed her daughter's company that she decided to keep her at home and start her own little school, just the two of them. Although Melissa really wanted to be around other children, her mother's dream prevailed.*

The Too Precious Child may be the victim of excessive parental enthusiasm and ambition.

Overprotective parents are far more likely to say, "I know what's best for you" or "Let me show you how to do it" than "I'll stand back and let you learn for yourself." Indeed, the parent often has better information and an argument could well be made for the parental point of view. That doesn't much help the child who needs to "do it myself." The toddler's task is to meet the world and experience it, while the parents' task is to *understand* this impulse to separate and to offer guidance and encouragement while remaining in the background for protection and comfort.

Eating is a favorite battleground for the overenthusiastic parent and the child who wants some independence.

> Mother: I know what's best for you and these green beans will build a strong body and this milk will help your bones and teeth grow strong and this dessert is mmmmmm-mmmmm good and you can have it when all your other food has been eaten.
> CHILD: No!

Toilet-teaching may provide another major battle for autonomy. How many parents recall the high drama of those moments spent standing and waiting and wondering, "will he or won't he?" For some Too Precious Children, the struggle centers around retaining control; for others, the problem is one of discouragement. They have little incentive for mastery because their parents don't want to impose their will. On the potty for the fourteenth time that morning, the reluctant toddler is playing a waiting game that becomes another typical battle for autonomy.

The Too Precious Child has difficulty making developmental progress in a reasonably smooth way. Either too much or too little is expected.

Pearce's magical children travel when they are ready to move on. Not coincidentally, matrix shifts occur when children have the physical, mental, and emotional tools they need to go on to the next phase. When they don't, there are problems. For example, a three-pound preemie doesn't have the physical ability to take on the job of being a newborn without a lot of sophisticated medical care.

As children journey from matrix to matrix, from the simple safety of their mothers' and fathers' arms to more demanding and complicated environments—neighborhood, grade school, junior high, high school, college, and the great big world beyond—they must acquire more complex skills.

These transitions may be difficult for any youngster, but our Too Precious Child typically seems to have a harder time acquiring and using the necessary skills.

> *Jay was taken to preschool at the church when he was three. Every morning, when his mother Linda would leave, he would cry and cling to her. The staff worked with Linda to encourage her to make the transition period fairly brief, and this helped some, but still he continued his misery for nearly the entire preschool time. Both Jay and his mother were wretched. After several weeks, the consensus of everyone—it seemed they all had deep circles under their eyes—was that Jay should wait another year before trying school. He just wasn't ready now.*

After several weeks without school, Jay seemed happier, but his mother was frustrated with him for "flunking" preschool.

Linda had planned to have him attend nursery school so that she could begin work on her master's in public health. After all, he *was* three and she had devoted herself to giving him a model early childhood experience just as she'd planned. She'd been available to him twenty-four hours a day for three entire years.

When Jay made it apparent he wasn't ready for school, she felt critical of herself for not wanting to sacrifice her own plans for her little son's needs and even more annoyed at Jay for deliberately acting like a "baby," spoiling her image of herself as the perfect mother. She was just going to have to make him grow up. In fact, she was sacrificing them both to her double agenda: to have freedom for herself and to begin Jay's schooling right on schedule.

Linda didn't realize how much she was asking of her son. She was so impressed with her own generosity in devoting herself to him that she had not looked ahead and sought ways to make the transition from home to school less abrupt.

She'd accustomed him to her around-the-clock availability, then demanded that he willingly separate from her—and at the same time learn how to get along in an entirely new setting. No wonder he'd cried and protested when she left him at school.

She took a hard look at what she'd been doing, then resolved that in the future she'd try to make transitions more gradual. She began by hiring a baby-sitter for short periods of time, and when Jay became more accustomed to being with another care-giver, she took him to a twice-weekly play group, so that he could begin to interact with other children.

The same year Jay got to stay home, thousands upon thousands of his three-year-old peers hit the nursery school interview and testing circuit because their anxious parents were convinced that the "right" school now would mean Harvard or Yale or Princeton down the road. The race for the top begins early, and it is not unheard-of in competitive Manhattan for parents to apply to ten or more schools.

Once enrolled, these young children have just begun their struggle to fulfill parental expectations. Some parents are disappointed to learn that their children don't appear to miss them, don't cry and demand to come home. Others expect their children to tolerate the separation without tears, to be a "big boy" or a "big girl." Parents who have either set of expectations are giving their child the message that he or she cannot be authentic or real but must always guess about and respond to parental agendas.

> *Seven-year-old Leah loved kindergarten and first grade, but she had her doubts about second. She enjoyed playing with the other children. She loved snacks, she loved coloring. She didn't much love memorizing the alphabet or learning to add, but since she was such a pleasant child no one until now had noticed that she wasn't really making progress. During a consultation with the school psychiatrist, it became evident that Leah was Too Precious. She was an adored youngest child and very little was expected of her. At home, she was still treated like a three- or four-year-old. She loved it and so did her*

family. But she didn't have the "oomph" to move forward
in school. Her parents' solution was to offer to take Leah
out of school for the rest of the year. They said they would
just as soon have her at home to play with and cuddle.

Neither Jay nor Leah was ready for school. Jay's parents were pushing too hard for early maturation; Leah's parents seemed indifferent to the fact that it was well past time for Leah to move ahead. Both sets of parents needed to rethink their plans and goals and to begin to prepare their children for the next great leap forward.

The Too Precious Child may develop too much or too little initiative.

That great illuminator of human development, Erik Erikson, presents the preschool years as a time when children either learn to exercise initiative (the capacity to start something), or, failing to do so, experience guilt. As young children begin to crawl, open drawers, climb out of bed, and explore their world in all its possibilities and limitations, they walk a thin line between "do" and "don't do." Too many "don'ts" may make them feel guilty about their attempts; they may display less curiosity and energy and become reluctant to continue their explorations. As parents, our goal is to instill enough of a sense of right and wrong to protect them but not enough to paralyze them.

Rex awakened each morning about 5:15 and lay
quietly in his crib singing and babbling. Hearing him,
his mother would smile, pull the covers up to her ears and
savor the time she had left before he got out of his crib

and the day began. She had about three minutes to blast-off. At 5:18, Rex would begin to scream and yell and rock his crib across the room. He WANTED OUT! He WANTED FOOD! He WANTED HIS DIDIES CHANGED! He WANTED ACTION!!! The rest of the day was enough to make a pentathlete drop. He walked, he ran, he climbed, he fell, he jumped, he dunked the kitties in the toilet, he pulled the plants out of their pots, he emptied the cans from the cabinet, he crawled in the kitty litter bag, he pulled the magazines off the table, he took the records out of their jackets. He had a marvelous time. By now it was 7:00 A.M.

Rex was a great initiator, and as he grew and developed, he remained energetic, curious, and ready to explore and try new experiences. His mother's task was to encourage his initiative while protecting him from its excesses. If Rex were to run into the street, start a fire in the garage, jump into a lake without being able to swim, or put a fork in the cat's rump, his mother would have to stop him. The trick for parents of young children is to find a good balance between too much control and too little.

Too Precious Children may be exposed too early to a great push for learning and skills.

In the past few years, we've seen an explosion of interest in early learning, something we call "cognitive overkill." There is a tremendous emphasis on early acquisition of formal learning skills and a corresponding devaluation of free play and fantasy.

Some of this interest has had valuable and important results by helping to create Operation Headstart and early-intervention programs for children who need more stimulation from their environment. But because some early learning is good for some children, more is not necessarily better. What concerns us here is the predicament of children who are being pressured into becoming performing monkeys by parents who are anxious to make sure that "my child doesn't lose out or fall behind."

In questioning parents whose very young children are involved in a ceaseless round of lessons and activities, two things seem apparent: the children's activities fill a void in the parents' lives and the parents often have had a major hand in choosing the activity.

Although a few three-year-old children do teach themselves to recognize letters and words and sometimes even to read, most young children are not developmentally ready. They do not yet have the initiative and interest that will make learning so much more rewarding for them later on.

There is something absurd about parents who spend two or three hours a day prodding their preschoolers into early reading. Yes, Johnny can be taught to read at age three, but is there any long-term advantage?

Pediatrician and author T. Berry Brazelton relates what happens to children whose parents push them into reading.

> They didn't seem to comprehend the words they read, but they could read ahead of their classmates, and they easily became the teacher's pets. But by second grade, this ability to read was no longer so precocious, for the other children were rapidly catching up. By third grade, the others *had* caught up, and a surprising phenomenon began to appear: The early readers were not learning new, flexible techniques for reading or other learning skills. They seemed to be "stuck" in that

rather flat, lifeless way of reading and of learning in general.

Not only were they unexcited about learning, but as they fell behind their classmates, they also lost the teacher's approval. That proved disastrous, for they had come to depend on adult approval for their self-confidence. When they lost it, they were left without any way of fueling themselves for future learning. They fell behind in school and began to have emotional problems.... It seemed to me that in early childhood they had become accustomed to being "special" to adults, and when they lost their "star status," they were in trouble.[3]

When we overemphasize the acquisition of abstract skills before children are developmentally ready, we devalue the important "magical phase" that helps prepare the soil for cognitive seeds to fall upon. Pearce's imagery describes the innate quality of growth:

The cycle of growth unfolds automatically, rather as though there are so many spins around the sun and, lo, the next set of molars appears, the next brain-growth spurt takes place, logical processing shifts, and we move into the next matrix...the next stage unfolds regardless. Baby teeth arrive pretty much on schedule as do six-year molars and so on; this physical timing is not dependent on diet (or the good graces of a dentist), although the quality or efficiency of those teeth might be. Genital sexuality unfolds around adolescence whether or not the young person (or God knows, the parents) is prepared for that unfolding. In the same way, matrix shifts take place automatically, whether or not a proper response and structuring has taken place to prepare for that shift.[4]

In other words, babies are born with their own lesson plans. It is a parent's job to attend to the unfolding, to aid it as much as possible and to refrain from meddling too much with the brilliant design.

We're not opposed to all early-childhood education. Young children are eager to learn, and they often enjoy going to classes. Tumbling lessons might be wonderful fun when a child is ready to tumble, or music lessons when a child shows a response to music. What we need to remember is that our children learn not only while they are in a class but also from their own free play.

The Too Precious Child may have trouble with rules, especially outside the home.

"Sit down."
"Take turns at the slide."
"Don't hit your neighbor."
"No talking while we listen."

Too Precious Children may have difficulty following rules, or they may be excessively compliant and worried about obedience and performance. So some of them will always sit down and take turns and never hit anyone, no matter how provoked to do so, nor talk out of turn; while others can't seem to do what anyone else is doing.

As children move from home to school, they enter a new phase and must struggle with new tasks. Erik Erikson characterized this new phase as "industry versus inferiority." During these years, typically the elementary school years, children attempt to master knowledge and organize information, learn to read and write and follow the rules. Self-esteem is up for grabs in all these areas. Some Too Precious Children, the overcontrolled ones, tend to look like little scholars at age five. Others may fail to learn the rules and master the inhibitions necessary to "play the game." Children who have had very little experience in controlling their impulses in the Too Precious Home are in for a rough ride at school.

> *Sam, a first grader, loved to play in the sand at recess. Sometimes other children would try to play with him, but they never stayed for more than a few minutes. Sam would hit them; a fight would ensue; the teacher would intervene; and Sam would claim it was everybody else's fault.*

Sam's parents met frequently with the teacher to little effect. They remained convinced that Sam's teacher just didn't understand their boy's special need to play alone and be protected from the other children. Finally, they pulled him out and enrolled him in a more permissive private school.

The Too Precious Child risks feeling inferior if he/she tries anything too new and different.

The great risk for many Too Precious Children during the school years is the development of feelings of inferiority in learning to deal with work. These feelings may lead to an endless spiral, where increasing difficulties in experiencing success further heighten a sense of inferiority. Many adolescent behavior disorders have their roots during these early school years, as we point out later when we discuss the phenomenon of Too Preciousness in adolescence.

> *Amy spent a lot of her time in school daydreaming about how her Barbies would look in their new outfits. The teacher seemed so mean because she always made Amy pay attention and do her work. Amy didn't like homework and didn't try very hard to do it. What she loved were dolls and fairy tales. Amy was glad her mother was so nice and so willing to play with her for hours. Amy's mother didn't make her do things she didn't like. Instead, her mother said things like "You're only young once," and "Don't let school stop your dreams," and "Isn't play more fun than work?" Amy thought it was and was glad that her mother was her Very Best Friend.*

The less work Amy accomplished and the less she learned, the more incompetent she felt. The other kids made her feel stupid because they knew the answers to questions. She tried taking ballet lessons, but as soon as the teacher challenged her to work hard and to make an effort, Amy dropped out. Her dolls became her constant refuge from the outside world.

Amy's mother was sensitive to her child's need to play, but could have been more helpful by adopting a balanced approach. By supporting her daughter's desire to play and suggesting that she could do this after she had finished her schoolwork, she would have helped Amy deal with the reality of the outside world.

The parent of the Too Precious Child may have difficulty assuming the role of the "bad guy" and may insist on always being the "good guy."

The first time you hear the child you dearly love shriek, "I hate you, you're mean" is not one of life's great moments. Some parents have so much difficulty being disliked that they will do anything to avoid it. If Baby gets upset because Daddy moves a magazine out of reach, Daddy will change the rule rather than stand firm and tolerate Baby's expression of anger. Somehow, Daddy's desire to read an unshredded magazine becomes less important than his fear of displeasing his child.

Preschool children and adolescents really put parents to the test with their inconsistent behavior. They never seem to be satisfied, no matter how many concessions are made. During both these phases, children may be clinging and, at the same time, fiercely independent as they try to tantrum their way to adulthood.

Parents need a lot of support during these two major separation phases, and there are a number of ways to get it. Certainly, husband and wife can help each other, with love and sympathetic listening. Talking to other parents or reading child guidance books can be a real comfort. When you find out that the uniquely awful thing your four-year-old did is what his friend Evan did last week (or, God forbid, learn from your mother is what you did at his age), you can relax a bit. Organized parent support groups are useful and often reassuring. What's important is to learn that there is no way to be effective parents without saying no sometimes. Even though you may feel like a monster, limit-setting is a basic parental task.

Too Precious Children may find parents unable to deal objectively with their willfulness.

Enthusiasm and energy and determination are all hallmarks of a healthy child—and all these wonderful qualities can at times be irritating. Rigid parents, unable to tolerate a display of independence, may identify their child's expression of will as "a manifestation of the Devil" or, in more modern fashion, as a "psychological problem." Permissive parents may be unable to set necessary limits to excessive behavior, leaving the child at the mercy of his or her temper. If parents realize that a child during this phase is experiencing a drive to feel powerful, they can avoid exasperating power struggles while firmly setting limits.

Power struggles might as well be called "powerless" struggles. They occur when neither parent nor child feels in control, so both vie for the upper hand. In such situations, parents do best by first checking to see if they actually have the ability to enforce their rule. "No smoking at home" is enforceable; "No smoking" is not. Next check to see whether the rule is *worth* enforcing. "You must come directly home from school" may be enforceable, but may not be necessary. A better rule would be: "If you're not going to be coming home directly, you must call." If you can avoid being arbitrary and can present a reasonable and enforceable rule, chances are it will seldom be ignored.

The Too Precious Child may sense parental fears about the dangers of the outside world and lose initiative or may resist restrictions and leap unprepared into dangerous waters.

Lincoln's conception was a "miracle" to his parents. They had tried to have a child for six years and had begun to believe they would never succeed. The pregnancy was healthy but nerve-racking because neither parent was willing to relax until the ninth month. His birth was a breeze, and both parents were convinced that their "miracle" baby was the Second Coming.

What happens when Lincoln grows up a bit and wants to go sledding or ride a horse? Will his parents allow "the miracle baby" to go out for football in high school?

When six-year-old Nell got a bicycle for her birthday, her mom and dad sat her down and explained all the dangerous things that could happen if she didn't ride extremely carefully. Day after day, they waited for Nell to try out her beautiful new bike, but she always had an excuse for not wanting to learn.

Nell's parents were disappointed at their daughter's lack of enthusiasm for her birthday gift. They felt they had been extremely wise to caution her thoroughly and never made the connection between their approach and her fear of the bike. Craig's parents, on the other hand, would have welcomed a little fearfulness.

Craig began to tune his parents out after the hundredth admonition to "stand up straight or you'll get a curvature of the spine." They warned him endlessly about scuffing his shoes, sitting too close to the TV set, riding his skateboard without a helmet, crossing his eyes. After a while, nothing they said seemed of special importance. If he listened to them, he wouldn't ever get to do anything he wanted to do. One morning Craig crashed into a car at the bottom of a steep and busy intersection. He was rushed to the hospital with a fractured skull. Craig hadn't bothered to wear a helmet.

As we discussed the perils along the path to growing up, our underlying argument has been to *allow* children to experience what is normal for their age and stage of development. A child is not a *tabula rasa,* a smooth, clean slate to be written on as and whenever we choose. Like a cell, which contains the genetic program for its own growth, the young child carries within a similar program for maturing at the right rate. Our job as parents is to respect those instructions and provide the healthiest possible environment to incubate our children. As the old Zen saying has it: "Don't push the river."

From Adoration to Separation

They await the birth of their child with eagerness and some trepidation. "Will I be able to make the transition back to work after my leave of absence?" asks Kim. "How will I feel about being a part-time house-husband?" wonders her husband, Pete, who has arranged to work half-time for the next six months. But when six-pound, three-ounce, pink and silky-haired Dana arrives, reason flies out the window. Kim and Pete, a sophisticated Chicago couple in their early thirties, now spend a good portion of their time, Polaroid at the ready, arranging photo opportunities for their daughter. She's only two weeks old, but she has a portfolio that would be the envy of an experienced model: Dana in her white dress with the yellow duck from Aunt Laura, Dana in the pale pink snowsuit and hat from Mom, Dana with a bunch of daisies on the couch. . . . They adore her; they worship her.

What's going on here? Will Kim and Pete spoil their baby with all this attention? Absolutely not. Infancy is a time for parents to adore, cherish, coddle, indulge—to absorb themselves completely in the wonder of their new baby's being. Later in the course of their relationship, when parent and child have difficult times, they will have these early roots of adoration to anchor them.

New parents are fascinated by every aspect of their baby, every burp, and smile, and sneeze, and no one finds this especially surprising. But as children grow older, this fascination gives way to a more balanced view. Each little noise or gesture does not require the utmost adult involvement, and while parents still think their child is wonderful, they begin to give a little more space, to pay a little less attention. They also begin to be more objective about what their child is really like.

The parents' progression from intense absorption to a more moderate interest is a normal one. When baby takes her first step, parents are excited. They tell their friends. They take a picture or record the date in a baby book. The second and third steps are wonderful. The eightieth or ninetieth are nice, but by now there's less applause and wonder. Fortunately, just as parents are becoming less enthralled, children are beginning to grow out of this period of attachment and to need a little more distance.

Normal as it all is, this transition from adoration to separation doesn't always progress smoothly. There are times when children want to be babies again and times when they demand more distance and independence than they can handle.

In this chapter, we will explore the route children take from birth through the first phase of separation, for it is during this period that the Too Precious Child is born. By understanding the importance of attachment for future development and the equal importance of separation, parents who tend toward overinvolvement may begin to seek the delicate balance between too much fusion and too much separateness, between too much adoration and too little support, between idealization and devaluation.

NO NEWBORN CAN BE TOO PRECIOUS

From their earliest moments with one another, parents and children begin by drawing together, forming a powerful bond that will last a lifetime. The baby's task is to make its parents feel special and unique; the parents' is to do the same for the child.

Adoration and preciousness are so necessary at birth that nature has endowed the newborn with a complex set of skills to elicit caretaking responses. The rhythm and reciprocity of this infant phase is a crucial building block in the foundation of trust between baby and parents. When little babies cry and are picked up and comforted, or when they yell with hunger and are fed, they learn important positive things about the world.

The experts of the not-so-distant past would have disagreed. Mothers were told to feed babies on a rigid schedule and to let newborns cry themselves to sleep, so that the babies would learn discipline. Swaddling prevented close contact and free movement. Breast-feeding was discouraged, and the bottle promoted.

According to the most widely read expert on child care, Dr. Benjamin Spock, some of these practices were the result of a medical belief that carefully measured feedings given at regular intervals would ward off disease.

During the first half of this century, babies were usually kept on very strict, regular schedules. Doctors did not know for sure the cause of the serious intestinal infections that afflicted tens of thousands of babies yearly. It was believed that these infections were caused not only by the contamination of milk but also by wrong proportions in the formula *and* by irregularity in feeding.[1]

One of the earliest proponents of on-demand feeding was a famous patient of Dr. Spock's. Margaret Mead had noticed in Samoa that the babies were nursed whenever they cried and that there was no attempt at regularity. She was interested in trying this approach and when she gave birth to her daughter, Catherine, persuaded her somewhat reluctant pediatrician that it might be a good idea.[2]

Nowadays, flexibility in early feeding is the norm, and most of our experts counsel more intimacy, more physical closeness, more touch, and more emotional and intellectual involvement with our children. But how much is enough, and how much is too much? What do children need from us in order to grow? Perhaps if we listen and watch, our babies will give us some important clues.

THE AMAZING COMPLEXITY OF NEWBORN SOCIAL BEHAVIOR: HOW OUR BABIES MAKE US ADORE THEM

Early students of child behavior described newborn infants as automatons that nursed and soiled and slept. As such, they needed physical care but the particular care-giver didn't much matter. A wet nurse, a maid, or a succession of helpers could do the job. In truth, the more we learn about babies, the more complex we find them to be.

The scientific community only recently has begun to acknowledge what doting parents have known, probably forever: that their babies could do many wonderful things.

> Kim and Pete were wowed by Dana when she was born, but the pace of their infatuation with her increased; she seemed to grow cuter day by day. Gratified by her alert gaze, they talked to her and showed her brightly colored toys. Hearing her cry, they would decide she wanted comforting and pick her up.

Dana has a surprisingly extensive repertoire of behaviors that very effectively draw her parents to her and engage their interest. Far from being a helpless "automaton," she's sensitive, communicative, and responsive. Like other newborns, she has remarkable abilities.

Seeing. Although mothers have always known that their babies could see, science has finally demonstrated the ability of the newborns to see, to follow, and to indicate visual preference. What do they like to look at best? The human face. Dana's parents gaze at their daughter and frequently find their gaze returned. Dana follows them with her eyes as they move about.

Imitating. At birth, babies can mimic the facial movements of adults. This ability fades somewhere between four and six weeks of age, but while there, it's a strong and fascinating response.

> Dana's parents were enthralled by this. They would widen their eyes, open their mouths, and wonder of wonders, Dana did it too! Kim and Pete congratulated one another on their daughter's obvious intelligence.

Hearing. Newborns respond to sounds (especially the female voice). They show distress in experimental situations when they are presented with a discrepancy between auditory and visual information such as seeing their mothers in front of them but hearing their voices coming from a loudspeaker to one side.

When people talk, babies listen. Researchers have discovered that, like adults who nod their heads and move their bodies, babies too have a rhythmic pattern of response to human conversation.[3]

> *"Isn't she an extraordinarily good listener?" Kim and Pete remark. "She even nods her head when we talk to her." As a result of this perception, they talk to her throughout the day, as they change her, feed her, take her for a walk in the park.*

Crying. All cries are not the same. Mothers, once again, have had the jump on researchers by many millennia. But now, thanks to spectrographic analysis of baby cries, four distinct configurations have been formally identified: hunger, anger, frustration, and pain.[4]

In fact, in cultures that encourage more communal responsibility for children, people learn to make distinctions without benefit of spectrograph. For instance, Betsy Lozoff, a pediatrician and anthropologist at Case Western Reserve, reports that among the !Kung of the Kalahari, a baby's cry of pain will bring a response from the entire community, while a cry of hunger elicits a response only from the mother (only she can feed it).[5] In our own culture, new parents haven't practiced distinguishing one cry from another, but they soon learn.

When Dana cries with hunger, Kim quickly picks her

up and feeds her. Later, when she is fussing, her parents comment that "she's mad because we won't play with her anymore." Now, instead of rushing to her side, they take a few moments to go to her.

Quieting. Anneliese Korner studied the many ways in which parents soothe their children: talking, caressing, cradling, rocking, etc. She found that using the voice alone was least effective. What babies seem to like most is to be picked up and brought to shoulder.[6] Why? It may be that this action taps into the greatest number of body systems, including the vestibular system, the balance center in the inner ear.

Dana has quickly taught her parents that she likes to be walked with her head on her dad's shoulder. She not only quiets down, she also looks around with great interest.

Right from the start, Dana, for all her apparent helplessness, is amazingly competent. She draws her parents to her when she's hungry, encourages them to spend time with her when she wants stimulation, and teaches them how to soothe her when she's fretful.

BABIES ARE DESIGNED TO BE PRECIOUS

There is something about the way babies *look* that elicits a protective response from adults. In one of his entertaining essays, author-scientist Stephen Jay Gould has made some intriguing observations on the physical characteristics we respond to, by tracing the evolution of Mickey Mouse from his first appearance as a "rambunctious slightly sadistic fellow" to his final large-eyed, short-legged, more juvenile form.

"Many animals," writes Gould, "for reasons having nothing to do with the inspiration of affection in humans, possess some features also shared by human babies but not by human adults: large eyes and a bulging forehead with retreating chin, in particular. We are drawn to them, we cultivate them as pets, we stop and admire them in the wild, while we reject their small-eyed long-snouted relatives who might make more affectionate companions or objects of admiration."

Somehow, says Gould, Walt Disney and his artists intuitively knew, or gradually learned, ways to make their creatures utterly appealing. How? Give them infantile characteristics: big eyes, full cheeks, and short, floppy limbs. Consider the charm of Mickey and Dumbo, Bambi and Thumper, the Three Little Pigs, and all the rest of those endearing and enduring critters. Babies all. It's as though infants came with labels: "From the Studios of Walt Disney."

Indeed, human response to babies appears to be instinctive and predictable. Gould cites Konrad Lorenz, the famous animal behavior expert, who was struck, when he turned his attention to human young, by what he referred to as their "babyness," all those qualities that tend to elicit a caring and caretaking response.

Lorenz pointed out to us nature's ingenuity in designing babies to appear and behave in ways that elicit caretaking behaviors. This design would insure that the newborn, a helpless and dependent creature, would not be left to its own devices but would be attended to initially in very devoted ways that would ensure its feeding, soothing, protecting, clothing. In other words, the first thing an infant must do for its very survival is to be so precious that its care-givers become attached.[7]

How well this strategy works is attested to by Roberta Israeloff, a writer who has vividly described her profoundly protective feelings for her new son.

> His perfect tininess was breathtaking and impossible, but it also hinted of terror. He was so brave, so valiant, every muscle in him straining toward awareness, some elementary kind of mastery. His vulnerability brought me to tears; his rawness, his entirety overwhelmed me, pierced through my consciousness as nothing else ever had.

When other people feed or hold him, Israeloff realizes that she feels jealous.

> I wanted every moment of my son to myself, convinced that no one else felt for him what I did.[8]

CHILDREN NEED LOVE TO GROW

Several important studies lend scientific respectability to what we all sense at some deep level. Children need more than just physical care to survive—they also need loving parents.

René Spitz, a French physician writing in the mid-1940s, recounted a chilling tale of the effects of feeding the body but not the soul. He studied two groups of babies and made a documentary film of his subjects. The first group was raised in a hospital by nuns from an adjacent convent. The babies were well nourished, clothed, and sheltered. They were cleaned but not cuddled, fed but not soothed. Though they received excellent hygienic care, these babies failed to grow and develop normally; many died.

Spitz then compared these little ones to a group of babies whose mothers were prisoners and who were being raised in prison. The differences were revealing: the babies raised by their own mothers were thriving.

At about six months of age, as part of prison policy, the babies were taken away to be raised outside the prison. Spitz's documentary shows the babies undergoing a pitiful transformation, becoming sickly and sad, losing many of their abilities—until reunion with their mothers induced a joyous and dramatic recovery. Both in his writing and in his documentary film, Spitz provided evidence that love, attention, and affection, like a mysterious elixir, are vital to a child's well-being.[9]

CHILDREN NEED TO BE CLOSE TO THEIR CARE-GIVERS

During World War II, great efforts were made to evacuate children from London to the safety of the English countryside. Many children, however, were forced to remain with their parents, enduring the terrors of the intensive bombing raids.

Follow-up studies compared the emotional impact of the war on both groups of children—those who were sent to the relatively peaceful countryside and those who remained with their parents, crowding into dark shelters, subsisting on meager food, and enduring the noise and terror and constant threat of annihilation. Contrary to expectations, children who had experienced the Blitz in

London were in better psychological shape than those who had been sent to live in a calmer environment. What made the difference? Quite obviously, it was that the children who remained in the city were united with their parents.[10]

PARENTS WANT CLOSENESS

While death and destruction create separation willy-nilly, the traditional family unit is sometimes intentionally broken up in order to explore new forms of child-rearing and to promote social goals. In the long run, though, there seems to be a strong tendency to want to reestablish the parent-child bond.

In his 1969 book, *The Children of the Dream*, Bruno Bettelheim, the famous and controversial child psychiatrist, described child-rearing practices in the kibbutzim of Israel. Bettelheim pointed out that many of the founders of these idealistic communities had themselves been raised in small Eastern European families where the "Jewish mother" was less a cultural joke than a social reality. Here was a chance to raise children in a new way in a new country. Instead of the intense and overinvolved style of their families of origin, the early kibbutzniks sought a more horizontal layering of society. Child-rearing was centralized. From infancy on, children lived in special children's homes with a staff of care-givers and teachers, seeing their parents on weekends and special occasions. Children of the kibbutz would be proof of the excellence of the new system. They would carry on the work; intrinsically valuable, they did not need to be adorable to elicit a caretaking response.

Communal child-rearing offered great practical advantages. Adults, particularly women, had more time to spend on community work. But while the setup seemed rational, many parents began to miss everyday closeness with their children. Some of those who disliked the kibbutz child-raising methods left; others stayed and tried to change the system. These days, kibbutz children tend to have more contact with their parents.[11]

Similarly, founders of the communes that sprang up across the United States in the 1960s and 1970s deplored the suffocation and antisocial self-involvement of the nuclear family and wanted to create new social forms. John Rothchild and Susan Berns Wolf, in their book *Children of the Counterculture*, describe the efforts of several counterculture groups to create new and better methods of child-rearing.

Guided by principles of cooperation and noncompetition, most of these planned communities assumed that communal child care was desirable. But, not infrequently, children were more valued in theory than in fact, and eventually many groups split up when parent-members insisted on living in more conventional nuclear families. To the surprise of quite a few of these committed flower children, what drove them from the commune was neither political nor sexual differences of opinion but profound disagreements over child-rearing practices.[12]

Why do most experiments with alternate patterns of family life end in a gradual return to some form of nuclear family? Our assumption here is that the ingredient missing from community child-rearing is the intimate relationship that both parent and child seek.

Clearly, involvement, even adoration, is especially important in the first year of life, and because so much of our book explores the process of separation, we want to be certain that we explain just how critical this first "attachment" phase is to later stages of development.

ATTACHMENT IS THE FIRST STAGE OF GROWTH

When we discuss later stages of development, we'll look at problems children experience when there is an excess of attachment, but as we explore what goes on in the first days and weeks and months, we find that it's not only natural and healthy but also vitally important for every young human being to have a unique and special relationship with a care-giver.

What do we mean when we talk about "attachment," or its synonym "bonding"? What do babies do that let the parent know he or she is special?

Kim watches the baby-sitter attempt to console a crying Dana. Sure enough, when her mother holds her, Dana stops crying. Kim and Pete have noticed that Dana follows them with her eyes when she's in a roomful of people. She smiles more with them, too.

One researcher, Mary Ainsworth, listed as many as fifteen separate behaviors she had observed and that new parents may notice consciously or understand intuitively.[13] These include such behavior as crying when the mother leaves and joyful greeting responses when she comes back, and the way in which infants who are beginning to crawl make forays from their parents, then return. Frightened or feeling insecure, they rush back to the parental side, burying their face in Mom's or Dad's lap.

These behaviors, many of which make us chuckle to

watch or recall, all tend to strengthen the attachment bond like an elastic net around the parent and the infant. Not only do these actions express attachment, they also induce attachment. "Not only is this baby incredibly dear to me," says the parent, "but I am incredibly, undeniably, and irresistibly dear to him [or her]."

ATTACHMENT IS A TWO-WAY STREET

Most of this early research was concerned with the ways in which children became attached to their parents. Little attention was paid, however, to the ways in which parents become attached to their children—possibly because parental involvement appeared to be such a "given" that there seemed to be nothing to explore. Parents become attached to their children because they are parents—or parents become parents by becoming parents, a tautology if ever there was one.

Some researchers did begin to explore the influence of early life experiences on both babies and their parents. Angus McBryde, a pediatrician at Duke University, studied the effects of "rooming-in," the practice of keeping newborns with their mothers rather than taking them off to the hospital nursery. His study revealed some important practical outcomes: mothers who had closer contact with their babies made fewer calls to their pediatricians and were also more likely to breast-feed.[14] This early closeness, it appeared, gave new mothers a sense of confidence and competence.

REDISCOVERING THE BOND

Rainbow Babies Hospital is an institution in Cleveland with a reputation for excellent care. In the 1960s, John Kennell and Marshall Klaus, two pediatricians who practiced there, were deeply disturbed when they found that the newborns they had worked so hard to save were being readmitted to the hospital months later with evidence of neglect, failure to thrive, and physical signs of beatings. What was going wrong?

Kennell and Klaus decided to try to observe the heretofore unobservable. Their goal: to discover what factors promote healthy attachment between parent and child and what factors tend to work against it.

As they began their investigation, they asked themselves if something was interfering with the ability of parents to feel like parents to these tiny survivors. Was the same system of medical care that was saving these babies also tampering with the evolution of normal parent-child interactions? The two pediatricians looked at Angus McBryde's earlier study and compared practices at their hospital with his results. The standard childbirth procedure at Rainbow Hospital was to show the baby to the mother immediately after delivery, then take it to the newborn nursery. Typically, the mother would not see her child again for six to twelve hours, and thereafter only for feeding.

The two doctors constructed a simple experiment in which the control group followed this standard procedure. In the experimental group, however, the baby was given naked to the mother for an hour after birth and then for five hours a day for the next three days.

Follow-up studies done when the babies reached one month of age showed that mothers in the experimental group were more attentive to their babies, less likely to leave them with another caretaker, more soothing when they fed the babies, and more likely to look at them in the *en face* position (with the mother's and the baby's face in the same vertical plane of rotation).

When the children were two, several mother-child dyads were studied. The researchers were intrigued by the discovery that mothers who had had increased contact with their babies for that brief period around the time of birth had a measurably different way of relating to their children. They gave fewer commands and instead asked more questions, a style of interacting that helps children to develop greater skill in handling decisions independently.[15] Even more intriguing was a five-year follow-up that showed higher IQs and better language skills in children who had received just a bit of extra attention in the newborn period.[16]

Subsequent experiments in different areas of the world by other researchers have tended to support the notion that early contact is beneficial, good for the mother, the baby—and the pediatrician. Babies who experience early contact are less apt to suffer from infectious disease in infancy, are breast-fed longer, and are more intellectually able. Some of the studies have shown that even a few minutes of early contact produce significant effects!

WHAT ABOUT FATHERS?

Until recently, little attention was paid to the needs of fathers, and they were routinely excluded from childbirth. Our culture has assigned them a secondary role in child care, and that role remained unexamined until the women's movement began to ask some basic questions about family life.

Why, for instance, is it only women who become intensely involved with their new infants? Why not men? In fact, researchers have discovered that when men spend time with their newborns, holding, examining, and interacting with them, the new fathers begin the process of bonding just as new mothers do, and the experience has long-lasting consequences. In addition, researchers demonstrated that even a very limited amount of contact produced beneficial long-term results. A father who undressed his newborn twice and logged one hour of eye contact during the first three days of life was more likely to take care of his child after leaving the hospital.[17]

The notion that men cannot be expected to take much of an interest in their new babies may be more a cultural than a natural phenomenon. One study of fathers' responses to their new babies described powerful reactions. Fathers thought their babies were "perfect," felt elated, and reported an increased sense of self-esteem.[18] Bonding is a parental, not just a maternal, process.

IT'S A FLEXIBLE PHENOMENON

During the past decade, research on the importance of early attachment has created confusion about a process that merely needs to be allowed to occur. Bonding is not the latest chic thing to do; it's as old as the human race. When, at some hospitals, mothers in labor are asked whether or not they "want bonding," as though it were an item on a menu, they are not being offered a reasonable choice. What the research offers is a scientific endorsement for what new parents are demanding from medical institutions: support, noninterference, and the encouragement of autonomy.

Writer Roberta Israeloff captures the intensity and complexity of this first phase of attachment:

> That I responded to him as quickly and thoroughly as I did, that his call roused me as urgently as it did, was surely a form of love. It simply wasn't a type of love with which I was acquainted. This was a love on a cellular, biological level. Intimacy, I began to understand, is rooted in the corporal. It has to do with the distance between bodies. None separated mine from my son's. We had both been swallowed by the cave I used to fashion for myself under the covers, that safe, familiar space which traps the odor of your own body—milk, blood, tears, sweat all mingling. This wasn't the romantic intimacy between adults, but an earthbound, often tedious kind, which is undertaken, no questions asked.[19]

She then goes on to explore her ambivalence during the process of bonding and questions the wholly positive experiences her friends and relatives report. For her part, she feels a deep connection to her son and, at the same time, a sense of being burdened by his dependency. For parents who are less aware or less willing to acknowledge their conflicted feelings, the resultant guilt over resenting one's own baby may lead to an overreaction, producing overprotection or overattentiveness.

The mystique of the "bonded" childbirth experience has led to some disappointed expectations. Instead of the joyous "natural" childbirths they'd been learning about in Lamaze class, many women have had long and wearying labors, cesarean sections, and sick babies. Many have mourned the loss of a much heralded "peak experience" and worried about their supposed failure to "get bonded" in some stylized and predictable manner. And, as we have seen, some new parents who feel disappointed may become unhealthily involved with their child in an attempt to make up for what they perceive as their failure.

Attachment is such a powerful phenomenon and occurs as a result of so many interplaying forces that we suspect it can occur through steel doors and across long distances. Witness adoptive parents who take children of all ages into their homes and hearts. Devoted and adaptable parents can overcome odds and attach in the face of illness, separation, catastrophes of all kinds.

> Lola and her husband, Ian, are horrified to learn that their apparently healthy eight-pound son is suffering from respiratory distress. Lola cries; Ian holds her hand. Together they peer through the nursery window where their little baby must be kept in an isolette under special lights. Lola longs to hold him, while Ian desperately wills him to be well. Their son, dear at birth, is even dearer now that his health and life are threatened. As they watch him sleep, they imagine that he looks pinker, healthier.

A strong bond with the parent prepares the way for future emotional and intellectual development. Before children can begin the struggle to define themselves as individuals, they need to experience a period of unconditional love and acceptance. We think it's important to understand that it is the very strength and security of the parent-child bond that allows for the necessary steps of separation.

Because this book concerns itself with the dangers of overattachment and the inability to let the child go, parents need to remember that *attachment can exist apart from the particular behavior of the moment.* Many of us can talk intimately with a friend we may not have seen for a year. Even though we haven't been in touch, the bond is still there.

When it comes to our close family relationships, it is natural that there are times when we can comfortably tolerate separation and that there are other times when we "can't get enough of each other" and seek proximity at every turn.

Looking at attachment behavior in children, we find that it is heightened during situations perceived as threatening. When children sense a separation—and that separation might be caused by distance or even by the diversion of attention—they cling. Watch what happens during telephone calls. As the parent becomes more engrossed in conversation, younger children step up their requests for juice while older children may ask for help with homework or attempt to provoke a dialogue on the relevance of sex education in public schools. Then watch what happens when the parent hangs up and wants to spend time talking to the child. Suddenly, television or the great outdoors beckons.

This kind of behavior is normal, but Too Precious Parents may draw the guilty conclusion that their child's clinging and nagging show that they have done something wrong, that they haven't been loving or attentive enough, and that the separation was all a terrible mistake, never to be repeated again. A healthier way to view this behavior is simply to realize that attachment has gone well because the child is showing visible signs of a bond with the parents.

Indeed, although being securely attached facilitates exploration, being too attached interferes with exploratory activities. A confident, playful baby will venture in ever-increasing circles of exploration away from its mother, but an anxious baby will not venture forth or will only explore in fits and starts.

NOW THAT I'VE GOT THEM, HOW DO I GET RID OF THEM?

Babies are skilled at getting us to approach them, but how do they tell us when they've had enough? Parents may learn the cues that say, "Pick me up" more readily than the ones that say, "Put me down and let me be." It's very important for parents to become attuned to the behavior that says, "I'm tired" or "I'm overloaded."

New parents determined to be perfectly loving and perfectly attentive may have a hard time realizing that their baby is trying to give them a message. The crying and fussing make them feel like failures, and so they redouble their efforts to soothe, rock, walk, or nurse the baby into silence.

Roberta Israeloff offers her first-person account of how burdensome this approach can be. Terribly fatigued and still feeling uncomfortable in her new role, she meets a Lamaze-class acquaintance on the street, who is "wearing makeup and a dress." Israeloff is intrigued. "I was in maternity pants and David's stained down jacket and was unable to recall the last time I had seriously looked in a mirror." The acquaintance reveals her secret discovery: you can, on occasion, let the baby cry.[20]

In fact, some babies need to cry in order to get to sleep, and there is nothing to do except to *stop* doing. Contemporary experts have seen the pendulum swing from always letting babies cry (otherwise you're spoiling them) to never letting them cry (you'll inflict deep psychological damage). Nowadays, parents can turn to a good child-care book for sound and balanced advice on when to soothe and pay attention and when not to interfere.

Parents who have exhausted their repertoire of tricks—burping, changing diapers, soothing, singing, rocking, and walking—may notice that their child has predictable periods of fussing and crying. In *Dr. Spock's Baby and Child Care*, authors Spock and Rothenberg suggest that mothers and fathers pay attention to those particular patterns and needs. Some babies, they observe, are susceptible to rocking in a bassinet or crib and may be helped during stressful periods by being walked or rocked in a rocking chair. They suggest that a child who has been fed and is crying at the end of a wakeful period be put to bed. "Let her cry for 15 to 30 minutes if she has to. Some babies fall asleep faster if left in the crib, and this is the method to strive for in the long run."[21]

In *Infants and Mothers*, T. Berry Brazelton also stresses the infant's need to release tension: "Some infants need to cry themselves to sleep; for them, crying is the last evidence of disintegration before sleep can be achieved. These patterns are of great importance, and one sees this behavior repeated in the middle of the night when an infant comes up to semi-consciousness and must get himself back down to deeper sleep again."[22]

Parents need to adapt their demands to their baby's state and to discover when to offer stimulation and attention and when to taper off. Usually, the signs are fairly obvious once you realize what they are. Babies who need peace and quiet start to fuss, cry, turn away, or just fall asleep. Later, they get away by getting away—by crawling, walking, even running. (Still later, they get away by borrowing the family car or getting a car of their own.) These are the early roots of the separation process to which we will be referring again and again. This is a rehearsal for the big plays that are to follow. Most parents quickly get the message.

The seeds of separation are here in these first encounters, and one useful way to prepare the soil for a healthy process of separation is to pay close attention to early signs of individuality. The more parents can appreciate their child's particular nature, the more they will be able to nurture its own unfolding—and the less likely they will be to push for preconceived parental agendas.

BABIES ARE DIFFERENT RIGHT FROM THE START

When a highly respected professor of psychology had her second child, her graduate students noted her every move. She was the kind of teacher who was involved with her students, taking them out for coffee or inviting them to her house frequently. Now she withdrew for a while into her family. She never brought the baby to campus, and requests to visit the newborn at home were gently deflected. She seemed to shelter and protect her new child from any contact with the world for several months. One of her students who was about to be a father approached her one day with a big question. Was this sheltering absolutely necessary, he asked, or did she think it might be all right occasionally to expose an infant to new faces? "Why of course it would be all right," answered the professor. "But you've never brought your new baby anywhere," he replied. "Wouldn't this go against your theory?" The professor was surprised. "What theory?" she responded. "I used to take my daughter Katie to class during her first few months, and she slept like a log. Mark is the kind of baby who needs to take things slowly."

What this psychologist did next was to lend her student a book that we think would be helpful to any new parent. It is called *Your Child Is a Person* by Stella Chess, Alexander Thomas, and Herbert G. Birch, and is a study of the psychological development of a group of 231 children from infancy onwards, and an examination of the interplay between the child's "givens" and the parents' expectations and personalities.[23]

Many factors interact with an infant's basic temperament: among these are parental fatigue, the presence or absence of siblings, the state of the family finances, and illness. One crucial factor is the "goodness of fit," the way an infant's temperament meshes with parental wishes. "Fit" can be good, bad, or in-between. Even a seemingly "good" (i.e., easygoing) temperament may be a bad fit for a given family because they are looking for a baby with more independence, more "feistiness," more challenge.

Here are four different babies, with brief descriptions of their family environments.

Zachary was an active, restless, irritable baby. His hardworking young parents, both executives with demanding jobs, found it difficult to respond to him when they came home from work exhausted and found him fussing. They were dismayed because they had been sure that babies slept most of the time. Zachary, however, was usually awake.

Gerry Lee was a quiet, undemanding baby. Her parents were tired and overwhelmed when she was born and were relieved that she wasn't the kind of "difficult" baby her brother and two sisters had been. She didn't cry much, fuss much, or ask for much. By six months of age she weighed only ten pounds and was hospitalized for "failure to thrive."

When Barry and Leslie had a baby girl, they were thrilled: they imagined her wrapped in pastels and softness. But Anna was fussy, never seemed satisfied, tolerated almost anything new very poorly, and cried at the drop of a hat. She would wake frequently throughout the night and take a long time to quiet down. Their pediatrician said it was just "colic" and nothing to worry about. Leslie tried not to regard motherhood as a big disappointment. Barry just felt tired.

The boys were in grade school when Felicia was born. Her parents were less than thrilled when the pregnancy was confirmed. They weren't sure they wanted to be new parents again, especially now that they were heavily involved in soccer league and school activities with their sons. But Felicia . . . ah! She was so special, so mellow, so sweet, so easy! Everyone wanted to hold her and play with her. She was so different from her boisterous older brothers.

From the moment a baby is born, parents can become alert to his or her characteristic ways of responding to the world. To give you some idea of what we're talking about, we'll use the methods described by researchers Chess and Thomas to take you through a kind of "temperament analysis."[24]

1. *Activity level.* Does the baby lie still or twist and squirm?

> *Zachary was active night and day, a chore to keep up with from the beginning. He kicked in the nursery, he stood up and ran rather than walked. He seemed never to be still.*

> *Gerry Lee, by contrast was so quiet, so inactive that she seemed "lazy" to her parents.*

2. *Rhythmicity (regularity).* Some babies develop their own schedule; others are far more unpredictable.

> *Anna exhausted her parents, and they were always on the alert. Long after other babies slept through the night, Anna was still waking and crying to be picked up.*

3. *Approach or withdrawal.* What is your child's first response to something new?

> *As a baby, Zachary fussed every time a new food was introduced. He protested whenever he was given a new toy. Later he would continue this pattern of protesting every time some new situation came up, whether it was going to play group or to the Grand Canyon.*

Felicia greeted each new event and person and stuffed animal with glee! She was a delight to buy presents for and such fun to take places.

4. ***Adaptability.*** How difficult is it to change an established routine? Can your child learn to accept changes in his or her environment?

Anna kicked up a fuss when her parents moved her into the nursery they had been readying for months. She finally calmed down when she was moved back into the little crib in her parents' room.

5. ***Threshold of responsiveness.*** Some babies startle easily; others take loud noises or bright lights much more easily. Some babies will accept being wet, and others won't.

Felicia's family gave a New Year's Eve party, and she fell asleep in her godfather's arms. She stayed asleep through the party, not even waking when the group sang a noisy version of "Auld Lang Syne."

6. ***Intensity of reaction.*** How energetic is your child's response, either positive or negative?

Once Zachary was awakened, he was a terror, screaming loudly for hours.

Felicia woke up gradually and greeted her parents with a cheerful smile.

7. ***Quality of mood.*** What percentage of the time is your baby pleasant, joyful, or showing friendly behav-

ior compared with the amount spent in unfriendly behavior or crying?

*Gerry Lee seemed often to be "in between," neither
happy nor sad, neither pleased nor upset. She was
friendly enough, but it took her a while to respond.*

8. ***Distractibility.*** How easy or difficult is it to alter your
   baby's behavior?

   *Zachary couldn't nurse if there were conversations
   going on. His mother liked to listen to music on the public radio station, but if an announcer came on or the
   sound level changed, Zachary stopped nursing and
   began to fret.*

9. ***Attention span and persistence.*** How long will your baby
   try to reach a toy that is out of reach? How hard
   will he or she try to resist something undesirable,
   such as nail-trimming or face-washing.

   *Gerry Lee was quiet, but she would keep playing for
   hours, it seemed, with the pots and pans under the sink.
   Her persistence even in the face of apparent overwhelming distractions was one of her most notable traits.*

The kinds of behavior we've pointed out are responses that parents can observe in their own infants and
children. By making note of many of these bits of behavior, parents can see patterns that will help explain what
may seem like puzzling or disturbing reactions.

If, for example, parents observe that their baby
characteristically withdraws in new situations, they may be

less upset when that same child takes a bit longer than his or her peers to make the transition from grade school to junior high school. How parents respond to their child's particular nature may make a big difference in the way that child learns to cope with it.

Zachary, now ten years old, was born to parents who value structured schedules and organized lives. He always seemed "out of synch" with them. He would never maintain a schedule, never wanted to enter into a new situation, and once there, protested leaving. His parents labeled him "difficult" right from the start, and his subsequent problems with school have confirmed their worst fears. They have not succeeded in adjusting their vision of how they wanted him to be and are therefore unable to be very effective in finding ways to help him. Gerry Lee's parents were financially and emotionally overburdened, and though they found her undemanding nature somewhat uninteresting, it was also a relief. They didn't have much in the way of time or extra energy to give her. Gerry Lee didn't learn to assert herself and sometimes got left out or left behind. Anna's parents struggled through her difficult early childhood. They certainly would have preferred a more even-tempered child, but as she grew older, they began to enjoy her friendliness and fostered her outgoing nature by including playmates for Anna in their family plans. Felicia's parents, both of them high-energy outgoing types, were first puzzled, then delighted, by their easygoing, relaxed daughter.

For potential Too Precious Parents, the Chess, Thomas, and Birch study offers a timely warning: don't expect to mold your child to preconceived patterns. You may have dreamed your child would be like friendly, outgoing Felicia, but if what you've got is a sensitive, hyper-alert Zachary, you need to try to foster his strengths, not deplore his weaknesses.

In our experience, as parents become more aware of their children's innate differences of temperament, they may feel a great sense of relief, particularly if they have a child whom they find difficult. Said one mother in surprise, "You mean it's not us? I thought Danny was fearful because we were terrible parents." Now, instead of devoting their every waking moment to the boy's needs, she and her husband accept the fact that his negative, fearful approach to new situations is not their fault, and look for ways to make transitions easier.

WHEN THE ADORED STOPS BEING ADORABLE

While some parents don't need a psychological study to alert them to early differences, others remain so enmeshed with their pride and joy that they fail to realize during the attachment honeymoon that there are boundaries between adoring parent and adorable child. Sooner or later, though, the scales fall from the parental eyes. Between infancy and adolescence, something happens both to us and to our children.

Although new parents may eagerly share anecdotes, pictures, and tales of the exploits of their infants and toddlers with almost anyone who will look and listen, rarely do those same parents thrust the latest snapshots of their adolescents at friends and acquaintances. Or, as a corollary, how many couples have been known to say, "Oh, honey, why don't we get married and have us a teenager?" From a time when we think we couldn't live a day without them, we come to a point when we would gladly matriculate them, marry them off, or fund them on a long expedition.

> *Leonard and Gina realize with mixed emotions that their sweet little infant is growing up fast. Troy scoots around the floor, picking up fuzzies along the way. He goes from room to room, scrambling back to his mother from time to time. Gina remembers how he used to gaze adoringly up at her as he nursed. Now she feels a twinge of sadness as he pulls away from her breast to watch the dog eat and the boy next door mow his lawn. She thinks he's precious, but he doesn't seem to need her as much as he used to.*

What we're looking at here is this first period of transition in the lives of parents and children. Troy is doing what healthy children do. He's turning outward, toward the world, actively seeking an end to his adorable/precious/helpless/dependent stage. He's on the threshold of a new phase, and with each passing month and year he will work to find a more realistic appraisal of his place in the world. He will move beyond the warmth and safety of home to the excitement of "the great beyond."

As parents, our job is to progressively relinquish our biased in-love view of our offspring and watch with approval as that flawless and angelic creation, with his tiny perfect fingers and toes, becomes a real human child who throws food on the floor, whines, shouts, runs away. We must remember that in the process of letting go, we continue to offer our support and encouragement—with an awareness that this is not a linear process but rather more like a dance with steps that sometimes advance and sometimes retreat. Like most adventures, the one of being a parent is often scary, and our feelings are frequently ambivalent. The process may be painful, for we may have to revise daydreams of what our child will be, or how natural and easy it is to be a parent.

> *Karen and Paul conceived their child in love and felt that she was special and blessed. From the time that Allison was born, they tried to make her world perfect. Only natural fibers, wool and cotton, were allowed to touch her perfect skin. They played her baroque music and hung her room with crystals that shattered the light into rainbows. She was to be raised with sensitivity and tenderness. Someday, they thought, she would be a creative person, drawn to beauty.*

Allison, however, didn't share their ambitions. When she first began to walk, she sought out not the light but all those interesting things that toddlers seek: cigarette butts, dog food, dirty socks. Her parents felt they had failed and wondered who could help them understand what had gone wrong.

SIGMUND FREUD, ANNA FREUD, AND MARGARET MAHLER: THREE WISE ELDERS

Where do today's parents, struggling with their own fears, turn for insight and encouragement as they strive to help their children begin the long, arduous journey to independence? Time was, they would have turned to their parents or, better yet, their wise old grandparents. But Karen's and Steven's elders, like those of so many couples, are not available. Her mother lives in a condo in Boca Raton and plays bridge; his parents bask in the desert sun in Arizona.

Lacking our own elders, who can guide us as we seek a deeper understanding of our children? When we hit bad patches in our relationships with them, who can reassure us? We do have sources of wisdom to whom we can go for instruction as we go about the task of raising our precious young—the great psychologists, educators, and psychiatrists who have devoted their lives to studying the ways in which children move from infancy to adulthood, from adored to not-so-adorable, from protected to independent.

SIGMUND FREUD BRINGS CHILDHOOD OUT OF THE GARDEN OF INNOCENCE

Nicky is Janet and Will's first son. Will had worked long hours at his law firm when his two daughters were infants. Now that he had an easier schedule, he was eager to help take care of his youngest child. In truth, the whole family was enthralled, and they became accomplished baby-watchers, staring intently at Nicky in his bath, Nicky as he drank his bottle, as he slept, when he soiled. They were all struck with the intense pleasure he had at just being. As he grew older, they all watched with fascination as he discovered the different parts of his body: his mouth, his hands, his penis, his muscles. He loved to be touched, except when he didn't want to be. It was obvious to all that Nicky was a pretty complex guy.

Eventually, though, baby-watching became less beguiling. The first to lose interest was his six-year-old sister; his nine-year-old sister soon followed suit. "Mommy, he doesn't do very much. He's just boring," they complained. Later, even his devoted parents wearied of delighting in his every burp and bowel movement. They were distinctly *not* delighted when he managed to smear the contents of his diaper all over his crib. In fact, they were shocked and upset with themselves that they could feel so repelled.

In an earlier time, these parents might not have simply wrinkled up their noses as they scrubbed Nicky and the crib he had so joyfully ornamented, but Janet and Will were aware that this behavior is quite natural for a child of this age.

Until Sigmund Freud began to explore the unconscious and to fashion his revolutionary theories about human nature and human development, parents had very little to guide them except their own reactions. And those reactions, based on unconscious needs and fears, were often unhelpful or emotionally damaging.

In Freud's view, Troy and Allison and Nicky are responding normally to internal urges, and their behavior is prompted by biological instincts that propel all human beings toward seeking satisfaction. Thus, Troy's drive toward maturation is just about unstoppable. At first, his pleasure in nursing was so great that it superseded all else. But as he becomes a toddler and can begin to move around, the pleasure of locomotion is so wonderful that it preempts everything save the hunger drive that preceded it.

Allison, he would explain, is at a stage in her life when putting things in her mouth is her major mode for experiencing the world. Nicky, he would add, like all children of his age, is fascinated by his bowel movement and sees no reason not to play with it.

To those Too Precious Parents who are disinclined to set any limits on a child's behavior, he might point out that theirs is the job of communicating to their children the attitudes of the culture at large. Allison and Nicky must learn that it is not socially acceptable to eat cigarette butts or to smear feces.

ANNA FREUD: THE DAUGHTER ILLUMINATES THE FATHER'S WORK

The famous daughter of a famous father, Anna Freud elaborated and expanded on her father's work. But rather than deriving information about childhood from adult patients, she based her theories of child development on her direct observation of children. Her work can help us to make sense of what might seem ordinary pieces of behavior—whether we find them cute or exasperating—by showing us how what we think of as mundane moments of child-rearing may actually be key events in human growth.

When little Corey takes one sip of her beloved chocolate milk, then pours the contents of the cup onto the freshly washed floor, her parents may scream, or laugh, or threaten never to give her chocolate milk again. But, thanks to Anna Freud, they may now realize that their daughter's act was neither defiant nor comical, but that it resulted from Corey's developing curiosity about cause and effect.

Anna Freud posted a series of signposts along some

half dozen developmental tracks and described in each of her categories a range of behavior from immaturity to maturity. Using her concepts, we can show how some parents interfere, with overprotection or overindulgence, while others help their children's progress toward greater self-mastery.

From Dependency to Emotional Self-Reliance and Adult Relationships

With amazement, his parents listen as David seems to be talking to himself. His chatter gets softer; there are brief interludes of quiet, and then...silence. Unbelievable! Their one-year-old son has put himself to sleep. For one painful moment, David's mother realizes that he doesn't need her to soothe him any longer.

Four-year-old Sheppard's mother has always enjoyed taking care of her youngest son. What a surprise when one day he refuses to allow her to wipe his nose. "Hey, it's my nose," says Sheppard. Obvious as that statement is, it reminded them both that he had certain responsibilities and was ready to handle them.

From Suckling to Rational Eating

Bridget loved her bottle, but she was also eager to start on solid food. Now, as a toddler, she'll eat anything that can conceivably fit into her mouth. At this stage, her parents put locks on the cabinets and maintain a state of eternal vigilance for small, easily swallowed objects.

Stephanie has always been a fussy eater. From an early age, mealtimes were tense and exhausting. Mom urged her to eat vegetables, whole grain bread, organ meats; she worried when Stephanie picked at her food. As an adolescent, Stephanie has developed anorexia nervosa.

From Wetting and Soiling to Bladder and Bowel Control

Shaun's big day has arrived. He's three years old, and he's graduated to big-boy pants. He proudly shows them to anyone who will look.

Rachel was trained at age three, but began soiling when she started kindergarten. Her parents feel she's under too much pressure and decide to keep her home a year and start her in kindergarten later.

From Irresponsibility to Responsibility in Body Management

Olivia is bright and energetic. She's learned to ride her trike after lots of scrapes and spills. She's ridden into the "big road" once, but her mother taught her to stay within bounds. Now she slows down, then turns around when she approaches the street.

First Drew learned to take off his socks. With delight, he learned to take his clothes off, and, later, to put them on. By the time he started kindergarten, he was able to dress himself, but he still likes his mom to pick out his clothes for school.

From the Body to the Toy and from Play to Work

Nika's thumb and fist were for a long time the most soothing things around, next to her bottle. Gradually her

Busy Box and the pile of toys in her room became interesting to her. Now she enjoys playing by herself or with her friends. In school, she's able to do her work well and keep her attention on the task at hand.

From Egocentricity to Companionship

Neal loved to play in his crib and be held by his mother when he was hungry or unhappy. As he grew and developed, he liked to play near Mom's feet and then to play in a toddler group. These days, he seems to be totally immersed in his friendships with others. He rushes in from school to ask if he can go outside and play with his friends.

Anna Freud is an important resource in understanding human development as a *continuum*, in which one must reach point A before going on to point B. Before a child can walk, he or she must learn to crawl. Obvious? Maybe, but it wasn't so long ago that mental-health experts and educators used chronological age as the most important indicator in evaluating the state of a child's development. For example, until relatively recently, it was commonly assumed that if a child reached the age of six, he or she was automatically ready to begin reading.

Some Too Precious Parents may want to suspend their children in a cocoon of safety; others may attempt to push them to emotional or intellectual feats beyond their abilities. But by using Anna Freud's vision of child development as a continuum through which individuals proceed at their own pace, parents may find it easier to allow their children to develop naturally, rather than to retard what must come next or force what is yet to come.[25]

MAHLER: THE PSYCHOLOGICAL BIRTH OF THE HUMAN INFANT

The work of the Freuds helped to map out the grand design of human development, but to explore the task of separation—the central issue of our book—we need the help of that extraordinarily insightful child psychoanalyst Margaret Mahler, who became fascinated by the process of individuation that begins when an infant is about four or five months old and continues to somewhere between two and a half to three years of age. During this period, children learn that their bodies and selves are separate from their parents. How parents handle this phase is extremely important, and will reverberate throughout the lives of their children. Mahler's observations on this key transition bear directly on the plight of many of our Too Precious Children as they and their parents flounder through difficult terrain and sometimes become stuck.

Joshua was long-awaited by his parents, Carolyn and Bill. He was the only son of an only son. Both sets of grandparents flew to see him twice in his first three months. When Joshua was eight months old, Carolyn's parents returned. Joshua refused to even look at them or allow them to hold him. He would scream in terror whenever they approached. And he would cling intensely to Carolyn, who in turn was mortified at Joshua's behavior. She felt apologetic and wondered if Joshua might be spoiled. When her parents weren't around, Joshua seemed to ignore her and spent his time exploring the house, crawling from room to room, down hallways and even into the closets. Carolyn began to feel like a rotten mother with a rotten kid. Bill would come home from work and wonder why Carolyn was so tired and the baby so irritable.

Molly's parents were grateful she was such a sweet baby; she adapted to almost any change in her environment. But when Molly began going to day care, she would cry painfully every morning when her mother dropped her off. When Mom, filled with love and yearning for her adorable child, would come to pick Molly up in the evening, she got the cold shoulder; Molly was aloof and disinterested. Her parents were worried. Their sweet little baby seemed so different, so unlike herself.

All parents go through these experiences, with varying degrees of ease or pain. What Margaret Mahler offers us is a keen and sympathetic vision of how common and how necessary they are.[26]

She begins by differentiating *biological* birth ("a dramatic, observable and well-circumscribed event") from *psychological* birth ("a slowly unfolding intrapsychic process"), during which the baby begins to experience its own separateness from the mother. Next, she envisions this gradual birth of the individual human being as a process that is subtle, mysterious, and sometimes frustrating to child and parent alike. In a sense, the newborn baby is like a precious egg that the mother "hatches." As we have seen, "preciousness" appears to be a built-in survival tactic, a genetic plan to get us to fall in love with our babies so that they will be cared for and will survive.

Mahler's terms for the initial phases of a newborn's life are "the normal autistic phase" and the "normal symbiotic phase." Both of these phases are precursors to separation. At first, her seeming disregard for the newborn period and the first few months of life seem puzzling. We know that babies do a great deal more than just vegetate!

What her phraseology and focus tell us is that the earliest phases of life may in some sense be most important for parents, while the later phases are more important to the baby. As Mahler points out:

> Separation and individuation are conceived of as two complementary developments: separation consists of the child's emergence from a symbiotic fusion with the mother...and individuation consists of those achievements marking the child's assumption of his own individual characteristics. These are intertwined, but not identical developmental processes; they may proceed divergently with a developmental lag or precocity in one or the other.[27]

Mahler divides the separation process into four subphases, each with its own tasks. There are no set ages at which each subphase begins and ends.

1. *Differentiation and the development of the body image.* This is the phase of "hatching," marked by a certain new look of alertness, persistence and goal-directedness that appears at about four months. At about eight months, some, but not all, babies begin to show marked signs of "stranger anxiety." Joshua clings to his mother and won't go to his grandparents. He doesn't necessarily perceive them as strangers, but they are certainly "not-mother" and consequently scary.

    A second behavioral change that appears during this phase is the need for a "transitional object," a special something (often a baby blanket or stuffed animal) that serves as a bridge between being totally dependent and being independent, between the world of the mother and the world of the child.

Cassie had been easy to put to bed until recently, but now she refuses to sleep without the blue plaid quilt her grandma gave her. This quilt has become such a cherished object that it even has its own name, "Wiltie." Whenever someone new—especially a baby-sitter—comes over, Cassie's Wiltie is in her arms. At nap time, she falls asleep on the sofa or under the kitchen table or sitting by her mother, with Wiltie covering her. Her parents know this is important, and even though the quilt is becoming dirty and tattered, they don't interfere.

2. **Practicing.** Now there's an endless series of moves away from the parent and back. These first forays trouble some parents, who may then interfere with the youngster or express annoyance that their precious little child would want to leave them.

Joshua starts to spend the better part of each morning running away from his mother, going out the door into the backyard. Once, he even managed to get out the gate before his mother apprehended him. She was angry and scared.

Cassie, with her Wiltie in tow, scoots around exploring her environment. Her mother has made the environment safe and fairly "childproof," although the stereo is still in territorial dispute.

3. ***Rapprochement.*** Mahler used the word *rapprochement* to label a phase during which children learn that all is not lost when they are separated from their care-givers. When parents and children come back together, the energy that existed in the relationship will be restored. This new phase appears at a time when young children realize that even though they can't see their parent right in front of their eyes, he or she is still there. (Psychologists call this "object permanence.")

Peek-a-boo is an important game now and a good way to test this new piece of learning. Children can close their eyes and open them and, sure enough, Mommy or Daddy is still there. During this period, there's a lot of venturing forth and running back, and for some parents it is an especially trying time.

Now Cassie runs away, then just as readily comes back. If her mother wants to go do chores, Cassie protests. She's happiest when her mother stays put. When her mother sighs and sits down, Cassie wanders away. Her mother begins to wonder why she wanted so desperately to become a parent. When her husband comes home, he finds the house a mess and wonders what his wife has been doing all day.

Molly really gets a test for her "object permanence" when she goes to the Day Care Center. She doesn't see her mother all day. She plays the same games that Cassie does, but instead of Mom, it's Mrs. Anderson, the Director of her day care center, that Molly darts away from. Mrs. Anderson is sensitive to the developmental impor-

tance of Molly's behavior, so she pats her each time she returns, many many times a day.

4. *Consolidation of individuality.* At this stage, children develop a sense that they have an existence separate from their parents and can sustain a sense of their own identity when they are left alone for a while.

     Cassie can spend time now—still with Wiltie by her side—out of eyesight of her mother. She frequently keeps a patter going between her mother and herself, somewhat like a radar with its blips and bleeps keeping the mother ship in contact.

     Joshua will stay by himself in another room for a few minutes, sometimes in his playpen, sometimes out, without going on a frantic search for his mother.

     Molly gradually gets less tearful when she's left for the day and begins to greet her parents with joy when they come to pick her up in the evening.

In these four subphases, we've watched Molly and Joshua and Cassie give birth to themselves as separate individuals. In order to do that, they must move away from their parents and put an end to the fused ecstatic precious state of infancy. Parents who delighted in the intimacy of caring for a newborn now need to find ways to take pleasure in signs of separateness and independence as they watch their babies grow into *people*, with sometimes very fierce convictions about what they should be able to do and when they want to do it.

The constant theme as we study the experts on child

development is their insistence on an inner timetable for emotional maturation that must be respected and allowed to unfold according to its own design. When parents are attuned to their children's changing needs, their children will have a far easier time as they face the demands both of their inner and outer worlds. As that innate timetable pushes them to seek greater mastery, their parents offer support without demanding a return to complete dependence. As we go on to explore the specific problems of Too Precious Children, we'll see that at the root of Too Preciousness is the inability of parents to give up the closeness and fusion of attachment and become the guides and protectors of their children's journey to independence.

CHAPTER FIVE
The Vows of Love

The Too Precious Child is surrounded by an all-confining parental love that interferes with his or her ability to adapt to the demands and relationships of the outer world. Individual growth is suffocated by a blanket of overconcern. And, yet, how are parents to know how much love is enough and how much is too much? How is it possible to have a meter running on love?

As parents, we struggle to master our role in each new phase of child development, and the last thing we want to do is to create difficulties for our beloved children. Most of us set out to be good, and maybe even great, parents—but in our efforts in this direction, we may sometimes overshoot the mark.

When we first thought about having a child, how many of us imagined the conflict we would come to feel? How, for example, we might want to throttle the little creature for whom we would gladly sacrifice our lives.

Most of us, instead, vowed that we would love our children (more than we had been loved), and promised ourselves and our future progeny that we would be wonderful, caring parents. Many of our pledges echoed a central theme: we would be sure not to repeat the mistakes of our parents. We would, instead, be consistent, generous, patient, and would *truly love our children*. The vows we made probably went something like this:

1. I will never spank my child.
2. I will never yell at my children.
3. I will always be consistent.
4. If they want it, then they need it, and they shall have it.
5. I will never say no.
6. I will always attend to my children whenever they need me.
7. My children will lack for nothing.
8. My children's needs will always come first.
9. We will never quarrel or disagree in front of the children.
10. I will always be patient and persevering.

Notice how the promises we made have the same refrains: "always" and "never." The old saw goes that *always* and *never* are never always true. If your children are two or older, how many of these vows have you already broken? As any experienced and honest parent knows, such promises may sound nice but are impossible to live up to.

Many of us began to decide what we were going to do as parents while we were still children ourselves— often, still stinging from a rebuff or a denial or a scolding, we would run to our rooms to get away from our depriving and mean parents and make promises to our future children. We thought we meant very sincerely what we vowed, but, in truth, none of us knew what we were talking about. We committed ourselves to a path as parents before parenthood was a reality.

The inevitable day comes when the vow is broken.

There is a terrific disappointment and sense of failure. We were never going to yell; now we find ourselves thundering at our children to clean their rooms and threatening them with lifetime grounding if it isn't done now, on the double.

What a nightmare! We've gone beyond identifying with the aggressor; we've *become* the aggressor.

> *Lauren was surprised by her feelings the morning four-year-old Jeb defiantly dumped his paints on the kitchen floor, then stubbornly refused to help clean up. She was furious with Jeb, not so much for the paint trick but for bringing her face to face with her parental shortcomings. How could that loud, angry voice be hers? She'd promised herself never to yell at her child. Overwhelmed by this unflattering glimpse of herself, Lauren couldn't shake a lingering annoyance all day, and her son responded with unusually grouchy and clingy behavior.*

Pediatrician T. Berry Brazelton, points out the ambivalence parents feel as they begin to perform the difficult balancing act that raising young children requires.

> It is a valuable and even crucial time. It may also be a painful one. But if parents can see it as a vital bridge to the next set of achievements, and not just an assault on them by a miserable child—it may be easier for them to participate with pleasure as well as pain.[1]

These moments of crisis when we experience the distance between our expectation ("I will never be angry") and reality ("This child is driving me nuts") are important. The greater our commitment to being perfect parents of perfect children, the greater the danger that when the dream is threatened, we will fall to blaming someone else. Our parents used to be the "meanies"; now we'll attach the label to our kids.

Parents and children often view these situations as dramas of blame. He said this; you did that. You failed to respect his dignity. She invaded your turf. They yelled first. The problem with this world view is that it oversimplifies the complex interplay of family life.

> *Freddy and his mother were both really stubborn. She would say "do" and he would say "no." An explosion was inevitable and invariable. One day, Freddy cracked a joke in the middle of one of their arguments. They both started to laugh—and they stopped fighting. Freddy quickly learned how useful humor could be. Freddy's mom was amused by his new tactics, and encouraged them. As the tension lessened, mother and son began to enjoy each other more.*

By focusing on whom to blame in a given situation, we may fail to consider the contributions of our child's temperament, our own temperament, standards and level of patience, our spouse's reactions, and all the interactions that occur for good or ill, for pleasure or for pain in the context of any reciprocal relationship.

Plans, goals, formulas, and ambitions decided on in advance of a child's arrival can create a thorny dilemma. It's hard to give up a dream of how it's all supposed to be. Faced with a real and very individual young human being who had no part in our elaborate planning process, we suddenly realize we've neglected to get informed consent. Now our choice is to abandon our cherished vows, however reluctantly or angrily or sheepishly—or abandon our child. By and large, vows and children don't mingle well.

> *Everett valued independence and couldn't bear whiny, clinging children. He vowed that his infant son, Mark, was going to be brave and self-assertive. Maybe a major-league ballplayer. But Mark turned out to be a shy child who needed tremendous encouragement to try new things. Everett became increasingly annoyed with Mark and found himself berating the little boy for his lack of courage and initiative. Overwhelmed by his negative reactions and disapproving behavior, Everett talked about his feelings with his wife and together they explored Mark's real needs as opposed to his dad's image.*
>
> *In the months that followed, Everett began to work hard to see his son more clearly as a real person. Instead of pressuring Mark to learn to catch a ball, Everett planned relaxed outings and delighted in the wealth of details, sounds, and colors his attentive son noticed when they were out walking together. Things that Everett tended to overlook, he now began to appreciate as he looked through his child's eyes. He began to regard Mark as someone special, someone unique, someone surprising.*

In an earlier chapter, we mentioned the psychology professor who protected her newborn infant from the outside world because she was sensitive to his particular need for a quiet, predictable environment. Her students had mistakenly assumed this must be the "proper" way to raise a baby and would have begun to sequester their own more adaptable infants had one of them not asked why the professor kept visitors to a minimum. Instead of adopting formulas, we have the more challenging task of remaining open to surprise and responsive to individual needs.

VOWS REVISITED AND RETHOUGHT

Let's take another look at that list of vows with an eye to making some more-reasonable promises. This new sampler may lack the bold grandeur of certainty, but it aims to satisfy our ambition to improve on the handiwork of our parents while respecting the importance of a vital reciprocal relationship with our children. Finally, we need to respect our own very human responses to stressful situations. After all, if we expect too much of ourselves, chances are we will expect too much of our children.

Vow #1. I will never spank my child.
Revow #1. I may spank at times, but if I spank when it is inappropriate, I will try to understand myself and my child and how we "lose it" with each other.

Perhaps no disciplinary technique is as often discussed as spanking. There are some parents who seem almost pleased with the opportunity of getting in a few wallops; others proudly announce that they don't believe in spanking and then proceed to yell viciously at their children.

A slap is a great attention-getter and may be the only tool we have in dangerous situations. Its powerful tactile reminder can be used to anchor the message. Some messages that may need to be anchored include: Look before you cross the street; don't unbuckle your seat belt while the car is moving; don't put ropes around your neck; and don't stick your fingers into electrical outlets.

Beyond these limited situations, physical punishment isn't either useful or effective—and it isn't really discipline; it's an indication of the failure of discipline. When parents resort to blows, they have either lost their cool or run out of methods for teaching their children self-responsibility. Children who are routinely spanked don't learn how to behave; they learn how to avoid punishment, and they are likely to conclude that their parents don't mean what they say unless it's accompanied by spanking. This leads to more undesirable behavior, not less, and to more spanking. In addition, parents who spank feel guilty, and they may then overcompensate with presents, extra attention, special treats. Now what have their children learned?

Parents may lose their cool for any number of reasons; some have more to do with how they feel about themselves and how they were treated as children than with their child's particular misdeeds. Often, children who were spanked, even though they hated, and felt degraded by, the punishment, grow up and spank *their* children.

One reason parents may "lose it" is that they feel helpless. They really don't know what to do once they've asked or demanded that their child behave and the misbehavior continues. But there are ways, somewhere in between mayhem and capitulation, to set limits. First, we may need to realize that our children really do want to please us and that they don't want us to be angry at them. How we choose to communicate our displeasure will depend on the age of the child and the seriousness of the misbehavior.

Parents can quickly intervene to prevent a young child from doing something wrong or dangerous. If two-year-old Jack wanders too near the edge of the duck pond, pick him up, say "No," and set him down farther away. Take the nail clippers out of three-year-old Antonia's hand, tell her that the clippers are not a toy, and offer her something else to play with.

Parental perseverance and consistency pay off. If four-year-old Lainie repeatedly asks for a third helping of cake, and finally succeeds in getting one because you've run out of steam, she'll learn that bugging you pays off. She gets cake.

Of course, you need to adjust your expectations to your child's ability to behave. It may make more sense to respond briefly to a young child's request for attention than to expect there will be no interruptions at all. When you do respond, you can make it clear that you are going to return to what you were doing.

When a child is out of control, parents can say something like "What you are doing is unacceptable and you must stop doing it. If you are unable to stay here and behave properly, you can go to your room."

Most parents don't feel very good when they've lost control of their temper and hit a beloved child. To those who are overcome with remorse, we offer the reminder that their relationship with their child is shaped by thousands of interactions over the years—and there will be many opportunities to respond in an effective way.

Vow #2. I will never yell at my children.
Revow #2. I intend to learn more about myself and my children whenever I yell at them.

Yelling is seldom the best way to deal with a problem; but when we're hassled enough, we hassle back. The rising decibel level is often a pretty good indicator that parents and kids are out of control. Now's the time to ask a few questions: Could I have prevented this situation from getting out of hand? Is there something I could do next time that would prevent a similar situation from arising? How can I handle things next time in a more constructive way?

> *Billy was quite a kid—in fact, his nickname was Billy the Kid. He was up in the morning early and would fight going to sleep at night. In the hours between, he was a whirlwind of activity and mischief. His mother, Colleen, chased after him and yelled and screamed to get his attention. He ignored her. She began to spank him and found the spankings, like the yelling, increased in both severity and frequency. Like yelling, spanking also decreased in effectiveness. She couldn't get his attention once he was beyond her reach.*

Colleen was fed up with Billy for ignoring her and disgusted with her own behavior. She talked about the problem with her pediatrician, and together they worked out a plan. Colleen would focus her effort on correcting just a few of the worst behaviors and she would experiment with ways of getting Billy's attention that did not involve yelling and screaming. Much to her surprise, she discovered an instant way to command Billy's attention: whispering.

Vow #3. I will always be consistent.
Revow #3. I will try to be consistent, but I know that flexibility is also important.

When we are inconsistent about important matters, we put an unfair burden on our children. They don't know what to expect or how they are supposed to act. Discussing rules openly and clearly or putting them down on paper—making rules overt rather than covert—helps children understand what is expected of them. This process tends to begin around eighteen months of age when a child's "no" behavior meets parental "no" behavior— when a bite is met with a stern comment: "Don't do that!"

As children grow older, they can engage in progressively more complex contracts, or agreements, with one another, with teachers, and with their family.

If we expect ourselves to be consistent in every detail, we will expect the same from our children, an expectation that won't help us grow as a family. As children develop and change, we may need to reexamine the rules. Not illogically, family crises often occur when it is time for a rules revision.

In sixth grade, Wally began a pattern of coming home late from school. His parents were frustrated. Their only tool—grounding—produced compliance, but Wally was sullen and miserable. His steady defense, "All of my friends play basketball after school" was falling on deaf ears. Finally, Wally's parents, who were suspicious of the "all-of-my-friends" line of talk, decided to call his bluff. They talked to his friends' parents. Jolt of surprise. Wally was right! Now his parents had to look at two issues: one was when he got home, the other was how little input they allowed Wally into decisions about his life.

These periods of reexamination may be painful ones for parents. First, there's the acknowledgment that they were wrong (or at best not totally right) and, second, the recognition that their child is growing up.

Dean, a management consultant, felt guilty that he had so little time to spend with his fifteen-year-old son, Roy. When Dean wasn't on the road, he made careful plans for the two of them to go fishing, go to ball games, take in a movie, just father and son. Lately, though, Roy didn't seem to have any time for Dad. He was always busy, either with his school Debate Club or with friends. Matters came to a head one night when Dean, away again, tried to call home and got a busy signal for two hours. He lashed out at his son ("What if this had been an emergency?"), and was then even angrier (as well as rejected and disappointed) when Roy told him he was planning to go to the movies with his girlfriend on the evening that Dad would be returning home. Dean announced that he was going to lay down the law. "You're irresponsible, inconsiderate, and immature," he announced to his startled and unhappy son, "and to teach you a lesson I'm canceling your phone privileges for a month." When Dean came home, Roy was distant and sulky. Finally, his father confronted him with his behavior, and Roy exploded: "You don't want me to grow up and have friends and do things on my own. You think I'm still your little eight-year-old son, waiting to do anything you want."

Dean was startled by his son's passionate attack, but over the next few days he realized there was a great deal of truth to it and that he had overreacted. He wanted his little boy, not the independent young man who had begun to shave and would soon be going off to college. Dean, who had always prided himself on the fact that he meant what he said, was faced with the prospect of backing down. Management consulting was easier, he concluded, than telling your child that you'd made a mistake.

Dean faced the music, and acknowledged that taking away telephone privileges for a month was too harsh a punishment. Roy agreed that he would limit his calls to half an hour on the evenings his father was out of town. Dean then explained how much he valued the time they spent together, and the two worked out a plan based on both their schedules, not just Dad's.

We parents walk a thin line between lack of structure and rigidity. But if we don't stay open to change, then our children become frozen images in our minds, like pre-served flowers or mementos we keep to commemorate some special event. Kids aren't mementos, and they resist all our efforts to keep them static and overly precious.

Eda LeShan has pointed out that consistency in child-rearing is impossible.

> It seems to me that instead of trying to turn them-selves into machines, parents ought to set reasonable goals, try to live up to them—and then allow for the times when they can't measure up. It is good to have standards, but they must be temporized by a sprinkling of human fallibility.[2]

Vow #4. If they want it, then they need it, and they shall
    have it.
Revow #4. I will do my best to give my children what they
    need and help myself and them learn to distinguish be-
    tween "wants" and "needs."

Parents can find it difficult to distinguish between
wants and needs, and sometimes it truly is a tricky business. Children who want freedom often need limits; children who want material goods often need security and
affection. Not knowing what they really need or how to
satisfy it, they may grab at whatever comes to hand as a
"want."

An uneasy indulgence is one of the hallmarks of Too
Precious Parenthood. If we fail to give our children
everything they ask for, we are not negligent parents—although the kids can go a long way toward convincing us
of that. If they seem to be succeeding, perhaps the following observation from comedian and writer Bill Cosby will
help restore parental perspective.

> A parent quickly learns that no matter how much
> money you have, you will never be able to buy your
> kids everything they want. You can take a second mort-
> gage on your house and buy what you think is the
> entire Snoopy line: Snoopy pajamas, Snoopy under-
> pants, Snoopy linen, Snoopy shoelaces, Snoopy co-
> logne, and Snoopy soap, but you will never have it all.
> And if Snoopy doesn't send you to the poorhouse,
> Calvin Klein will direct the trip.[3]

When we're tempted to give because it's demanded,
we need to remember that to be totally adored and indulged in every whim is misleading and deceitful: it suggests to a child that he or she is all-important. It

emphasizes getting and underemphasizes giving. It leads children to expect a reward for no effort, an expectation that will not be met by the outside world.

Newborns and infants and little children by and large get gifts simply for *being*. They receive and aren't expected to give. But as they get older, they begin to acquire things through personal effort (saving their allowance for a ten-speed bicycle or doing extra chores to earn the money to pay for it). They are also increasingly expected to give: to give effort for reward, to work for money or a privilege, to give gifts as well as to receive them. Too Precious Children, on the other hand, continue throughout childhood (and often beyond) to feel entitled to things without any reciprocal obligation. And that feeling of entitlement may cause them great bitterness when they learn that the rest of the world doesn't see things through their parents' eyes.

Vow #5. I will never say no.
Revow #5. I will say no a great deal and will pledge to understand and share when appropriate—and when I want to—my reasons for saying no.

"No," is a powerful tool, but to use it well you need to understand why you're employing it. When you use "no" indiscriminately, your children may begin to ignore it. Often, sharing the reason for a prohibition is helpful and opens up a discussion. It may be that your child has more information—about how safe or inexpensive or significant something is—that might influence your decision. It may be that as your child shares his or her anger or hurt or disappointment with you, you will understand just how much the issue means.

These discussions can clear the air by allowing the participants to express what they feel, think, and want; and when parents allow this kind of interaction, they are encouraging the essence of communication. By setting ground rules—for example, we won't interrupt, we won't yell, and we'll try to stick to the subject—parents offer children a constructive model for how to resolve conflict.

There are moments, though, when even the most thoughtful parents find themselves saying no without being able to give an immediate justification. They may lack either the energy or the desire to explore their reasons, and they may be called selfish and unreasonable. Maybe they are, but they know that somebody has to make the rules—and when you're a parent, the buck stops here.

If we don't give ourselves the freedom to say no as often as possible for good and stated reasons but sometimes "just because," then we turn our families topsy-turvy and place the children in the position of being in control. Many of us have absorbed the notion that our children's self-esteem is a very delicate thing and that even a single poorly timed denial might ruin it forever. This "fragile ego" concept leads to a false indulgence whereby we allow the presumed fragility of their egos to be the bullies of our conscience, thereby undermining our authority and responsibility as parents. All too frequently this is the setup in an overly precious home.

Charlotte felt awful about the pain she'd caused when she divorced Suze's dad. She was determined to make it up to her daughter by being understanding and generous. This program, however, did not guarantee harmony or happiness. Suze was sullen, demanding, angry. Charlotte felt like a failure as a mother, and redoubled her efforts at patient understanding. One day, Charlotte went downstairs to deliver some clean laundry and knocked on her teenager's closed door; Suze refused to open it, demanding her right to privacy. Upstairs once again, Charlotte felt a surge of accumulated anger: her fourteen-year-old daughter was giving her orders. She marched back down, demanded entry, and found Suze attempting to hide a scantily dressed young man in her closet. Charlotte had had enough. She handed him his clothes, told him to get dressed and get out and announced firmly that he was too old to be a part of her daughter's life. Suze cried and yelled, threatened to run away, steal cars, commit either suicide or murder, but her mother stuck to her guns. As a reformed permissive parent, Charlotte at first swung to an authoritarian extreme, but in a year, when the dust had settled, mother and daughter were having a much better time. There was more laughter, less sarcasm and fighting—and no more boys in the closet.

Vow #6. I will always attend to my children whenever they need me.

Revow #6. I will do my best to give my attention to my children when I feel they need it.

This could be a real heartbreaker. Who would feel comfortable with the notion of not attending to one's child in a time of need? But, as we've seen, need is often a matter of opinion. Does four-year-old Sandy really *need* boysenberry juice at a quarter to one in the morning? Does five-year-old Timmy really *need* to have Mom come and see every single time he hangs upside down on the monkey bars? Whether or not he truly does, he will wake up one day to find that his parents simply don't have the energy, the interest, or the patience to attend to his every wish. There will also be a time when we fail to respond—and our child really did need us. We hope they'll forgive us just as we've forgiven them for the occasional false alarm. An apology helps if it's truly felt. ("I'm sorry I didn't come when you called. I didn't realize how scared you were.") Not only is this the truth, but it also models ways for people to behave when they've made mistakes.

One of the important developmental tasks of childhood is to learn, step by step, to handle one's own needs and not simply to shout to parents or the universe to take care of them. "I'm hungry; feed me" is an appropriate cry for an infant or young child, and the request will usually be responded to right away.

As children grow, we can begin to explain more and expect more in the way of self-regulation. Young children can begin to understand messages like "Dinner is in twenty minutes; don't eat now or you'll spoil your appetite." When they're old enough to spread peanut butter on bread, they can be told, "If you're hungry, you can fix yourself a snack." Similarly, by the time a child is four or five, we expect him or her to be able to wait a few minutes (four or five) while we finish a phone call, put away the groceries, finish taking a bath. Again, by the time they are ten, we expect they will be able to wait a while for attention. (Perhaps about one minute per year of age would be a nice arithmetical rule of thumb.) Parents who assume that they must respond to every expressed need can interfere with their children's developing mastery. Too Precious Children become adults who expect the world to be ready to satisfy their needs, moving through life shouting their demands for clean clothes, food, sex, money, constant attention, and entertainment.

BOREDOM: IS IT INSIDE OR OUTSIDE?

Parents who are overdevoted have difficulty accepting that any moment of life may be anything less than pleasurable for their children. When they hear the familiar cry, "I'm bored," they respond with frantic efforts to find things to do, toys to play with, wonderful projects to undertake. If these efforts aren't satisfactory, the parents may give up what they're doing and become playmates. Caring parents want their children's lives to be interesting and fun, and within reason try to provide imaginative toys and stimulating experiences. They're willing to spend time singing nursery rhymes, or reading stories, or teaching their children to make an origami bird or a paper-bag puppet. But when parents become the entertainment committee, they reinforce their children's belief that entertainment comes from without—like a program beamed into a TV set—rather than from one's own efforts to find things of interest in their environment.

Dr. Bruno Bettelheim, the noted child psychiatrist, points out the dangers of a childhood in which all entertainment and learning come from without.

Developing an inner life, including fantasies and daydreams, is one of the most constructive things a growing child can do. The days of most middle-class children are filled with scheduled activities—Boy or Girl Scout meetings, music and dance lessons, organized sports—which leave them hardly any time simply to be themselves. In fact, they are continually distracted from the task of self-discovery, forced to develop their talents and personalities as those who are in charge of the various activities think best.[4]

Children who expect to be entertained, who rely on having their time scheduled and structured by others, don't learn either how to survive the inevitable boring stretches or how to make things better for themselves. When they arrive at adulthood, they're poorly prepared either to take initiative or to put in the necessary time waiting for the right career opportunity or the right spouse.

Vow #7. My children will lack for nothing.
Revow #7. My children will have everything they need and many things they want; however, I will make judgments about what is important.

Opportunity and Privilege and Toy and Gift are showered on Too Precious Children. They are crown princes and princesses who learn neither moderation nor gratitude in this atmosphere of excess.

But when do you give and when do you utter the "no" we've just been discussing? For parents with money to spend, the answer is often difficult. If you could readily afford to buy all the junky toys that are advertised on TV, why not go ahead and buy them? If you drive a BMW and your spouse tools around in a Mercedes, why wouldn't you say yes to your nine-year-old's request for a snazzy Honda four-wheeler? If you're a happy customer of Nordstrom or Lord & Taylor or Saks Fifth Avenue, why wouldn't you hand over your charge card and send your teenager to stock up on the latest trends?

Some parents say yes to all the above; some are outraged at the very idea that children would be allowed such privileges. Where do you stand and how indulgent would you like to be? Perhaps the best way to begin to answer those questions is to examine your own motives for giving. Are you saying yes because you don't want your child to be angry at you? Are you saying it because you're afraid your child won't be able to tolerate the disappointment of a no? Granting requests based on either of these impulses has far more to do with your own needs than with those of your child.

Perhaps after looking at your own reasons for giving, the next thing to do is to gather some information about whether what your child is asking for is unusual. Does every five-year-old in town have the overpriced doll your youngster is clamoring for? Whether or not you decide to buy the doll, you may understand better why you're hearing so much about it if you find that it's a staple play item in the neighborhood.

Is what your child wants appropriate to his or her age and skills? If your five-year-old demands to wear stockings and high heels to kindergarten, you won't have any problem turning down the request. What about the sixth-grader who wants you to buy her lipstick? If you don't feel that sixth-graders need lipstick, you may decide not to provide it, even though you see bright red lips on every eleven-year-old girl you pass in the street. If your daughter really wants lipstick, she can save up her money and buy it herself.

Is what your child wants safe or dangerous? The nine-year-old who wants a four-wheeler may have to wait a few years to discuss it, because four-wheelers are not recommended for children under twelve.

Is it something that will be used with pleasure for a year or for half a day? If, for example, your five-year-old wants the expensive doll—and you can afford it—the fact that practically everyone has one and that it will offer hours of absorbing fun may make you decide that it's worth it.

As children grow older, you may set more conditions. If your sixteen-year-old wants a car and you're willing and able to provide one, you may require good grades in school both as a precondition and an ongoing requirement.

Finally, when you begin to hear too many requests for things, you may decide to set some limits and turn over as much decision-making to your child as is appropriate.

> *Every trip to the supermarket was an ordeal for Wayne. His four-year-old daughter, Sandra, scouted the aisles for goodies and made endless requests. Wayne hated to say no; after all, it wasn't Sandra's idea to go to the store, and a little child couldn't help it if she wanted things. But when Sandra threw up after eating three candy bars, two slices of pizza, and a soda, Wayne decided to put the brakes on. He told Sandra she could choose one treat, and this solution worked well. Sandra put her energies into deciding what she would get, and there was much less whining and fussing.*

We parents don't have to feel like monsters when we decline to provide our children with every item on their wish lists. By going out of our way to indulge all of their whims, we deny them the usual opportunities life offers to learn some very necessary skills, such as how to wait and how to do without, skills that will help them to mature and become adult.

Vow #8. My children's needs will always come first.
Revow #8. I will provide food, clothing, and shelter for my children, and I will love and protect them.

We fathers and mothers have needs apart from our children—for private time as a couple, for adult conversation with friends, or for solitude. We can't meet our own legitimate adult needs if we always put our children's demands first. Should we do so, we create an unhealthy imbalance in our families, with everything going to the child—attention, time, toys, love. Our Too Precious Children may grow up to be difficult spouses or uncooperative fellow workers to whom consideration for the needs and feelings of others is a foreign concept.

Single parents have an especially difficult time balancing their own needs with those of their children. Stress and guilt are constant companions. If you're raising a child alone, you need to make sure you have some time for yourself and for adult companionship and activities.

Vow #9. We will never quarrel or disagree in front of the children.
Revow #9. We will show our children both sides of some of our discussions or disagreements so that they can learn how families make decisions and struggle to communicate and work together.

Of course, adults have personal issues they do not discuss with their children—for example, their sex lives or their financial problems with ex-spouses—but some of us want to protect our children from all dissension. At best, it's an impractical, if not impossible, goal because the only way to avoid conflict in relationships is not to talk. The Too Precious Child who hasn't seen how parents resolve their disagreements has no concept of the normal give and take involved in a committed and healthy love relationship and may grow up to view conflict as the other person's fault.

Jeanne grew up in a family in which no dissent was ever directly expressed. Her mother would occasionally criticize her father when only she and Jeanne were home —but the criticism was never to his face. When Jeanne married Stuart, she was shocked by what felt like frequent angry attacks: he told her he didn't enjoy clothes shopping with her, he expressed annoyance that she was always late getting ready to leave for a party or a movie, he was unhappy with the state of the refrigerator. Stuart, for his part, was puzzled. All he had to do was try to tell her what was on his mind and she would burst into tears! Did she want him to lie?

After a few visits to their respective in-laws, something dawned on the couple. They came from families with completely different styles. Jeanne agreed that the strong undercurrent of displeasure in her parents' house was chilling. She said she would prefer a more direct approach—and she'd try to listen without bursting into tears. Stuart agreed to lower his voice when he offered his opinions.

Vow #10. I will always be patient and persevering.
Revow #10. Patience is often but not always a virtue; perseverance is. I will never "give up" on my child.

Patience is a wonderful goal, but children are better at trying our patience than we are at keeping it—especially when their intention is to exceed our limits and get us upset. Why? Maybe they're upset and want company. Maybe they want to know the limits. Maybe their energy is boundless and ours isn't. Too much patience is the province of the martyr.

Perseverance, on the other hand, is crucial. Even when we run short of patience, we can persevere. Even though we are temporarily upset or furious with our children—and we may need to go to our separate spaces for a while—we won't abandon them. It may take us time to let our rage or weariness subside, but we will always make the effort to respond. It may be a few minutes, an hour, a day, or even a week later, but we'll try to discuss what's at issue:

"Jimmy, I want to talk with you about what happened last night."

"Meredith, I had a lot of feelings about that topic [sex, drugs, rock 'n' roll] and I imagine you have a lot of feelings about what I said to you."

"Kurt, I'd like to hear what you were going to say before I got so upset."

Sometimes we have to persevere in actions, not just in words. That may mean persevering in our intent to have children become more responsible. If, for example, our children are heedless about doing their chores, we can continue to insist that they do them and look for new ways to see they get done—a list on the refrigerator or a bonus for all chores done on time without reminders. One mother, tired of hearing her own angry voice berating the children for being slobs, started an allowance-deduction program, charging a nickel an item for everything she had to pick up and put away. The first week, her children didn't believe her. The second week, they did. By the third week, she was back to paying their full allowances.

In the homes of the Too Precious Ones, we often see an extraordinary patience. Nothing the child can say or do leads to parental irritability. Sound great? Maybe, at first. But it is false.

As children grow, they begin to act upon the environment and get feedback. Do you like this? How does this sound? Is this fun? What does the cat do when I pull its tail? What does my brother do when I go into his room?

Too much patience interferes with this feedback process. Many overly precious children are described as "spoiled." They're whiny, demanding, unresponsive to the needs of others. That's because they aren't given clear feedback.

CONDITIONAL AND UNCONDITIONAL LOVE

Unconditional love offers itself without expectations or regard for gain; conditional love sets terms. Unconditional love is the love we all seek, then challenge to death to see if it really *is* unconditional. Conditional love is the love we more frequently express—"I just love you when

you're cheerful and happy like this"—while unconditional love is more silent, less often expressed.

> *Jenny and Stephan were finally asleep. Their par-
> ents, tired by a long day with their energetic offspring,
> tiptoed into their toddlers' room to make sure they were
> properly tucked in. As they gazed upon those two peace-
> ful, beautiful little faces, so sweetly exhausted, the couple
> forgot all the petty annoyances of the day and just let
> them all go with a deep exhalation. They felt an inrush of
> love, a deep connection to each other and to their chil-
> dren.*

The wellspring of some of our more unrealistic vows
is "unconditional" love, freely given without regard to any
return. It is that rush of feeling that Jenny and Stephan's
parents feel as they look in on them, knowing that whatever happens they will love them totally and forever. It is
the underlying deep feeling that keeps us going during
the stormy periods in our relationships.

Conditional love establishes expectations. All of us
have heard or spoken sentences in the following style: "I
love you because you are my child, but I'd love you even
more if you would get an A, make the soccer team, clean
up your room, stop the sarcasm." Because we value unconditional love so highly, we are sometimes uncomfortable with the everyday bargaining of conditional love.
Difficult though it may be to identify, there is a point at
which we start asking things of our children: to tell the
truth, to do their homework, to keep their voices down
because we have a headache. Granted we don't necessarily
stop loving them when they disappoint us, but we do
make it clear that we're glad to have their cooperation.

When children are young, we smile at the gestures they make at helping perform chores around the house. As they near sixteen (or twelve or twenty-one), a gesture by itself is no longer much appreciated. We expect them to meet some conditions in order to earn our respect and liking. By having and expressing our own expectations, by setting terms, we introduce our children to those that the world places on us all.

MOM, I WANT TO BE AN ASTRONAUT

As children grow and develop, we find ourselves altering what we ask of them, and we translate everyday reality in ways that are appropriate to their stage of development. Suppose your child announces, "I want to be an astronaut when I grow up." What would your response be?

1. *The Young Child.* You might express unsparing enthusiasm, remarking on how much fun it would be to fly and float in the sky.
2. *The School-Age Child.* While you continue to enjoy the imaginative possibilities of this desire, you could begin to use it as an opportunity to encourage the "student" in your child. You might wonder what astronauts need to know: for example, how to operate and fix their vehicles, how to calculate their routes and speeds, how to carry out experiments in space, how to identify stars and planets.
3. *The Young Adolescent.* You'd share in the excitement of the idea, but you'd go on to discuss with your child what actual and specific steps would be nec-

essary to prepare for this career. Would you need Algebra II? What kind of physical shape would you have to be in? What kind of college training would be necessary? What about preparing for the SATs?

Similarly, if your child wants to play in the Philharmonic or compete in the Olympics, your response would vary, depending on whether you're talking to a child of three years or of fourteen. But even as you begin to point out the barriers that must be overcome, remember that no matter how old your children, they never outgrow the need for your blind faith and support, for the kind of encouragement implicit in comments like "Anything's possible," "The sky is the limit," "You can do anything."

Some parents demand that too many conditions be met and expect their children to give up too much of their autonomy. These "overconditioned" little boys and girls are darling and clean and well mannered. Their favorite lunch spot is The Plaza. They don't muss their clothes or roll down hills, and they always color inside the lines. Later on in life, they will look back on childhood as a time of learning to be good.

But in dealing with overpreciousness, we are concerned not only with overcontrol but also with the dangers of undercontrol, of bringing up children who take too little care, who are careless rather than carefree. With undercontrol comes a sense of unease, a feeling of lack of competence. It's wonderful to feel that your parents love you unconditionally and will forgive you when you make mistakes; it may be even more wonderful to feel that you really know how to get along in the world, that you know how to moderate and express your wishes and needs within relationships, that you can manage both give and take. Parents who strive to express only unconditional love may forget one of their primary parental responsibilities: to prepare their children to live independently in a world that demands some measure of control, some balancing of individual needs with those of families and communities.

CARING AND OVERCARING

How do we find the right balance between caring (the way we demonstrate our love through concern, help, protection, attention) and overcaring? Should there be limits to our solicitude? Consider the old TV commercial for Excedrin that humorously dramatizes a classic and utterly familiar situation. We see a harried young mother turn to her own too helpful mom and say, "Mother, please, I'd rather do it myself!" Obviously, at some point, parental help and concern become intrusive. Overcaring leads to a paradoxical situation. Eager to help our children, we rob them of the pleasures of their own accomplishments and interfere with their opportunities to learn from their own mistakes. Stepping back sometimes feels like withholding help, and it isn't always easy to do. It's difficult to watch your child struggle with a task you could do easily or better. It's also difficult to be accurate in your assessment of what your child has the ability to do.

> *Eight-year-old Maggie argued long and hard with her mother every time the topic of cleaning her room was broached. The spat would go on until her mother would give up and do it herself. Finally, after an especially long*

argument, the reason for Maggie's refusal to clean emerged. Sobbing, the child explained what her mother had not really understood. Maggie didn't know how to go about cleaning her room if her mom wasn't there to help her. Maggie's mother realized her daughter's refusal to straighten up her room was the result of confusion and fear of failure. She and Maggie cleaned the room together, and over time, Maggie learned to do more and more by herself.

A little preliminary parental investigation can prevent some of these misunderstandings.

Ten-year-old Travis wanted to take scuba lessons and asked his mother to sign him up. She asked him some basic questions: Where and when were the classes? How much did they cost? Blank looks. Realizing that her son didn't know how to find out the answers, she sat down with him and they brainstormed about places that might teach such a course. Then they studied the Yellow Pages together and identified a few that looked good. Travis agreed to make the calls after he and his mother rehearsed what he wanted to ask and even wrote down a script. After calling three places, Travis learned to his disappointment that he was still too young to take lessons, but he had also learned a lot about how to find things out.

Travis's mother might have told her son in advance what she suspected: that he was too young. Or she might have made the calls for him and then given him the information. If she had done so, however, the results wouldn't have been so helpful to him and so satisfactory to her. He learned through his own efforts what he needed to know. He wasn't angry at his mom for telling him he was too young. He was far better able to accept his disappointment—and he'd learned one more piece of the giant puzzle of how to get along in the world.

> *Sixteen-year-old Jackie wanted new bookshelves for her room. She didn't know how to measure for them or where to buy materials for them or how to put them together. She also didn't know how to ask for help because she felt as though she ought to know. So when her dad asked her why she hadn't gotten going on her project, she snarled at him, then started to cry. After her father figured out why they were fighting about the shelves, he went over the "how-tos": how to measure, how and where to buy materials, how to build them. What a treat for both of them when she went to the lumber store by herself and bought the right supplies, then put them up without any help. Both Jackie and her father were proud of her accomplishment.*

One of the oft-quoted definitions of maturity is "the ability to tolerate frustration and postpone gratification." Overcaring leads us to be uncomfortable with the struggle our children go through. Perhaps our own frustration level is on the low side when we intervene. Maggie's mother was angry at herself because she knew she was cleaning her daughter's room to avoid fighting about it. Travis's mother had to bite her tongue just as she was about to say, "You're too young to go scuba diving." Jackie's father started to offer to install the shelves himself before he realized that his daughter was old enough to carry out the task. By offering the right amount of help, these three parents avoided the pitfalls of overcaring and overinvolvement, and they aided, rather than interfered with, the maturation of their youngsters' skills and ability to postpone gratification.

THE LESSONS OF FAILURE

Not only must parents learn to stand back and let their children struggle with difficult tasks, but sometimes they even have to watch them fail and allow them to experience the consequences of that failure. For Too Precious Parents, the idea of failure is catastrophic. When a child doesn't succeed at something—whether it's academic, athletic, social—they fear that doors to their child's limitless future are slamming shut. Instead of teaching that child to try again, these anxious parents create a tremendous pressure and a sense that it may be better not to risk anything that's new or challenging because the danger of failure would vastly outweigh the pleasure of success.

Thirteen-year-old Michaela was adventurous, resourceful, and responsible. She was a natural leader and always had good ideas for new ways to do things. Her parents valued these qualities, but they were terribly worried about her academic performance. They had always imagined that she would become a lawyer or a physician, but she was barely managing to bring home C's on her report card. When the school counselor at her prestigious private school suggested that Michaela, who had some learning disabilities, might do better in a less-demanding school, her parents were deeply upset. As they discussed the situation, though, they began to see that they needed to help their daughter build on her real strengths rather than mourn the loss of the imaginary future they had created.

The lessons that Too Precious Children learn don't prepare them to deal with the inevitable frustrations of life or teach them to take the necessary steps toward attaining a goal. Here are two contrasting incidents that illustrate two very different parental approaches.

Chris had been sickly as a small child, and his mother recalled this scary period every time he cried. She remembered how she and her husband would drive Chris to Toys 'R' Us to distract him from his misery. Now that he was in the fifth grade, he was miserable once again. He was expected to do some homework every night and every night he would protest. His parents sat down and did the work with him from beginning to end. In addition, they often called the teacher to complain that Chris was "too young" for homework.

Lynette loved her Barbie dolls. She got more Barbies and more Barbie clothes and accessories at holiday and birthday time. When her friend got the newest Barbie fur coat, Lynette just had to have it. For days, she talked about nothing else. Her parents offered her some suggestions as to how she might plan to save up for the coat. They told her they would pay a bonus of twenty-five cents for special extra chores and helped her figure out how long it would take to pay for the doll coat. Lynette had wanted her parents to treat her to it, but decided that the only way she was going to get it was to wait and work. Seven weeks later she had the money.

SPECIAL BUT NOT IMPORTANT

During a community affairs class on "wellness," the teacher raised the topic of "importance." "Were you made to feel important when you were young?" she asked. "How?" Several of the class members had come from large farm families, and one woman in particular described in rich and colorful detail a powerful childhood memory. She had spent hardworking summer after summer riding in the back of a big farm truck with her sisters and brothers and cousins, harvesting stalks of corn. "I never felt special as a child," she said, "but I always felt important."

She acknowledged that she doesn't want her children to have to work as hard as she did. At the same time, she was aware that the hardships she had endured had had some positive features. Now, she said, she worries that although her children feel very special, they do not feel *important*.

What a difficult challenge: to make our children feel both special *and* important. Some would argue that children already feel special and that it's up to us to teach them to be important. Nevertheless, we are living in paradoxical times. As children's economic importance to their families has decreased, their specialness has increased. In her provocative book, *Pricing the Priceless Child*, Viviana A. Zelzer points out that in 1900 one out of six children between the ages of ten and fifteen was gainfully employed (a statistic she believes is low because the figures don't include children helping their parents in sweatshops and farms, before or after school hours).

Zelzer then goes on to discuss the "profound transformation in the economic and sentimental value of children," and asserts that "the emergence of this economically 'worthless' but emotionally 'priceless' child has created an essential condition of contemporary childhood."[5]

Because we value our children so highly, we're willing to spend large sums of money to house, feed, clothe, educate, and entertain them. Professor Zelzer observes that "the total cost of raising a child—combining both direct maintenance costs and indirect opportunity costs—was estimated in 1980 to average between $100,000 and $140,000." Rather than expecting a direct return on this sizable investment—that children as they grow older will take on an increasing amount of the work of the household or that they will eventually become a source of financial support—many parents hope for a less tangible reward that may ultimately put a far greater burden on the child.

There are those who spend far larger sums of money so that their children can have all the "right" social and cultural and educational experiences, and these parents often expect a payoff. They're putting their money into the creation of a winner! Like an expensive car, an "investment" child ought to look terrific, perform exceptionally well, and attest to the highest standards and good taste of the owner-parent.

The competitive style that is a hallmark of the Yuppie game demands that players always seek and acquire the best—whether it's a car, a kitchen stove, a dog, or a handbag. When parenthood becomes part of the game, the child must ride in the sleekest stroller, enjoy the most creative birthday parties, attend the top schools. The *quid pro quo*? I'll give you the best, but you had better *be* the best.

And so, youngsters today are pressured to get into the right nursery school, the right computer camp, the right college, yet they are rarely required to do anything that would be truly important in the real world.

*Marya and Van couldn't understand why their fif-
teen-year-old son, Carter, was such a disappointment.
They'd devoted so much time and energy to him from the
moment he was born. He'd had all the recommended
child-guidance toys, an outstanding nursery school, and
nine years of expensive prep school education. They'd
taken him to France and Italy and Japan, and they'd
sent him to special tennis programs and computer camp.
The result? Carter was a sullen, resentful, under-
achiever, who wouldn't lift a finger to help his parents
around the house and didn't really have any skills that he
could put to practical use. He seemed to spend most of his
time aimlessly watching MTV or fooling around with an
electric guitar that he never bothered to learn how to
play.*

Carter knew that he was supposed to be "special,"
but the knowledge was more of a burden than an incentive to him. He felt that he was supposed to do something
glorious, something brilliant, in exchange for the privileges that had been lavished on him, but he would gladly
have settled for public school and being "ordinary."

IMPORTANT AND SPECIAL: A BIT OF BOTH

Rather than overburdening their children with inflated expectations, what can parents do to help children
develop a sense of purpose and importance? One way to
begin is with the concept of owing something back to the
community from which they receive. When they are
young, that community is their family. As soon as they are
capable of helping, children should be encouraged to par-

ticipate in the tasks of family life: food preparation, cleaning, picking up after oneself. These are not tasks for which any family member is paid; they are the dues we pay to be part of the family. Often the chores themselves are quite small; a young child might be responsible for putting the napkins on the table or bringing in kindling every night for the fireplace. Many children grumble about performing their chores and mutter darkly about slavery and indentured servitude, but their efforts to be released from the tasks should be lovingly ignored ("Thank you for sharing with me. Now please put a glass at each place").

One mistake many parents make is trying to change too much at once. If they feel their children do too little around the house, they will set new standards that are excessive and not likely to be met (e.g., "Not only will you do the dishes but also the laundry—and you will keep your room straightened and mow the lawn"). It's better to introduce new tasks progressively and gradually.

A child should be able to understand that a task must be done at a specific time and should have the skills to accomplish it. In the beginning, he or she may need patient reminders and assistance from parents.

> *It was four-year-old Philip's job to feed Tinu, the family's Akita, and he sometimes needed to be reminded to set out the food in the morning. His parents kept the dog food on a low shelf and provided a stool so he could reach the tap to fill the dog's water dish.*

Once parents relinquish their unrealistic vows to be all-giving, they can work to create a more reciprocal, more cooperative kind of family life. And children who learn to pitch in and do their share will grow up feeling more competent and successful than children whose parents have vowed to overindulge, overprotect, and, in effect, underprepare them for adult life.

CHAPTER SIX
Learning to Be a Not Too Precious Parent

Loving enough but not too much, caring but not interfering, helping when help is needed but respecting the value of struggle and enterprise, requiring the right amount of cooperation without overloading the child with excessive demands—how in the world are parents supposed to do all that? How are we ever going to manage to fine-tune our performance to the precise requirements of our child's developmental needs? And yet, over time, through a process of trial and error, with great efforts at empathy and a few flashes of inspiration, that's what we strive to learn and to do. And we carry out our very complex task without much in the way of preparation.

None of us received training to be a parent, except during the childhood course we took from our own parents—and how many of us as adults would sign up for that parenting class again? In fact, many of us decided to do things very differently: to be kinder, more consistent, more generous, more patient, and so on and so forth.

How shocking then to hear that familiar accusing voice issue forth when our guard is down and our beloved child has forgotten for the third time to take out the garbage: "Some people think they're too good to help out around here." (Oh my gosh, it's my mother.)

When it comes to developing the sensitivity and skills to raise a child, Too Precious Parents are at a disadvantage: they are so intoxicated with the *idea* of being parents that they don't pay enough attention to what their child is really like and really needs. These are the parents who are so fearful of bruising their child's self-esteem that they are unwilling to scold little Bruce, even when he's busy putting his wooden blocks inside the toaster-oven. These parents may function well during their child's infancy, when their role is to adore. Later on, though, when their toddler refuses to go to bed or whines constantly in the grocery store, they don't have the flexibility to respond to the requirements of the situation. These parents remain attached to their rigid list of vows: "I'll never spank, criticize, nag, or compare."

If it's difficult to find the right balance—caring but not *over*caring, protective but not *over*protective—when things are going well, how much more difficult it is to establish that balance when illness, death, divorce, or the rigors of adolescence intervene. Add to these the demands that contemporary society seems to make on parents—and you have an enormously unstable emotional and social context for bringing up the young.

One of the special situations that we previously identified that makes parents vulnerable to Too Preciousness is that of the divorced single parent. Such a parent is especially susceptible when it comes to the question of vows made and vows broken.

Whitney was sixteen when she was admitted to the adolescent psychiatry unit of a large metropolitan hospital. She had been unmanageable since her parents' divorce two years earlier and had stopped attending school because it was "boring" and the teachers were "hassling" her. Her mother thought of herself as her child's advocate and felt that if Whitney were to take a year off, she might start feeling better and could get a fresh start in school the next year. Mother and daughter took an extended vacation. They explored the West and Mexico. To ease Whitney's return to her old routine, her mother bought her a Mustang convertible. The two enjoyed spending their time together on weekends driving around town and going out to lunch.

A single mother raising an only daughter may find she has an unusually stormy time. The typical stresses and strains of the mother/daughter relationship may become suffocating without a father or sibling around to run interference.

When Whitney's school attendance record again became unsatisfactory, her mother was genuinely surprised, then angered; she and her daughter fought more often and more bitterly. Finally, bringing matters to a head, Whitney took an overdose of aspirin. During her subsequent hospitalization, Whitney, with the help of her psychiatrist, learned to be the child and her mother was urged to reassert the role of parent. It wasn't easy for either of them, and they both were honest enough to state that they had had a lot more fun riding around town in the convertible.

Disturbed and set adrift by her parents' divorce, Whitney needed someone to set limits. Whitney's mom, however, was so eager to show how concerned and caring she was that she had abdicated the more unpleasant role of rule-maker and rule-enforcer.

Like divorce, death means loss—and in a sense the

unanticipated and tragic breaking of a vow to join together as a couple to care for and raise a child. Often and understandably, the surviving parent is unwilling to cause the child any further pain.

> *When Joel was six, his father died. He never cried, not at the funeral and not later, and he would always leave the room whenever someone would mention his father. His mother secretly worried about him and wanted to "make it up" to him somehow. There were toys when he was little and bikes as he got older and then stereos and TVs. When he hit adolescence and holed up in his room with his electronic playthings in typical teenage fashion, his mother felt like a failure. "I'll buy you a computer," she offered, "if you'll just come to the dinner table every night."*

Steeped in her son's pain over his father's loss, Joel's mother failed to notice that some of his behavior was fairly typical for his age and was related more to developmental changes than to grief. He needed structure, not another gift. Both Joel and his mother remained caught in their sorrow and were unable to move forward.

> *Elena and Jason visited their father often after their parents' divorce. In fact, they saw a lot more of him after the divorce than they ever had before. But the back and forth wasn't easy, and Elena began having stomach-aches and headaches when she returned home from a weekend with her father. Jason seemed to be getting along fairly well, but his mother worried because "he didn't talk" and rarely helped around the house. Both parents were reluctant to make demands or to criticize, because they knew how rough the divorce had been on the kids.*

Since the children always seemed to be going to the other parent's house, there was never a good time for discipline.

Fortunately, these divorced parents cared more about helping their children than blaming each other. They found a family therapist who felt that brief therapy would be useful. In their meetings, the parents worked out guidelines for discipline that they both agreed to enforce. They also had the children join them for several discussions, and ended up deciding that some weekends only one child would visit Dad, so that every so often each one could have a period of special attention from each parent. The new regime worked out well for everyone.

In the sixties and seventies, discipline wasn't a fashionable concept. Being "laid back" and displaying "openness" were the *summum bonum.* Parents were supposed to adopt a hands-off policy and let their children unfold, express their creativity, explore many options. That sounded wonderful until parents discovered that they'd raised kids who were too creative to do the laundry or their homework or to get a job.

Now, in reaction, we have books like James Dobson's *The Strong-Willed Child,* which pictures children as possessed by an excess of will that their parents must constantly struggle to subjugate. The Dobsonian world view, with its drama of the defiant, willful child and the stern yet loving parent armed with a switch, polarizes family life into a "them" (the willful children) and an "us" (the caring parents who are only punishing "them" for their own good).[1]

Similarly, we see the emergence of a movement like

Toughlove, which stresses limit-setting, toughness, firmness. Parents who have allowed their children to get out of control are remotivated to do their parental duty and to emphasize their right and obligation to discipline and make choices for their young. So far so good—but many Toughlove advocates approach their task with a ferocious determination to undo in one intense weekend all the excesses and indulgences of the past years.

Toughlove is an extreme solution, which may, in some circumstances, offer too much, too late. Some children are too fragile or troubled to respond appropriately to its aggressive agenda. More often, however, children whose parents join Toughlove are simply out-of-control youngsters in out-of-control families.

LIMIT-SETTING AND PARENTAL LOVE

How many people even consider discipline, rules, and punishments when they decide to have a baby? When you dreamed of having children, who was your fantasy ideal of the Good Parent? Maybe it was someone like Glinda the Good Witch in *The Wizard of Oz*, who is kind and gentle and grants wishes with a wave of her wand. In truth, most of us dislike depriving, negating, refusing, and declining, and would far rather permit, bless, and bestow. (Indulging exclusively in these latter three activities is what makes it so nice to be a godparent or a grandparent.)

What goes wrong? Why do we set out to be like Glinda the Good Witch only to end up feeling like the Wicked Witch of the West? We have generosity on our minds and in our hearts, and yet we end up being the "great deprivers." Our children ask us if they can go to Disney World (they've been twice this year) or buy a snowmobile (they're only six years old) or paint their rooms black. Interesting ideas all, but with little hesitation we say no. We say no to their requests to see R-rated movies at age nine, date at age eleven, or spend the weekend with a youngster we don't know.

> *Bridget asked her mother for a freshly baked choco-late chip cookie. Her mother gave her darling four-year-old a cookie. And another. And a third. When Bridget asked for yet another, her mother gave it to her with a warning: this was to be the last one. Bridget began to think that her mother wasn't very nice at all. And her mother wasn't very nice when Bridget demanded a fifth cookie. The answer was a much sharper no. Little Brid-get decided her mother was just possibly the meanest per-son in the world.*

While we're saying our no, however, part of us wants to say yes. We begin to resent our children for wanting so many preposterous things, without being willing to fulfill our simple and reasonable requests. Few of us realized that being a parent would involve saying no so loudly—and so often; yet, here we are with the job of setting limits, imposing authority, preventing the children (to whom we wanted to give the moon) from overindulgence in chocolate chip cookies, TV, fun, and sex.

And how terrible it is for us to find ourselves, in spite of our vows to be different, doing the same mean things our parents did to us. As we experience the irony of this situation—perhaps without our ever being fully aware that it's happening—our resentment of our own parents diminishes as we begin to understand what it was like to *be* them. Quite often, painful conflict between parent and child eases with the arrival of a third generation.

And what surprises await us when our parents come to visit. While we run around with a broom, chasing after the children to empty the dishwasher, our parents (those former paragons of strictness) say such unsupportive things as "Oh, honey, let her be. She'll only be young once—and, besides, she's much too pretty to have to do housework." What!!! Was this the woman who taught "Chasing Bad Children with a Broom 101"? She never thought *we* were too smart or cute or talented to do dishes.

To recall the reaction of comedian Bill Cosby, as he watches his TV parents "spoil" their grandchildren: "I don't know who those people are.... They're imposters.... They're surely not the same people who raised me."

SETTING LIMITS: PARENTAL STYLES

But though we long to be Glinda the Good Witch, we have an obligation to teach our young how to function in the world, and to carry out this task, we must provide them with structure. How we do it has a lot to do with how well the lesson is learned; yet, in our efforts to control and direct our children, we often tend to focus exclusively on *their* behavior, when in fact we might be more successful if we also were to examine our own.

To understand more about the ways in which our children respond to our disciplinary efforts, we might ask ourselves which of the three easily observable modes or styles of "parenting"—permissive, authoritarian, or authoritative—best describes the way we operate.

The *permissive* parent is all too well known to many of us. This is the parent who lets the children scratch the furniture, bite the cat, and interrupt adult conversation gratuitously, all in the name of freedom of expression. To their children, these parents' constant message is "Do what you feel like when it feels good."

> *Three-year-old Jake loved to color. After he'd colored the living room walls with his crayons, all visitors to his parents' home were given guided tours of Jake's "creations." In fact, no restrictions were placed on him. If he wanted to play outdoors, parents and guests moved outdoors; if he wanted to dance, then they all listened to "Mickey Does Aerobics," and were urged by his mother and father to participate with Jake.*

Curiously, those who castigate our "overpermissive" society have tended to lay blame at the doorstep of Dr. Spock. Rather, these critics have misread him—if they have bothered to read him at all. Instead, his advice to parents on the subject of permissiveness makes the greatest of sense: "The everyday job of the parent, then, is to keep the child on the right track by means of firmness. (You don't sit by and watch a small child destroy something and then punish him afterward.) You come to punishment (if you use it at all) once in a while when your system of firmness breaks down."[2]

In truth, underlying the surface tolerance of many permissive parents is the inability to endure conflict.

Their deep reluctance to engage in the unpleasant task of saying no may surface early in their parental careers.

> *The pediatrician called to find out how five-month-old Lee was recovering from a middle-ear infection and inquired whether he had finished the prescribed course of antibiotic treatment. "Oh, no, Doctor," explained his adoring mother. "We stopped that after two days because he didn't like the taste."*

When conflict arises, permissive parents handle it by trying to smooth things over. Rather than acknowledge the existence of a problem, they communicate "no problem."

The *authoritarian* parent, on the other hand, is one who says, "You will do what I tell you to when I tell you to do it" at all times. The child is made to submit to and accept under all conditions the superior position of the parents.

> *In the grocery store, little Tony ran a few feet ahead of his parents, who were making slow but steady progress down the aisles as they did their weekly shopping. The boy bumped into an elderly woman, who smiled at him, patted his head, and said, "Excuse me." Tony quickly returned to his parents. His father reached down with his big arm, grabbed him and spanked Tony vigorously several times, exclaiming, "Don't you ever do that again." "Do what again?" wondered Tony. "Bump into old ladies? Come back to Dad? Allow myself to be hit?"*

The goal of authoritarian parents is obedience, and the tools they use to achieve their results are force and fear. They may be successful in enforcing good behavior, but it is usually a very limited success. The children of "authoritarians" behave when their parents are present, but once out of their sight are often the worst-behaved, most-undisciplined kids on the block. The authoritarian mode of parenting is not well suited to instilling self-regulation because it requires the presence of a feared enforcer.

STRUCTURE AT DIFFERENT AGES

Both permissive and authoritarian parents tend to respond more to their own needs than to those of their children. The permissive parent may have wanted more gifts, more love, more approval as a child. He or she may not want to risk hearing the child say, "I hate you because you won't let me..." Authoritarian parents may simply echo what their parents did or said. Perhaps having themselves been raised without much affection or respect, or maybe needing a sense of power in a life that affords very little, they play the petty tyrant, without every considering what long-range effect this form of parental behavior will have.

By contrast, the *authoritative* parents are responsive to their children's needs. Their source of power flows from the natural authority of the parental role, from age and greater experience. The underlying message to the child is "Do what you feel is right; I will give you limits and let you know what they are."

Hillary and Evan were expected to visit for a few minutes when company arrived. They were allowed, even

encouraged, to be the center of attention for a little while.
Then they were excused to return to their play in the
family room, where they remained without interrupting
the adults.

The comparison of these three parental styles to
forms of political organization offers some useful insights.
The permissive parent creates a form of anarchy that so-
licits the opinion of the child as the most cherished
member of the family/society. The authoritarian parent,
demanding absolute obedience to his or her wishes,
creates tyranny. In this system, only the wishes of the tyrant are considered. The authoritative style is parallel to a
republic, where the majority rules but respects minority
rights—and is prepared to change as the situation requires.

Few of us would question the necessity for parents to
have absolute authority over very young children. We
know the kinds of opinions they have on such issues as
bedtime (cancel it), homework (cancel that, too), and
cleaning up (yup, that should go also!). Yet, as soon as
their children are ready to begin to assume more responsibility, authoritative parents, unlike their autocratic
peers, start to find ways to help their youngsters share in
family decision-making. Because they can comfortably set
limits, their children will learn how to set their own limits
when Mom and Dad are not there to pick up the pieces or
lay down the law.

FIVE TYPICAL SITUATIONS:
HOW PARENTS WITH DIFFERENT
STYLES RESPOND

How parents handle the minor crises of child-rearing offers insight into their basic styles of parenting. In the following five tests of parental limit-setting, permissive, authoritarian, and authoritative parents respond quite differently to the same challenge.

Situation 1: What would you do if your eighteen-month-old son, Kit, wakes up crying and wants to sleep in your bed?

Permissive parents would allow Kit into the bed night after night, even though they really didn't want him there. Authoritarian parents, by contrast, would immediately return Kit to his crib, without offering any support or comfort, and perhaps even with a spanking. Authoritative parents would briefly soothe and comfort Kit, then return him to his own bed. They'd remind him that they want him to sleep in his own bed and that he has the ability to stay there and go back to sleep.

Situation 2: Four-year-old Trina is a bed-wetter. She wakes up wet and crying almost every night. How would you handle this situation?

Permissive parents either allow the soaking child into their own bed or get up and change the sheets, murmuring, "That's okay, honey." They do not communicate any expectation that Trina should stop wetting her bed. They fail to promote maturation or the development of self-control. Authoritarian parents incline toward humiliating and punitive behavior. They make her sleep in the wet bed and hope she gets their message. They succeed only in making Trina feel bad, without offering any help or encouragement. Authoritative parents help the child change the sheets and adopt a neutral stance. They remind her that they are glad to help, but they know that she'll learn to control her bladder, so she won't always need their help.

Situation 3: Seven-year-old Bruce comes to you and says he has taken a pack of bubble gum from the drugstore. What do you tell him?

Permissive parents may cover for him by returning to the store and paying for the gum or may even tell Bruce that it's the fault of the store for putting the gum so temptingly within his reach.

Authoritarian parents react strongly and sternly. They lecture or spank. They may make a point of humiliating Bruce in public, a tactic that may be effective in the short run, while teaching him in the long run that crime is bad mainly if someone finds out.

Authoritative parents react more moderately. They tell Bruce clearly that stealing is wrong, explore with him why it is wrong, and then discuss how to make amends. They arrive at some punishment that seems to fit the crime.

Situation 4: Ten-year-old Justine won't do what she's supposed to do. She won't do her homework, practice the piano, or clean her room. How do you deal with her?

"What can we do?" permissive parents ask themselves. "Nothing," they sigh. So Justine goes her merry way, neither studying, nor practicing, nor cleaning. Her motivation to accomplish these thing continues to decline because she lacks her parents' continuing and firm expectation that she *will* do them.

Authoritarians get the job done with the usual tools of their trade: coercion and punishment. They have some success in making Justine do what she is told, but since her motivation to do so lies in her parents' commands, Justine doesn't learn how to make *herself* do things.

Authoritative parents have to work a little harder than their permissive or authoritarian peers. Their ultimate goal is to become dispensable. They want their child to feel pride in his or her own accomplishment and a progressive sense of responsibility for policing his or her own behavior.

They begin by offering friendly support when they discuss what needs to be done. For example, they don't implore or command Justine to practice the piano. They might say, "What time do you plan to do your half hour of practice?" They become more neutral and less friendly when they remind her that she has yet to accomplish her task. They don't throw up their hands in despair or shout orders like a drill sergeant, but they do persist in making sure that what needs doing gets done.

If Justine continues to have difficulty with these tasks, they are much more apt to reexamine the problems

individually than their permissive or authoritarian coun-
terparts, and to come up with flexible solutions:

1. You need to do your homework; let us know if
   you need a better place to study.

2. We don't want to pay for piano lessons if you
   won't practice. Let's rediscuss what you are
   going to do. But if you want to continue with
   lessons, you must practice.

3. When your room is a mess, it drives us crazy.
   But it is your room. If you want to keep it a
   mess, you have to keep the door closed. And if
   you want company, you have to clean it.

**Situation 5: Fourteen-year-old Gordon has permission to stay
out until ten. He doesn't get home until eleven-thirty.
What action do you take?**

When Gordon announces, "Everyone else can stay
out late," permissive parents tell him, without much conviction, not to do it again. Gordon feels the lack of parental authority and has little incentive to develop his own.
Authoritarian parents, by contrast, come down hard on
Gordon. They focus on his "crime" and dole out the max-
imum punishment (grounding for four weeks, restriction
of all privileges, the silent treatment). They place little
emphasis on discovering what lies behind his disobedi-
ence or on helping him to move toward self-control.
Authoritative parents make it clear that a rule has

been broken and establish a punishment commensurate with the crime (e.g., early curfew for two weeks). They use the situation to gather more information. Was Gordon late because of peer pressure or because he doesn't have a watch? Is he angry at his parents and looking for a way to get back at them? By discussing the issues behind the infraction, Gordon and his parents clear the air, learn some more about each other, and evolve a new solution for a new problem.

TOWARD SELF-DISCIPLINE

It would be easy to assume that when we talk of the Too Precious Child we are talking about a child with permissive parents, the kind of folks who dotingly turn over the helm to little peanut-butter-coated fingers, allowing them to steer through life with no charts or instruments. Too much permissiveness without structure is certainly destructive to the development of self-regulation. But so is too much structure. Many times, parents who are overinvolved with their children are quite authoritarian. Their teaching methods are deprivation, austerity, and denial of children's needs.

Is the antidote to parental tyranny a completely child-centered family? That is an equally despotic, equally unbalanced, system. The goal, we believe, is to find a point of balance between the rules of the parents and the wants of the children—between the desire of the child for no structure and the wisdom of the parent who knows that some structure is necessary.

HEALTHY PARENTS/HEALTHY FAMILY

In our work with families, we strive to remind parents that their relationship as a couple is the most important and fundamental relationship in the family. When a couple with a strong and loving relationship have a child, they feel as though *their* love multiplies. The child belongs to them both.

In many families, however, the birth of a child represents a real disruption. One of the parents (typically the mother) becomes more involved with the child, and the other parent feels excluded by this new intimate relationship. The parent who feels left out may either give in to feelings of jealousy, berating and belittling both members of the dyad, or may become aloof and relatively uninvolved in family life. The less-involved member often is the parent who has the major work obligation outside the home; the overinvolved one usually has the major commitment in the home. The result is often an intensification of the bond between the mother and the child, thus reinforcing and intensifying the imbalance.

Without correction, couples like this—typically with an intense, overinvolved mother and a distant, aloof father—either separate and divorce or become chronically unbalanced. As the situation deteriorates, as the parents grow farther apart, the mother feels more and more lonely and isolated, and she commonly tries to have her emotional needs met by her child.

Ilene, increasingly concerned when her son, Jeremy, began to do poorly in school, decided to seek consultation with a child psychiatrist. Even though Ilene argued that her husband, Rob, probably wouldn't come, the psychiatrist insisted that the whole family be present at the first session. Much to his wife's surprise, Rob came to the appointment and appeared very interested in Jeremy's problems. Although she was glad he was there, she couldn't help feeling a bit resentful that Rob came across as such a "good guy." She hadn't been able to enlist his help in raising their son, and now she actually took some pride in the fact that she had done it all herself. There were times when she wondered why she stayed married. The psychiatrist, sensitive to the issues affecting young families, emphasized how crucial the strengthening of Ilene and Rob's relationship was to Jeremy's improvement.

Finding time and energy to maintain a close relationship is a problem for many couples as they begin to have families. There are personal, cultural, biological, and familial influences that affect how involved a parent will be at any given stage in a child's life. Involvement is dynamic; it waxes and wanes from one developmental stage to the next. Often mothers are more intimately involved with their infants, fathers with their older children. Nowadays, though, many more fathers are finding out that babies can be great fun and are spending more time taking care of them.

To make raising a family even more of a challenge, children need the most attention at the very time their parents' careers require greater commitment. The young couple must juggle career and child-care demands—and somehow nourish their own relationship. It can be done, but obviously something has to give; after the children are born, the relationship between the parents does alter. Yet a healthy couple can tolerate the strains and pressures of child-rearing, and can find ways to insure that neither one of them will feel painfully deprived.

> *Every evening when Faith came home from work, Marcus would have iced coffee ready, and the two would sit together and chat for fifteen minutes while supper simmered. This was parents' time. Children who strayed into the kitchen were shooed back to their homework. Marcus and Faith counted on these few precious minutes together, plus bedtime and early morning and an occasional evening out. Often, the children tried to "cut in," but their parents stood firm.*

Therapists who work with families know that the greatest gift that parents can give their children is the gift of their parental relationship. As children witness their parents' affection, their struggles, their efforts to resolve conflict, they learn for themselves how to be married and how to be parents.

> *Martha and Bart had been very political in college, and both retained their strong opinions, though they were now settled and successful. They shared those opinions freely with their children, who were encouraged to participate in heated, animated dinner table conversations. When Martha and Bart raised their voices in hot debate, the children weren't worried because they knew these discussions were always resolved by dessert. The meal ended in laughter as the dishes were cleared.*

WHAT DO PARENTS NEED FROM THEIR CHILDREN?

We began this chapter with a discussion of the expectations we bring to parenting, sometimes even before we have children. Perhaps some of these expectations arise from the urge that Erik Erikson described as "generativity," the need to leave some legacy that will survive us. If Erikson is right, then we quite understandably dream dreams of what our gift to the future, our children, will be and do.

Given all our anticipation and hard work, we often assume that we're going to get some kind of satisfaction out of the experience. For healthy parents, the pleasure comes in seeing their children grow and be happy, leave home and marry—and eventually begin families of their own.

James and Lillian were proud of their three teenagers. Jamey was enjoying his sophomore year at the university; Kara was a popular high school senior; and Lisel, their baby, was now an independent seventh-grader, with a real talent for music. James and Lillian loved having their family together, but they also cherished spending time just with each other.

Sometimes, though, our idea of how wonderful parenthood should be is at odds with the realities of our child's nature or stage of development.

From the moment she was born, Gabrielle was an irritable baby, and her mother, Kay, was having a hard time experiencing the much-heralded joys of motherhood. When Kay tried to play and laugh with Gabrielle, she would be greeted with a sour puss. "It's my fault she's this way," thought Kay. "I must be lacking some vital maternal something." Kay felt guilty, cheated, angry at her baby, and just plain disappointed.

Kay and other parents of "difficult" babies learn at the outset that the next twenty years may not be a breeze. But even the "easiest" child may pose problems along the way. As children struggle to develop and grow, they inevitably clash with our images of what they will be and how they will reward us. Witness the bewilderment of parents as children enter adolescence.

> *When Cecily turned eleven, her parents watched her undergo an alarming metamorphosis. Although she continued to do well in school and to be actively involved with friends, the outgoing child who had enjoyed talking to her mother and father turned into an irritable and displeased creature. Her parents began to cringe when she came into the living room, feeling the atmosphere palpably cloud. They felt only slightly less tense when she lounged in her room, behind a closed door, out of sight but only somewhat out of mind. She seemed to have no use for them and refused to go anywhere with them. Worried and unhappy, they tried to talk to her about what was happening; but she would merely look at them with ill-disguised contempt, sigh in disgust, and leave the room.*

PARENTS HAVE NEEDS TOO

Cecily was suffering the pangs of early adolescence, and her parents were suffering right along with her. Nothing they did was right. If they pushed for more communication, she retreated. If they ignored her, they felt like lousy parents. Why had they poured heart and soul into raising this child, if she was going to turn on them like this?

We parents aren't totally altruistic beings, existing solely for our children's welfare. We have the usual human needs: to feel self-esteem, to find outlets for our creativity, to love and be loved. When we create children, we may imagine them meeting some of these needs and, up to a point, they do. They value us, want to be with us, love us and are delighted to have us love them.

But if we expect that our children are going to fulfill all our needs forever, that they will remain at the center of our universe, and we at theirs, we will either suffer a bitter disappointment or rob our young of their individuality. Often, it is precisely this dangerous soul-robbing expectation that lies at the heart of parental overinvolvement.

WHAT CAN PARENTS EXPECT
FROM PARENTHOOD?

First, let's look at what we *can't* expect. Larry Freeman, a family therapist and child psychiatrist, has observed that "people expect their children to make them feel better, but children really just make us feel *more*."[3]

Living alone, we can present the mask we choose to the world—serene, delightful, warm, witty, generous—but once we begin living in a family, the game is up. However beautifully crafted our persona, cracks appear in the façade. Our children may be our comfort; they may inspire feelings of love and pride and pleasure. But at times they arouse the beast. They may make us bad-tempered, petty, hassled, irritated, and impatient. They may be our hope for the future—and yet arouse in us a keen sense of our mortality and the fragility of life. So we feel more deeply, but we don't necessarily feel better.

Family life is rarely the Eden we imagine it will be. We often act our worst at home, yet it is a refuge and a haven. And if we are to create a home that will continue to be a refuge for us and for our children, it will have to be a complex, changing environment that meets our needs as parents without submerging the needs of our developing children. Creating such an environment is no mean achievement.

We parents are to love our children neither too little nor too much. We are to raise them with a sense of their own uniqueness coupled with a sense of their normality. We are to give them a good sense of self-esteem without letting them ruin ours. WHAT A BALANCING ACT! Yet, if we fail to create that balance, if we are unwilling to relinquish a fantasy of ourselves as always loving and generous and kind, and of our children as the always-willing recipients of what we want to give, we risk the lopsidedness that comes from a failure to push for growth and maturity.

CHAPTER SEVEN

Adolescence: A New Beginning

Adolescence is an extraordinary phase of life, a kind of developmental renaissance, bursting with energy, fraught with conflict and paradox. During this time, children mature not just physically and emotionally but also personally, intellectually, socially, and morally. As we watch our adolescents exercise adult skills—organize fund-raisers, throw parties, drive cars, write computer programs, or debate the great issues of the day—we may forget that these amazingly adept young people are removed from childhood by only a few years at the most. In a crisis, they may easily slip back into more childlike patterns.

If they do, their parents may feel both isolated and helpless. Somehow, that network of other parents that offered both practical help and moral support when the kids were young doesn't seem to be available anymore. Perhaps part of the reason is that parents are far more likely to discuss their toddler's bad behavior (refusing to eat anything but hot dogs, hitting other kids, throwing tantrums) than they are to share their teenager's problems (getting pregnant, taking drugs, binging and purging).

During difficult tearing-your-hair-out times, you might find some perspective by comparing the adolescent behavior that's upsetting you with your child's first struggles to separate. The toddlers we described earlier were atempting to metamorphose from infant to child. In adolescence, there is a similar challenge: to emerge from the cocoon of childhood, unfold one's adult wings, and fly.

Many parents feel that, because they've been teenagers themselves, they are qualified experts-in-residence. How disappointed they are when they attempt to share their own adolescent experiences to find they are as likely to be met with scorn ("That was then; this is now") as with interested appreciation. In truth, as difficult as it might have been a generation ago, there is no question that adolescence is even more complicated today.

Why is adolescence such a trying time? What's at stake for the child? For the parent? In this chapter, we'll try to answer these questions by looking at the challenges the adolescent faces in moving from the world of the child to the world of the adult. Compared with the wealth of printed material now available for the general reader on the subject of early-childhood development, there is relatively little on the subject of adolescence; so before we go on to examine the special perils that the Too Precious Child may encounter, we would like to explore the overall tasks adolescents must accomplish to grow up and the many stages and steps and subphases of this complex transition.

FROM THE FIRST PIMPLE TO PERMANENT EMPLOYMENT

As we begin to focus on the inner emotional and intellectual changes of adolescence, we must at least make reference to the obvious: this is a time of tremendous biological change—in every part of the body, not just the gonads. One easily observable change is that youngsters grow rapidly taller. Of course. But it's not so easy and obvious if you're the one who has suddenly grown ten inches and when you go to kick a football, you find your knee where your foot used to be. It takes some getting used to.

Sexual changes are just as striking and far less easy to talk about. "My, how tall you've grown," is a more socially acceptable remark than "Goodness, you've developed breasts." In addition to providing evidence that a child is becoming an adult, this transition to a sexually mature status has developmental consequences. The adolescent sexual drive gives impetus to the desire to separate from one's family of origin and ultimately leads to the creation of a family of one's own.

Accompanying the physical changes are intellectual ones. Inside the mind of the adolescent, striking cognitive changes are taking place that amount to a profound neuropsychological reorganization. Jean Piaget, the Swiss psychologist and grandfather of cognitive development, described this process as a shift from concrete to abstract thinking. Adolescents suddenly develop the ability to understand concepts of "infinity" and "forever." Because they can now think about thinking, and are capable of being truly *self*-conscious, their parents may notice the beginning of a new era of diaries, secrets, privacy.

During this time, there may be an explosion of creativity. Many great thinkers, writers, visual artists, and musicians begin to blossom during adolescence. But whether or not this creativity ever comes to benefit the world, it may be a wonderful way for youngsters to express and ease some of the pain of this confusing time.

Russ was sullen, angry, unwilling to talk to parents or teachers—none of whom knew what to make of his hostile behavior. He wouldn't talk and his basic mood seemed to be anger. What a surprise to discover that he was a musician and poet. He composed songs that expressed his sadness, his loneliness, and his worries about the future.

In addition to the physical and intellectual changes are the social ones. As they enter junior high and high school, adolescents must learn to cope not only with greater educational demands but also with more complex social environments. There are labels that they may either covet or dread—"jocks," "brains," "soshes," "heads," "nerds," "sleazes."

Leaving the safe world of the neighborhood school may create great and lasting apprehension. One boy who had always eagerly looked forward to his birthday turned pale when he reached fourteen and said he didn't have a lot to celebrate. He dreaded leaving his local eight-year primary school where everyone knew him for the anonymity of the large district high school. Sooner or later, most youngsters adjust, but we know a forty-four-year-old woman whose subconscious has a permanent record of this time. She has a recurrent dream every September. She's in the ninth grade; it's her first day in high school; and she is hopelessly lost, unable to find the next class on her schedule. Every door she knocks on is the wrong door. The people in the room look at her with superior, scornful smiles. They are tenth-graders.

How long does adolescence last? For some people, it never ends. The perpetual graduate student is an example of someone who has gotten stuck in a developmental rut. But for most of us, adolescence starts with the onset of the sexual changes of puberty (the word used to describe physical development into an adult) and ends with the establishment of an adult set of values and goals sometime during the early twenties.

Parental perspective is not easily come by during this early phase of adolescence. At times, maturation seems so steady and sure, so impressive, that we begin to believe we've got a thirty-year-old sophisticate under our roof. What a shock when the said sophisticate runs into problems and begins throwing tantrums like a three-year-old!

> *Competent, self-confident Aviva was, at fourteen, a top student, a soprano in the school chorus, and an active member of her synagogue youth group. She wrote long essays for her demanding honors English class, took buses by herself wherever she needed to go, and filled out an application to be a counselor-in-training at a summer camp. Yet, one evening when her mother reminded her to feed her cat, Aviva burst into tears, and began shouting, "I'm not a child. You don't trust me. Just leave me alone." It became apparent that she was doing entirely too much and was expecting too much of herself.*

Schoolwork now may and should require more long-range planning, more investigation, and more conceptual material, but too often schools, responding to pressures for higher-quality education, undertake an intellectual Great Leap Forward without a teaching staff that has the academic training or developmental know-how to accomplish it. "The teacher assigned a research paper on the origins and development of the English language, and we have to have at least ten footnotes," says an anxious eighth-grade boy to his parents. "What should I do? I don't know what she wants." That's not all he doesn't know. He doesn't understand what research is or how to do it—or what a footnote is for. He and most of his classmates will do the assignment by copying material out of encyclopedias.

A SECOND CHANCE

For parents and children, adolescence is a chance to relive and rework earlier issues. As adults, we tend to look back on our own adolescence with a mixture of chagrin and nostalgia. Wouldn't it be nice to be young again, just for a Saturday night—but, Lord, what idiotic chances we took then! We may think we have left our youthful selves behind, yet few of us truly have. A parent may come to an interaction with a teenager trailing the remnants, or shadow, of an adolescent self. All or part of the adult's unfinished business from that turbulent time may cloud the interaction, obscuring the real people and the real issues. In a family, quite a crowd may assemble during a heated interchange. There is the mother and her shadow adolescent, Dad and his unfinished adolescent, the real adolescent, possibly some older brothers and sisters with their shadows, and maybe even some leftover business from Grandpa and *his* adolescent, which then influenced Dad, and so on.

Lori was an effervescent sixteen-year-old, full of ideas and opinions, very involved in student government. She was a frequent participant in school assemblies and was asked to represent her school in statewide events. Yet, when Lori's mother got angry at her exemplary daughter, she'd refer to her as "you little tramp." Lori wasn't even going out with boys! What Lori didn't know was that her mother had become pregnant as a teenager and had relinquished the baby for adoption. She had never been able to mourn the loss of this first child. For her, Lori's adolescence led to a reawakening of painful memories that had lain dormant for many years.

Shadowy themes that span generations may emerge during this phase.

Gary had always been a good student who liked school, so when he got to tenth grade and started getting C's, D's, and F's, his parents were perplexed. Neither promising him rewards for good marks nor yelling at him seemed to work. Finally, they all entered family therapy, and as they explored their ways of interrelating, a definite generational theme became apparent. During their arguments, father was in the habit of announcing that son wouldn't amount to a hill of beans. This made no sense. Gary had lots of potential. Where did it come from? The therapist helped trace the accusation back through two generations. As a teenager, Gary's father had been badgered repeatedly with the same words and had left his family early to join the navy. His grandfather, too, had heard the same message; he'd been raised in a very strict home where he was told daily how bad he was.

While adults struggle with their shadows, teenagers are busy reworking conflicts that haven't been fully resolved at earlier stages. If separation was a problem at age two and a half, the same old separation, in a new guise, suddenly becomes a battleground in the teens. The toddler who wanted to take the escalator all by herself is now a teenager who wants to drive from Chicago to San Francisco with her sixteen-year-old boyfriend.

Looking ahead, we see that emotional and intellectual growth does not end with adolescence. Indeed, if our children fail to grapple successfully with separation issues in adolescence, those issues will return to haunt them as adults, and the shadowy influence of the past may obscure their own children's present reality.

TOWARD AN ADULT SELF

In order to understand the difficulties that face a Too Precious Adolescent, we need to know more about the emotional and intellectual transitions that take place during this period of life. Like early childhood, adolescence can be divided into a series of stages. Girls frequently begin the process about two years ahead of boys. Some girls as young as ten are beginning to exhibit not only early breast development but also the emotional upheavals that accompany puberty: the moodiness and stormy outbursts and anxiety that are typical of the teen years. Usually, however, the process begins during junior high school. An occasional youngster may get off to a late start in high school.

EARLY ADOLESCENCE: WHAT AM I?

Am I a boy? Am I a girl? A brain? A jock? An adult or a child? Is my body okay? Do I look like the other kids? Asking—and trying to answer—these questions are the preoccupations of this early phase. This period coincides fairly well with puberty, which is the *biological* transition from childhood to adulthood.

Young adolescents begin to take giant strides toward independence. They go downtown by themselves, go to parties without their parents, handle larger allowances, and receive more responsibility at home. Heady with freedom, or overwhelmed, they may make demands that can sound unreasonable to their parents—often substantiated by references to the infamous "everybody."

"Everybody I know can stay out until one in the morning," sniffs an aggrieved thirteen-year-old, the pitiful offspring of two hateful antiquarians in their late thirties. The antiquarians in question were surprised to learn that "everybody" was a very bright, very unhappy girl whose parents had dropped out of the parenting business.

Separation is the big issue, and there may be a lot of turmoil as parents struggle with a young teenager's demands for personal freedom. The youngster no longer wants to be part of the family unit; he or she may protest at having to go on family vacations or attend religious services.

Peer pressure begins to take over. Suddenly, parents find themselves doing battle with an amorphous "they" who appear to have unlimited influence. As the world of the adolescent becomes centered on self and peers (others who are "like me"), the process of separation becomes increasingly painful for parents (those who are no longer "like me"). So intense is the quest for identity, that any child who acts or looks "different"—who plays the violin, or comes from a foreign country or possibly even a different junior high—frequently feels isolated and set apart.

For many youngsters, especially girls, the separation process is a very dramatic and tearful one, with ringing cries of "You don't understand me" echoing throughout the household. The great vehicle for the establishment of boundaries is the slammed door. Underlying the *Sturm und Drang* is the theme of loss: loss of childhood, loss of innocence, loss of the time when things were (or seemed) much more simple. Because of this sense of loss, parents may see their early adolescents express sorrow, anguish, or anger out of all proportion to the outward events that provoke these responses.

> *"Why is Ted shut up in his room?" asked his surprised father. "He was just in here a minute ago telling me about his new Siamese fighting fish."*
>
> *"I think I did it," said Ted's somewhat stunned mother. "I asked him if he'd returned his library books."*

To soothe the pain of this phase and to achieve some control or mastery, the struggling adolescent may find that his or her peers help the separation and offer support outside the family group. The telephone is a mighty conduit to the world beyond, a link to the peer group. Rock music, played at full volume, reinforces the sense of self (youngsters identify with particular musical groups and styles) and delivers a sustaining message: "There is life away from home and homework and worry."

Telephones and rock music play a part in many power struggles between parents and teens. These fights may seem trivial or ridiculous on the surface, but underneath is a serious issue: the right to separate. No one is really arguing about five more minutes on the phone or five more decibels of radio noise. Parents sense they're being shut out, and they may react with grief or outrage.

MIDDLE ADOLESCENCE: WHO AM I?

Am I attractive? Am I popular? Am I smart? Is my poetry any good?

In middle adolescence, which usually coincides with the high school years, youngsters put a great deal of energy into exploring their personal values and identity. Peers, telephone, and music continue to ease the transition from the world of the family and help to answer the conundrum: Who am I? The car or the motorcycle becomes a powerful symbol of separation and freedom.

During this time, youngsters strain to escape, pushing at the gates of parental limits. Safety issues frequently involve bizarre dialogues between parent and teenager: the parent, frightened—no, terrified—that something horrible may happen, decides to work some tips on "defensive driving" into a coversation while the teenager stares off into the distance with an alarming lack of comprehension and an even scarier lack of interest. Because adolescents feel themselves surrounded by a sort of bubble of protection, it is extremely difficult to teach caution.

This sense of magical protection is at the root of millions of unplanned and unwanted pregnancies ("How could I be pregnant? We only had sex once, and I douched with Seven-Up"). While regressive forces within our society are actively working to restrict teenagers' access to information and contraception, the media continue to promote the glamour and freedom and fun of sex while banning any mention of sexual responsibility from the airwaves. Lovers in soap operas have active sex lives, but as they hop into bed, they're never heard to ask, "Are you using birth control?"

How can parents promote safety at this critical time? Remember that too many warnings will weaken your case, and your teenager will begin to tune you out. The teenage ear is deaf to an admonishment like "Wear wool socks or your toes will freeze," a message rightly perceived as relevant only to younger children. If your parting words to your son as he goes out the door are "Take your jacket or you'll get pneumonia, and don't drink, and comb your hair," your chances of being heard are minimal. Rather, your efforts will be more effective if you stick with the premier issue: "Don't drive if you drink."

This is a good time to sort out parental priorities and select only those safety issues that are most important to you. Throwing in a gratuitous "eat-your-spinach" or a "wear-your-sweater" message is going to lessen the impact of more major warnings. (And if your teens haven't learned to wear sweaters by now, they may never learn.)

Some parents have difficulty expressing a practical bottom-line concern about drinking or sex because they're afraid to say anything that will be interpreted as permission to do the impermissible. If this is your fear, you may or may not be consoled by realizing that teenagers are going to do whatever they do anyway.

We suggest you say something along the following lines:

> "Please don't drive if you've been drinking, Anne. It's much too dangerous. If, in spite of what

I say, you drink, please call me and I'll come get you."

"Steve, I don't think at sixteen you're old enough to have a sexual relationship, and I hope you will agree with me. But one thing is extremely important and that is responsibility: you must make sure you don't get a girl pregnant."

"Please call if you'll be home later than midnight; otherwise I'll be terribly worried."

LATER ADOLESCENCE:
WHAT WILL I BECOME?

During *late adolescence* (the post–high school years up through the early twenties), young people consolidate their values and goals. They decide on occupations and begin to establish responsible sexual-romantic relationships. This is a time for experimenting with one's newly solidified sense of self and for testing out one's dreams in the real world.

If parents have been successful, they will by now have put themselves out of business, having achieved the ultimate victory in the great separation wars: the creation of a mature, confident, competent young adult. If the timing is right, the young will leave the nest equipped for independent life away from the immediate supervision of parents. If separation occurs in an untimely way, then the youngsters may either separate prematurely—unequipped to deal with independence—or not at all, continuing to live at home until well into their twenties, still dependent on Mom and Dad.

THE TASKS OF ADOLESCENCE

"Why do you say these are the best years of my life?"
demands a fourteen-year-old. "If these are the best, being
an adult must be pretty awful."

We've suggested that adolescence is a difficult period, but in order to appreciate just how overwhelming it
may seem, we invite you to consider the formidable tasks
an adolescent must undertake—and succeed at—in
order to make the transition from the dependent existence of childhood to the independence of adulthood.

If you want to become an autonomous adult, you must:

- Find out who you are.

- Convince your parents you can take care of
yourself responsibly.

- Develop a set of ethical guidelines.

- Learn how to live with the rules that help you get
along in the world, neither accepting nor reject-
ing them blindly.

- Learn how to have close relationships.

- Learn how to deal with people in a practical way.

- Learn how to deal with your sexuality, both
physically and emotionally.

- Explore what you want to do with your life.

- Begin to acquire the skills you will need to be self-supporting.

- Learn to view your parents realistically and limit your battles with them to a necessary minimum.

- Develop realistic aspirations and find role models that embody them.

SAD TEENS: HOW TO RECOGNIZE
A SERIOUS PROBLEM

Once we're aware of the magnitude of the developmental tasks that adolescents face, perhaps we shouldn't find it surprising that they experience a good deal of misery as they struggle to grow up. Parents can expect their adolescents to experience some form of sadness; for most youngsters, though, that sadness will be temporary and will be caused by something that happens in the outer world—losing the student council race or a spot on the team. Some youngsters, however, may have inner difficulties that lead to a serious depression.

Too Precious Teens are apt to take their losses harder, since they've been taught to believe that the world is, or should be, their oyster. They may feel that their parents regard them as failures or that somehow the world has failed to come through and deliver—the way they've been led to expect it would.

As youngsters grow older, they're more able to deal with disappointment. A seventeen-year-old will be far more skillful in dealing with frustration and rejection than a thirteen-year-old who's trying to cope simultaneously with a new body, new friends, new feelings, and a new school.

If a youngster doesn't bounce back from a disappointment, can't seem to take an interest in anything or have fun, and continues to be sad and irritable, parents have cause for concern. The following eight symptoms are indicators of depression. If there are four or more of these symptoms—and if they persist beyond two weeks—you should consult with a mental-health professional.

1. Overeating or loss of appetite
2. Sleeping problems: sleeping long hours or being unable to sleep
3. Inactivity or hyperactivity
4. Diminished interest in activities
5. Loss of energy
6. Feelings of guilt and worthlessness
7. Impaired ability to concentrate
8. Recurrent thoughts of death or suicide (This alone is a reason to seek professional help.)

Children and adolescents don't always show their feelings in the same way as adults. Frequently, they allow their bodies or their behavior to tell the story. If your teenager exhibits symptoms such as recurrent headaches, stomachaches, drug abuse, eating disorders, problems with the law or with those in authority, school refusal, or sexual promiscuity, there's a reasonable chance that depression is at the root of the problem. Again, if you're concerned that your youngster may be struggling with depression, we suggest you talk it over with your family doctor and ask to be referred to a psychologist, psychiatrist, or family counselor who has been trained to work with adolescents.

"YOU HIT MY HAIR"

While serious and persistent depression is abnormal and may require professional help, serious self-centeredness is to be expected. What would be diagnosed as a personality disorder in adult life, in adolescence is normal. The technical term for this self-centeredness, *narcissism*, is a word that has acquired negative connotations. Yet, it is an ingredient of any healthy personality, and when we encounter it in someone who is caring and attentive to others, we approvingly call it self-esteem. What parents of a teenager need to remember is that this self-centeredness is both necessary and temporary. During adolescence, the scales are tilted toward extreme self-involvement as youngsters ask and attempt to answer those crucial questions about their identity—What am I? Who am I? What will I become?

During her high school years, Marnie was always busy when her parents needed some help, and she seemed outraged that they would expect her to interrupt what she was doing—or what she intended to do after she finished watching her favorite soap opera—to straighten up the kitchen or feed the dog. When Marnie came home from college for Thanksgiving break and offered to run errands, then asked, "Is there anything else I can do?" her mother and father were amazed and delighted. What had happened?

Marnie was growing up. The intense self-absorption of adolescence had served its purpose, and Marnie was emerging from that cocoon of narcissism as a reasonable and cooperative human being.

Because we've stressed the importance of teaching children that they do not always occupy the foreground, that they exist in a social context in which other people's needs may sometimes take precedence, we want to emphasize that all is not lost when a teenager begins to exhibit symptoms that in an adult would lead to a diagnosis of narcissistic personality disorder.

Adult narcissists enrage and alienate friends, fellow workers, and lovers. They are lonely and dissatisfied people. Therefore, when parents encounter extreme self-centeredness in their youngsters, they may experience not only exasperation with the behavior but fear that it heralds a miserable adulthood. But as we look at the chief components of narcissism and the ways in which they manifest themselves in teenagers, we need to remember that there is one important and consoling difference: in most teenagers, the behavior and mind-set is *temporary*.

What kinds of behavior can we characterize as "narcissistic"? How can we deal with them or at least understand them?

A grandiose sense of self-importance or uniqueness and a preoccupation with fantasies of unlimited success

Adolescents may imagine themselves as future stars. They are often self-important and filled with a sense of their own uniqueness, a sense that stems in part from their recently acquired abilities to think abstractly. This ability to think about thinking may be so exhilarating that it leads to intense creative efforts.

> *Noah had always been a great reader. Now, at the age of sixteen, he had decided to become a great writer. He set up his office in the neighborhood coffee shop and spent hours there, drinking Cokes and writing the novel that would reveal his singular vision. When his nervous parents suggested that he consider a backup career in journalism, say, or business communications just in case things didn't work out for him, Noah was outraged. Why didn't his parents share his confidence? What does practicality have to do with anything anyway?*

An exhibitionistic need for constant attention and admiration

The makeup, endlessly and painstakingly applied. The nonstop parading back and forth in front of one another at football games, at the mall, in the park. This constant primping and preening is fairly universal teenage behavior. Parents may not approve, but they're wasting their breath if they think that lectures on vanity will have any effect. They may, however, stress decorum ("If you want to clean your nails, you can do it in the bathroom, not at the dinner table"), and they also have the right to prevent grooming from interfering with their own plans or convenience.

A characteristic response to threats to self-esteem

How distant and aloof teenagers get when they think we don't like their best friend, or their hair. There is an amusing scene in the narcissists' teen opera, *Saturday Night Fever*, in which the character played by John Travolta, having devoted hours to showering, shaving, and blow-drying his hair in order to look perfect when he goes out, finally joins his family at the dinner table. During dinner, his father, angered by a smart remark, reaches over and smacks Travolta on the head. Travolta looks at his father in genuine shock and says, with a mixture of disbelief and disgust, "You hit my hair."

A constant search for admiration and attention: appearance is more important than substance

Parents try to tell their sons and daughters that it's not all that important to make the basketball or debating team. But their children know the truth of adolescent experience: being important, being recognized, is where it's at! Mirroring is more helpful than explaining that in a few years the whole incident won't matter. Parents may make statements like "I can see you are really upset. You were really looking forward to being on the team."

An inability to recognize and experience how others feel

The classic battle provoked by this characteristic erupts over safety issues. For the parent, the challenge is to let up on the reins, gradually giving the child more freedom. For the child, the problem is that he or she feels belittled by parental concern. Furthermore, teenagers see no earthly reason why a parent *would* be worried: after all, *they* know they're safe. This inability to take the other person's point of view, especially when that person is in authority, is striking and underlies many conflicts between parents and their kids.

An expectation of special favors without the assumption of reciprocal responsibilities

This one is legendary: wanting an allowance or a good grade but not feeling that parents or teachers have the right to ask for anything in return. Parents may think they've made a deal only to find that their youngster hasn't followed or understood his or her end of the bargain. "What's the matter with you?" is a less useful parental line than "I expect you to do what we've agreed to, and if I need to spell it out more clearly, I will."

DEFINING RULES AND VALUES: AN IMPORTANT PARENTAL TASK

Adolescents are narcissistic and, as we've seen, may behave in infuriatingly conceited, self-involved ways. Should parents simply shrug their shoulders, remember that this too shall pass, and decide to ignore the behavior? Should they let their kids live out their fantasies—line their rooms with mirrors, congratulate them on their skill with a blow dryer, and have their breakfast of cold pizza and cookies served to them in bed by a maid who will pause on her way out to adjust the lighting to the teen's cosmetic advantage? Is there any point, when we can expect either a fight or indifference, in trying to break through the wall of self-involvement and insist that teenagers eat with the family, not tie up the telephone all night, be more thoughtful toward those less fortunate, and have a more pleasant and cooperative attitude?

The answer is yes, absolutely yes. Parents have an important job to do during these years. First of all, teenagers live in the parental home, and there must be someone in charge, defining its rules and values. It is by the very act of definition that we provide them with structure, thereby simplifying the struggle for emancipation. (Don't ever offer this as an explanation for rules. Your teen won't understand a word of what you're saying.) The whole process is very reminiscent of the earlier parental power struggle with the toddler who wants to rule the roost.

It is much easier to answer the question "Who am I?" if parents are providing information about who *they* are. It can be exhausting to a parent to argue again and again that Carla can't wear her Madonna getup to Grandma's for Thanksgiving dinner. It can be discouraging to insist over and over that John must help around the house *and* have a good attitude about it. It can be appalling to watch Paula's intense self-absorption and the hours—and money—invested in hair and clothes and makeup. It can be frustrating to have someone in the house who insists on privacy but doesn't want to give it, who wants privileges but doesn't accept reciprocal responsibilities, who wants to be an astronaut but doesn't see any need to do homework.

Parents commonly find themselves irritated by their youngster's behavior—and may be surprised and somewhat horrified to find themselves screaming, "Me, me, me. That's all we ever hear. Can't you ever think of anybody but yourself?" Have they dealt a lethal blow to the narcissistic adolescent's tender ego? And, yet, parents, as representatives of the outside world, must be ever vigilant and remind the youngster that he or she is not the be-all and end-all. Without feedback ("Carla, that outfit is not appropriate for a family dinner" or "John, you're getting out of line"), the preconditions for the Too Precious Adolescent are established. Youngsters need reminding that their long-term goal is to reach a balance between the wants and wishes of the self and the wants and wishes of the interdependent world in which we all live.

Parents may make these reminders in a way that is sympathetic rather than destructive. Our goal isn't to tell our teenagers that they have no right to their desires to be beautiful and famous. What we're trying to do is set clear limits to self-involved behavior.

CONTRACTS INSTEAD OF CONFLICTS

Contracts may be useful: they're agreements that serve to codify the expectations of the parents (the guardians of external reality) and the wishes of the adolescent for freedoms (car, phone, friends, time, etc.). But this solution only works when there is an actual commitment made with established consequences.

PARENT: David, if you aren't home by midnight, you've had it.
TEEN: (Silence)
PARENT: Are you deaf? Did you hear me?
TEEN: Yes.

The problem here is that this is a pseudocontract. David may or may not be home by midnight. If he's late and you tell him he's grounded for two weeks, he'll protest with outraged innocence that you never told him you were going to do anything so cruel and unusual. And, in a way, you didn't. "You've had it" might mean anything from "I'll yell at you" to "You're grounded for life."

Here's a more workable contract:

PARENT: David, last week you came home after midnight, and I was very worried [or, that broke the rules]. I'd like to let you go to the party tonight, but I need you to promise that you'll be home before midnight. Will you make that promise?

TEEN: (Silence)

PARENT: If you can't make that promise, I can't let you go out.

TEEN: Okay, I'll be home by midnight.

PARENT: Good. I'm sure you'll be home on time, but if you're not, I wouldn't let you go out again for quite a while. Do you understand?

TEEN: Yes.

Now you have a contract. You have agreed that your youngster may go out. He has agreed that he will be home by midnight and he has indicated that he understands what will happen if he isn't.

Unless a teenager has a very bad track record, it's a good idea to allow for some negotiating.

PARENT: Meg, will you be home by midnight?

TEEN: Midnight! This is the biggest party of the year. No one else will leave that early.

PARENT: What time would *you* think is okay?

TEEN: Two o'clock.

PARENT: That's too late. Why don't you call Cindy to see if you can sleep over? I don't want you out driving that late. Twelve-thirty is the latest I'd agree to.

TEEN: I can't do that now! I think Cindy is still mad about something. I mean, maybe I can stay over, but maybe I can't.

(Teen and Parent pause to consider next moves. Parent resists urge to ask why Cindy is mad.)

PARENT: Can you call me from the party to let me know whether you plan to stay over?

TEEN: All right. I can do that.

PARENT: Then we agree that you'll call, say by eleven-thirty, to tell me whether you're planning to be home by twelve-thirty or to stay over at Cindy's?

TEEN: Yeah, I'll call.

This may look like a painfully detailed conversation, but we've found it's better to be absolutely explicit. The little things left unsaid may leave you pacing the floor at midnight, wondering what is supposed to happen next.

Parents frequently feel uncomfortable about asserting their primacy as parents: it makes them feel too bossy or authoritarian or simply too much like their own parents. But without clarity and rules and expectations, children lack a framework to grow in, a structure to struggle against in order to define themselves. When parents are unable to set limits, or identify themselves too closely with their separating teens, we begin to see the subject of our next chapter: the Too Precious Adolescent.

CHAPTER EIGHT
The Perils of Being a Too Precious Adolescent

Times of transition hold both promise and peril. We've seen how this is so in younger children as they move from phase to phase. But adolescence is an especially perilous time because the stakes seem so much higher. The four-year-old girl who decides to "play doctor" isn't going to get pregnant. The nine-year-old boy with poor marks in fourth grade may suffer internal blows to his self-esteem, but college admissions offices won't be looking at the record.

Adolescents still face all the perils of the younger child and may begin facing some of the perils of adulthood as adolescence ends. In between, the list is endless. There are perils with peers, perils with self, perils with family, perils with religion—perils going out, perils staying in, perils with eating, sleeping, and learning. Perils with perils. All of these are compounded by parents who cannot easily give leave to separate.

Too Precious Adolescents must struggle with an impossible dilemma. Their urgent need to separate is opposed by an unbearable fear of causing the parent to suffer. "My mother wants me to be her little child; and if I grow up, she will be miserably unhappy with me. Maybe I'd better stay little [i.e., anorexia] or disappear [i.e., suicide] or become so confused I don't know what to do [i.e., depression]." These extreme measures are attempts, however mistaken or self-destructive, to cope with the agonizing conflict they experience as they attempt to grow up.

Parents who have been overnurturing or overdemanding may unwittingly push their children to extreme behavior, and no parents are more stunned when forced to confront the fact that their children have serious problems. "Attempted suicide? Anorexia nervosa? Where did we go wrong? All we ever wanted was the very best for our children." That this painful situation had its roots in their overinvolvement, that it was out of their zealousness or adoration that the illness arose, is especially painful to acknowledge.

Yes, this is scary stuff, but one of our purposes in exploring this behavior and its dangerous consequences is to frighten you; some of the things teenagers do are life-threatening and must be quickly attended to by their parents. A suicide attempt cannot be ignored. The underlying problem won't go away if you pretend that nothing is really wrong.

Our primary goal, however, is to offer some insight into the mechanisms that are at work and some reassurance: that by making changes in their own responses, parents may become more useful to their teenaged children. By understanding some of the perils of a Too Precious Adolescence, you may be able to improve a bad situation rather than perpetuate it. Remember, too, that most teenagers will somehow manage the journey to adulthood. Despite the perils, they will arrive, perhaps scarred but still alive and functioning.

ANNA FREUD'S DEVELOPMENTAL LINES

Adolescent problems really ought to come as no surprise. Yet, though their roots lie deep in childhood, parents may ignore them or be truly ignorant that serious difficulties exist when their children are young. They attribute things that ought to worry them to childishness and wait for them to be outgrown. Some problems are outgrown and some aren't.

In Chapter 4, in discussing the process of attachment and separation, we talked about Anna Freud's helpful concept of developmental lines and of how those lines show motion and continuity through time. By looking at three of them now—eating, working, and sexuality—we can begin to explore why and how parental overinvolvement causes problems for teenagers.[1]

The Too Precious Adolescent may develop problems with eating.

"Rational eating" is Anna Freud's phrase for the successful culmination of a line of development that moves from suckling and dependency to the ability to choose foods and regulate food intake in a responsible way. As children grow older, they learn to make better decisions about how much to eat, when to eat, when not to eat, and what to eat. During the toddler years, battles over food are common and expectable; but when the struggle for separation reemerges in early adolescence, decisions about eating may sometimes be linked to a more desperate struggle for control which takes the form of eating too much (obesity, bulimia), eating too little (anorexia nervosa), or eating the wrong things (nutritional deficiencies, junk food junkies).

While only a very small percentage of teenagers with eating disorders end up in the hospital, difficulties with "rational eating" are fairly common. The roots of these problems find fertile soil in our present cultural climate. Spend a day watching television and you'll notice alternating and contradictory images: gorgeous sleek bikini-ed bodies bronzed by the sun are interspersed with advertisements featuring food and more food. Couples greedily ingest cookies, candy, pancakes, pizza; children use packaged cupcakes to make friends; father and son fight over the possession of a frozen waffle; families sneak off for bowls of ice cream; youngsters make it through piano recitals because visions of future burgers dance in their heads. These are hardly visions of what Anna Freud calls "rational eating."

Parents may wisely decide not to keep too close and critical an eye on what their teenagers weigh; their kids have a peer group that is already doing the job too well. Two researchers studying a group of high school students found that more than half the girls wanted to weigh at least 10 percent less than their normal weight. Although only 20 percent of the girls were actually overweight, 59 percent of them said they "frequently" thought they were fat, and another 14 percent said they "sometimes" considered themselves to be fat.[2] Remarks like "You seem to have put on a couple of pounds" only reinforce the constant message relayed by peers, TV, and magazines: "You could be thinner."

Problems with rational eating may seem to appear

suddenly, out of the blue, but they have a history in past failures—in the inability of parents to support, and youngsters to achieve, separation. Teenagers who have not succeeded in differentiating their needs and wishes from those of their parents may struggle for separation in ways that would be more appropriate for toddlers.

Two kinds of parental overinvolvement may contribute to eating disorders. Some parents overfeed their children as part of a general pattern of overnurture. You may recall Adonis, the only and long-awaited son, whose adoring parents would sneak cookies into his mouth as he crawled about the floor exploring. Would you be surprised to learn that fourteen-year-old Adonis overeats or that when the scale hit 230, his anxious mother enrolled him in a weight-loss program? She didn't want him to be overweight, just well fed.

Another kind of overinvolved parent may, by contrast, be exceptionally involved in the youngster's diet and "thinness." Here, the child is expected to play a role in satisfying the parent's narcissistic need to be pretty, successful, talented, or thin. In an earlier chapter, we gave the example of this kind of overinvolvement: Lizzie's mother was irritated with her plump daughter. She wanted a slender ballerina who would have the career in dance she had never achieved.

If both parents and children are perfectionistic, they may be providing fertile ground for anorexia nervosa, an increasingly common psychiatric disorder with extremely serious consequences.

Randi was adorable, a bright and capable youngster, who enjoyed spending time with her friends. But there was something puzzling about her. She seemed ob-

*sessed with exercise. Early one morning, after a success-
fully raucous slumber party at her friend Claudia's
house, she appeared fully dressed in the kitchen with her
bus money in hand and explained to Claudia's parents
that she had to get to an early-morning exercise class.
"Why not skip it, Randi?" they suggested. "It's Saturday.
Why not relax? Sit down and join us for breakfast." She
explained anxiously that she couldn't skip her class. If she
did, she would get fat. Her behavior was puzzling at the
time. In retrospect, however, it became clear. Two months
after the party, Claudia told her parents that Randi had
been hospitalized with a diagnosis of anorexia nervosa.*

Randi's parents were taken by surprise. They'd done
everything they could to be model parents. Mom ironed
all her daughter's clothes, even her nightgowns and
T-shirts, and Dad supervised every theme Randi was assigned to make sure that everything was correctly spelled
and neatly written. They had been so proud of her when
she'd taken top honors in her junior high school science
fair, and they'd spent a lot of money to send her to a
special summer program for gifted young scientists. It
was painful for them to listen to her anger when she
began to express it, hard to accept that their child just
wanted to be "regular," and deeply troubling to realize
that their behavior had played a part in Randi's illness,
but they also realized they cared more about helping their
daughter get well than they did about defending their
abilities as parents.

In a world in which every other person seems to be
on a diet, how does one recognize symptoms of serious
eating disorders? Anorexia is easier to spot than bulimia. Ninety percent of its victims are female. The classic

anorectic becomes progressively thinner while vigorously denying that she has a problem: "I'm not too thin. I'm not even thin enough!" Often, she'll exercise very strenuously, at least until she's too weak to summon up the energy. If parents suspect that their child is an anorectic, they need to seek the help of a professional with special training in dealing with eating disorders. The problem is serious and may become life-threatening. Treatment usually requires family therapy, and the victim of anorexia may need to be hospitalized.

Bulimia, too, is most often a problem of young women. One study of college students attending a summer session of a suburban liberal arts university found that almost one-fifth of the young women had bulimic symptoms.[3] Bulimia is generally not as much of a medical emergency as is anorexia, but if allowed to continue, it may have very significant health consequences, and it too may become life-threatening. Victims eat huge quantities of food, then induce vomiting or resort to laxatives in the hope that they won't gain weight. Any evidence of recurrent vomiting or regular use of laxatives may very well be symptoms of bulimia; if so, experienced professional help must be sought.

A high percentage of youngsters with eating disorders have parents who viewed them as "perfect" and compliant—until the problem developed. What these parents may not realize is the terrible price their children have paid. "Perfection" often means doing what the parents want.

> *When eight-year-old Lily saw the bright red winter coat with a black velvet collar, she wanted it right away. It was just her size and it was almost exactly like the navy*

one her mother picked out. "Oh, honey, you don't want that red coat," said her mother in a disapproving, disappointed voice. "You wouldn't really like it. You want this navy blue one, right? You look just precious in navy blue. You want the blue coat, don't you?"

Lily didn't make a fuss; she chose the blue coat. Her mother was gratified that her daughter had such good taste. Year in and year out the same pattern was repeated. After a while, Lily didn't know the difference between what she wanted and what her mother wanted her to want. But somewhere deep inside, Lily knew that in order to be loved, she was going to have to conform to her mother's wishes. When Lily developed a serious eating disorder, her mother was shocked and upset. Why all this crazy stuff about being thin from the one child who was always so easygoing and cooperative?

Sweet harmony isn't an ideal goal: separation involves struggle and dissent. Parents and children can expect to have disagreements, and they need to be able to deal with them directly and openly. Family conversations, meetings, dialogues, are all helpful.

The Too Precious Adolescent may become either an anxious overachiever or an anxious underachiever.

If some adolescents encounter problems along the path to rational eating, many more experience difficulties with Anna Freud's next continuum: "From body to toy, and from play to work." The beginnings of this second line of development are simple and natural. All normal babies learn to move their fingers, suck their toes, and grasp objects. As children grow older, their play becomes incredibly sophisticated as they manipulate tiny Legos to create detailed structures and make up increasingly complex games. The drive to play deepens over time to include the pleasures of studying and learning, building and working. One expects a toddler to spend time playing; one expects a ten-year-old or fifteen-year-old to spend time playing—but also to show progressive ability to work at chores, schoolwork, music, and basketball.

As children grow up, they discover just how much more is expected of them; their ability to handle the rigors and expectations of the outside world is severely tested. They begin to realize that within the foreseeable future, they will have to bear the unimaginable burdens of adulthood. If all goes well, teenagers come to accept the challenge of work. They learn to do their homework before they watch TV, or maybe even while they watch TV. Somehow, they manage to do what needs to be done without too much prodding. When parents are overprotective or overdemanding, however, teenagers may have to cope with some extra difficulties on the path that leads from play to work. Some anxious young perfectionists decide to satisfy the demands of work so utterly that there is no time for fun, for spending time with friends, for musing, for pleasurable reading, for hobbies of any sort.

Theo, an intelligent high school sophomore, worried incessantly about his schoolwork. Even after he'd spent three hours completing it, he'd put in extra time double-checking his algebra, asking his brother to quiz him on French verbs, or retyping a paper because the margins weren't wide enough. He worried about being able to go to sleep (he was always pretty wound up) and being able to wake up (he was exhausted in the morning). He wor-

ried about not getting into one of the "hot" colleges. Theo always looked pale and drawn, harried, anxious. He never read a book for pleasure or pursued a question that interested him. All his energy was invested in meeting the demands of his high school teachers, and he looked for all the world like a worried little old man.

Theo's parents had been grooming their bright son for a long time, preparing him to win big in the college entrance sweepstakes. From the time he was in third or fourth grade (and not quite sure exactly what college was), they talked about what he would have to do to get into an Ivy League school. His was a problem typical of adolescents who have been exposed from an early age to parental expectations and agendas.

Youngsters like Theo are highly responsive to parental worries. If their parents are high achievers, these youngsters may be acutely aware that they have big shoes to fill, or they may feel intensely the pressure of being "special." They can't manage a transition from childhood play to adult work in a balanced way. Here are the adolescent roots of Type A behavior, that driven, compulsive workaholism so inimical to joy and health.

In contrast to Theo, Siobhan is a classic *under-achiever:*

Siobhan is just as bright as Theo, maybe even brighter; however, her grades plummeted when she entered high school because she refused to do the required assignments. Her parents are baffled and worried by her resistance to work. They have bought her a computer, taken away her bedroom telephone, lectured her on the need to achieve; but no matter what they do, she stub-

bornly insists that it is her life and her right to do with it what she chooses. When they ask, "What about getting into a good college?" she has two standard replies: "What about it?" or "I'll worry about it when the time comes."

Siobhan is so busy fending off what she experiences as parental intrusion into her very "self" that she's unable to perform the necessary transition from play to work. She is stuck somewhere in limbo, since she doesn't have a lot of fun, either. Most of her energy seems funneled into *not* doing her homework. For many adolescents like Siobhan, the pleasures of success and accomplishment are diminished if they feel their parents are orchestrating the whole thing.

In adolescence, the need to "do it myself" echoes the "me do it" insistence of toddlerhood. Parents need to find ways to step back, without withholding their encouragement and love. They need to support without suffocating, steer without strangling, and inspire without stealing their youngster's sense of personal accomplishment.

THE BATTLEFIELD OF HOMEWORK

School performance is a loaded topic during adolescence, and it often turns into a battlefield for struggles between parent and teenager. How can parents be helpful without intruding?

Practice what you preach. It is difficult to expect your child to work hard in school if you don't work hard in your life. You don't have to produce a file folder of yellowing all-A high school report cards, but you do have to accomplish your own tasks well and efficiently if you are going to expect good work from your child.

In the last chapter, we discussed the issue of the "shadow" adolescent that each of us still carries within and that is evoked when we watch our own children struggle with issues we may never have resolved in our own lives. If school was oppressive to you as a teenager, your shadow remembers, and occasionally pops up in remarks or behavior that undermines your conscious belief in work and responsibility. Even though you think you're doing all the right things, your youngster may sense the message of your shadow and behave accordingly. Whatever you say to your child, however brilliantly you lecture on the need for self-discipline or the importance of good high school grades, the example you set by your own behavior when it comes to getting things done—on the job or at home—will be a far more persuasive influence.

Examine your expectations. Not everyone *can* be an A student, a varsity athlete, a performing musician; more to the point, not everyone *should* be. Do you expect more from your teen than he or she has the ability to deliver? High expectations generally raise performance, but impossible ones seldom do and, in fact, may have the opposite effect: "I know I can't do as well as my parents expect, so why even try?"

For Siobhan, our anxious underachiever, taking some of the heat off may be the answer. Parents often resort to the old saw that "anything worth doing is worth doing well," but this sort of expectation may lead to undue and unfair pressure.

As Eda LeShan has observed in *The Conspiracy Against Childhood*:

In the mad rush for academic acceleration, more and more nice, normal kids are being labeled as underachievers or failures without regard for the change in our expectations. We turn our schools into failure factories, insist that our children grow up according to an entirely new time schedule, demand a much higher level of achievement from nursery school to college—and then wonder why so many intelligent children cannot "live up to their potential"!

This book, first published twenty years ago, continues to speak to our present concern with "stress," especially as LeShan challenges us to imagine ourselves trading places with our children and living under similar pressures.

[It] has occurred to me that I do not know any adult who doesn't spend some part of every day underachieving.... Whether you are a lawyer, a housewife, a secretary or a salesman, suppose you knew that every Friday you were going to be tested on everything you were supposed to have learned during the preceding week. You also knew that you would be graded on what you had accomplished—not in relation to your own growth or development over a number of years, but in relation to everyone else around you in your office, or your community.[4]

This is a plea for perspective, not a commitment to underachievement, however. Our overall goal as parents is presumably to do our best to ensure that our children reach adulthood alive, healthy, happy, and successfully prepared to cope with the adult world. Some adolescents need more parental guidance and explicit expectations, some less. How can we decide which approach is best?

Stop, look, and listen. Gordon Deckert, a psychiatrist

and popular lecturer, uses an incident from his adolescence to illustrate the need to pay attention. He was driving a tractor with his great-grandfather when suddenly the engine stalled. Twelve-year-old Gordon tried to restart it. He then pulled out a wrench and repeatedly turned, thumped, and pounded on various parts of the engine without success. Finally, his great-grandfather offered a useful word of advice. "If something isn't working, take a look at what you're doing, *and at least don't do that*." In other words, if your teenager is doing well in school and is happy, fine. But if he or she is performing poorly and is unhappy, *stop* whatever it is that you've been doing, and *look* at your behavior.

Are you putting pressure on your teen? If so, maybe it's too much. Or do you have a *laissez-faire* attitude: "Peter is old enough to make his own decisions, so if he wants to fail math, what can I do?" Maybe Peter needs to hear that you want him to succeed. Perhaps you can offer to arrange for tutoring.

In any case, if you've *stopped* whatever you are doing that isn't working and have *looked* at your own expectations realistically, then your next step is to talk to your teenager about your concerns—and to *listen*. He or she is apt to welcome your honest effort to get feedback. You may find that listening—just listening—may be incredibly difficult and threatening; you may have to bite your tongue to keep from proving that you're "right" and that everything you've been trying to do is (after all) for your youngster's own good. Remember that this is your chance to gather information. If you are drawn into a power struggle, you may lose further chances to communicate. Sometimes, if you reach a stalemate and you and your youngster cannot seem to communicate at all, you may find it helpful to turn to a neutral third person. A few visits with a counselor or therapist who is trained in adolescent development may help get a dialogue going.

College is a means, not an end. There is a strenuous competition going on these days to get into the "right" college, and an illusion that acceptance guarantees "success" for the rest of one's days. Many parents feel that if their youngster doesn't make it into one of the "hot" schools, he or she is marked for a life of failure. With an average life expectancy of sixty more years, how can youngsters be failures at eighteen? They've barely begun to shape their destinies. The right college, from our point of view, is one that will be stimulating and intellectually exciting and suited to the needs of your particular youngster, and there's a long list of those. Or maybe no college is "right," and your youngster needs a different post— high school experience such as work or travel.

Again, it is always important to listen. If fifteen-year-old Justin says he wants to go to Harvard, Stanford, or Michigan, your advice about the need for good grades, extracurricular activities, and preparation for College Boards is helpful. If Alexa, who's at the top of her class, says she's only applying to State, ask why. Is it because all her friends are going? Is it because she has a boyfriend there? You might suggest she consider other schools as well. But if she wants to go because they have an excellent program in a field she wants to explore, she may be making a sound choice, even if State is not the sticker you wanted on your car.

Battles over school performance may enlarge to include the whole issue of The Future—and who "decides" what a teenager's will be. Before making pronouncements about your child's future, try asking yourself some hard

questions. Is my child really suited to a career in medicine
or law—or do I think that's the best choice because that's
what I did (or wished I had done)? Do I want some reflected glory? Am I so sure that I "know" what's best that
I've neglected to take a close look at my child as an individual?

Many are the tales of struggle over this question of
the future, and some of the most successful people have
had the biggest battles. Bob Dylan's parents, for example,
had high hopes for their son. But they disapproved of the
particular path he took to meet their goals. As Bob was
gathering the skills and definitions of his own brand of
ambition, music and life, in his parents' eyes he was just
being lazy and unresponsive, disrespectful and disruptive.
His mother, in an interview in 1968, said that if the family
had moved to St. Paul, "I think he would have been an
architect. He was cut out to be an architect....I would
have kept him so busy...that he wouldn't have had time
to decide for himself what he wanted."[5]

**The Too Precious Adolescent may have difficulty dealing
with sexual maturation.**

One of the tasks of growing up seems so obvious in
childhood that though it may cause difficulties, we often
don't stop to question its inevitability or necessity. Anna
Freud identified this as the line of development that concerns body management. We expect our toddlers to learn
how to control bowel and bladder. We tell them that they
can't play too rough in the house, that they can't run into
the road. We teach them to dress and undress themselves.
This line of development begins with the utter helpless-

ness of infants and extends to the complete responsibility of adults for control of their bodies.

Early adolescents' sexual concerns are focused on their new and changing bodies. What's the right way for this body part to look? What if one breast is larger? How does my body compare with everyone else's? In middle adolescence, youngsters become interested in the "facts" of each other's bodies. Boys want to know more about girls and vice versa. This is replaced in late adolescence with a greater interest in feelings—both "yours" and "mine." Now, at last, real consideration, responsibility, and love appear—behavior that wasn't developmentally possible in the early phases, when sexual exploration and activity serve more to decrease personal anxiety than to share sexual feelings.

In adolescence, the most dramatic issues—the ones that have parents in a frenzy—are those that surround sexuality. Although learning to be sexually responsible is an aspect of a larger task, parents tend to isolate it and surround it with their own agendas and fears. While adolescents wonder if they have the right body, adults worry about their authority and control: "Am I doing the right thing?" Many questions are reawakened for parents when their children's lives are transformed by puberty. How, for instance, can I resolve the inherent paradox between my own liberal *adult* sexual attitudes and my conservative views on sexuality for my child? Sometimes, we mingle these worries with our teaching about sex and transmit confusing messages about pleasure and responsibility.

All adolescents these days, precious or not, are vulnerable to the hazards of a popular culture that says "do" and "don't" simultaneously. On the one hand, our society seduces consumers with sexual imagery in product adver-

tising and in selling movies, television, newspapers, magazines, and music. (The message here is "Do it.") On the
other hand, it casts up regressive and puritanical television preachers and their political allies, who are out selling a nonexistent yesterday, when presumably nobody
"did it." We are a society that, on the one hand, preaches
that pleasure and responsibility somehow go hand in
hand, and yet, in practice, often assumes they are mutu-
ally exclusive. In scenes of erotic passion in fiction and
film, for example, you'll rarely find the characters using
birth control.

There is no clear and easy solution for solving difficulties with adolescent sexuality, no simple formula to
deal with our deep concerns about unwanted pregnancy
or sexually transmitted diseases. As the pendulum swings,
the excesses of the sixties are clearly being countered in
the eighties with arguments for responsibility and dis-
crimination from the sexual moderates—and for virginity until marriage and then sex only for procreation from
the extremists.

> *Two sophisticated "cool" students at an inner-city
> high school were being interviewed for a film about teen-
> age sex. They had been sexually intimate for about half a
> year. The young man was asked by the interviewer
> whether his girlfriend used birth control. He answered
> that he didn't know and certainly could never ask such a
> question because that was "personal."*

The consequences of sex without personal or social
responsibility are obvious: an alarming number of children are being born to mothers who are children them-

selves and who have little emotional help or financial support to assist them with their overwhelming task.

For the Too Precious Adolescent, the extra burdens of sexual maturation may be enormous. In addition to the societal conflicts we've discussed, they may encounter major problems at home as they attempt, often unsuccessfully, to separate from their parents. In some cases, when these teenagers have too much difficulty making their way through the sexual jungle, they may attempt to repress or deny their sexuality altogether. Although that may sound like a fairly safe solution to their anxious parents, young people who in desperation choose this approach may pay a heavy price.

> *Wesley was so disturbed that finally his distressed parents agreed to have him admitted to an adolescent psychiatric hospital in Massachusetts. He had hallucinations and a peculiar delusion: he felt that his penis was getting smaller. As the staff watched family interactions, they noticed two things: one, these were very loving and concerned parents; two, they denied by their behavior that their son was maturing sexually and allowed him no privacy. For example, they would insist that he leave the door open when he went to the bathroom!*

Sexual maturation in daughters, especially overprecious ones, can be particularly stressful for fathers. Independence, dates, and privacy itself are all symbols that the adorable little girl is becoming a woman.

> *When fourteen-year-old Susan began staying out late, Don, her worried and angry father, threatened to ground her for two months. Susan ranted and raved at*

*him, told him she had no use for his opinions, then fled
in tears to her room and locked the door. Enraged, Don
tore it off the hinges and told her she couldn't have it
back until she behaved herself.*

The opening and closing of doors during adolescence seems to be a recurrent theme: the closed door of the teenager's room, the slammed door that punctuates family fights, the forcibly opened door that deprives a youngster of necessary privacy. These doors seem to symbolize the struggle over separation that is taking place in the home.

The Too Precious Adolescent may behave in sexually precocious ways, not so much in rebellion as in response to hidden wishes of the parental shadow adolescent. Teenagers who wear sexually explicit T-shirts or dress in clearly provocative styles at the age of twelve, thirteen, or fourteen may be acting out parental wishes for sexual freedom. Parents who were repressed in adolescence may have vowed to make sure that their children never experience the same inhibitions.

*Madeleine was a devoted parent. She read books on
child development, helped found a cooperative nursery
school, and took parenting classes at every opportunity.
One day she proudly announced to her parent-child study
group that she had decided to teach her two-year-old
daughter Casey to masturbate (as though it needs to be
taught), so that her child wouldn't have to struggle to
learn about the sexual aspects of her body the way Madeleine had.*

Twelve years later, Madeleine is still ultraconcerned with her daughter's private sexual business. Madeleine had so many intrusive questions about who Casey liked and what she thought and what she wanted to do that Casey felt guilty and confused. She responded by withdrawing into books, avoiding boys, and dreaming of the day she could leave home for college.

In many instances, youngsters who are sexually precocious or inhibited are responding to unconscious messages from their parents. Perhaps the parents were somewhat "wild" in their own adolescence and have taken great pains to warn their youngsters about the dangers "out there." Perhaps the mother "had to get married" and vowed this would never happen to her daughter. Or, perhaps, like Madeleine, whose parents were exceptionally strict, the parents want their children to grow up "free" and "unrepressed" and "uninhibited."

> *Athletic and handsome, Joey became the focus of his parents' lives. When the main topic of conversation turned fourteen and wanted to spend his free time hanging out with his friends, his parents weren't too pleased. Now, at fifteen, he wants to spend much of that time with his girlfriend. "Why not bring her here, Joey?" they suggested. Now at least they knew where their son was—in the bedroom with his girlfriend.*

Joey wants distance from his family and they want closeness. Joey's parents tried to keep Joey home, using sexual license as a bribe to bind him. Other parents in this situation try to prevent separation by discounting their youngsters' new sexual interests, imposing too early curfews, and threatening to pack them off to strict boarding schools.

In our culture, sexual issues often promote separation. The customary rule in most American families is that, within the home, sexuality is confined to the marital dyad, and the adolescent cannot be fully sexually expressive until he or she has moved out. Nevertheless, as youngsters mature sexually, the boundaries of the family must open up and permit them to pursue new interests and activities—parties, dances, dates, or just spending time with a girlfriend or boyfriend. A father must acknowledge that his daughter is no longer "my baby girl," while a mother must part with her image of her "baby boy." A lot of conflict occurs as parents and teenagers struggle with this "next phase" in the life of a family.

Parents have the task of supporting the wanting as well as the waiting. Many teens (and especially some of the Too Precious Teens) are encouraged either to want or to wait, but not both. Some parents are so upset that their children want to do certain things—stay out late, have a steady boyfriend, wear tight, sexy clothes—that all they express is criticism: "How can you want that? What's the matter with you?"

It may help to let your child know you hear his or her wish to stay out late, go on car dates, or go steady. At the same time, you can make it clear that these desires are against the rules. Parents can help their teenagers best by guiding them toward behavior appropriate for their age. "As an eighth-grader, you can stay out until ten. When you are older, you can stay out later."

SEX AND DRUGS AND ROCK 'N' ROLL

Try as we may to understand the underlying conflicts and developmental problems teenagers face, we still have to live as a family day in and day out. And at least one of the people in that family is going to be a parent, issuing the usual parental orders to "Turn it down. Take that thing off. Watch your tongue." How much leeway is reasonable—and how far is too far?

Should parents have to listen to Twisted Sister at 180 dB night after night, with that loud, insistent beat pounding through the floorboards while they try unsuccessfully to sleep? Should parents who have already resigned themselves to "tacky" also endorse slave bracelets, T-shirts that advertise drugs and alcohol, or seminude and sexually provocative styles of clothing? Parents have the obligation to set reasonable limits: for example, "You may listen to Twisted Sister one day a week but only until midnight; wear one disgusting T-shirt but only around the house; buy a slave bracelet if you want but with your own money; and stay away from sexually provocative clothing because there are rapists and weirdos out there."

When it comes to the language your children use, you have a right to have your sensibilities respected. Times have changed, and words that you consider obscene may have lost their special power and turned themselves into common slang. Nevertheless, you may certainly insist that words that offend you not be used at home, whether or not every other kid in town says them.

THE SEXUAL BATTLEGROUND

As we've mentioned, sex is almost invariably the most difficult issue for parents who are trying to establish limits and set expectations. Many parents are uncomfortable trying to discuss their feelings about sex with each other, let alone with their children. In addition, our shadow adolescents often intrude with contradictory messages. We may say we believe that dating isn't important, yet push our children into early and inappropriate patterns because we wished we had more dates when we were young. Parents may also become overinvolved because they measure their own worth by their children's sexual attractiveness ("If I've been a successful parent, my son or daughter will have lots of dates"). There may also be a competitive element ("So-and-so's daughter has them lined up around the block, so what's the matter with mine?").

Many problems are intensified by contradictory messages: "Do it" from MTV versus "Don't do it" from parents. Or "Do it" from Mother versus "Don't do it" from Father. And what is "it" anyway? Dating? Kissing? Petting above the waist? Below the waist? Is intercourse okay, but not pregnancy? Is abortion acceptable?

When messages are contradictory and confusing, responsibility flies out the window. The high school senior who is head over heels in love with her boyfriend may be rushing headlong toward losing her virginity without allowing herself to consider contraception. If she gets a prescription for the Pill, she would be acknowledging that she intends to become sexually active. Rather than assume responsibility for behavior she's been told is wrong, awful, or sinful by her parents, she copes with the contradictions by pretending to herself that she's not really going to have sexual intercourse with her boyfriend.

It may be difficult to give advice to parents about school, but it is almost impossible to offer any specific guidelines about sex. When it comes to school grades, for instance, at least most of us feel A's and B's are better than

C's and D's, but we have less social agreement on acceptable sexual behavior. Some parents feel that intercourse before marriage is okay; others still demand that their daughters—and maybe sons—be virgins. Furthermore, we know about the A's, B's, C's, and D's because the school sends us report cards. It's the rare teenager who gives us a detailed account of his or her sexual adventures. What they do or don't do is rightly part of their private world.

The least reliable source of specific information on what is appropriate is your own precious child, who may be engaged in an active campaign to convince you that everything he or she wants to do—and more—is being allowed by everyone else's parents. Paradoxically, at another level, your youngster may be the very best source of information about what he or she wants to know or do or what limits need to be set. The procedure we outlined for dealing with school performance may come in handy here.

Practice what you preach. It's going to be difficult to tell your teenage daughter to remain a virgin if you're a recently divorced parent who occasionally has a lover sleep over. The difference between a sexually experienced and responsible adult of forty and an immature youngster of fourteen may be apparent to you, but parental *behavior* is a stronger influence than parental words.

Examine your expectations. Perhaps you understood that "premarital sex" would break your mother's or father's heart. Maybe, spurred by sexual longings, you married at nineteen, virginity technically intact. Do you really want your teenager to marry that young?

Perhaps an earlier generation's fear of premarital sex had to do with their attitude toward young women: there were good girls and tramps—and one certainly didn't want one's daughter to be classified as the latter. Perhaps, too, much of the fear had to do with the risk of pregnancy. Now that contraception is widely available and abortion is legal, young people need not be forced into parenthood or an early marriage.

What do *you* think and what have you merely absorbed without reflection? If you truly believe that premarital sex is a sin or a terrible mistake, you will obviously insist that your teenager abstain from sexual activity. If, on the other hand, you are more concerned with preventing pregnancy or sexually transmitted disease, you may be more effective if you emphasize the importance of safe and responsible sex, probably a more obtainable goal these days than "no sex."

Parents who came of age in the late fifties and who were exhilarated by the sexual liberation of the sixties may discover their shadow adolescent selves ready to endorse their youngster's sexual adventures. Having escaped from repressive times, they may not realize that "too much too soon" is more of a problem now than "not enough too late." Whatever our expectations, teenagers still seem determined to learn what they want to know, not what we want to teach. Perhaps this is their way of avoiding the perils of being Too Precious.

Stop, look, and listen. Again, if what you've been doing isn't working, stop doing it and look at what's happening. If you've given your sixteen-year-old daughter a ten o'clock curfew, talked to her about how important it is that she remain a virgin until marriage, and now you learn that she's just had an abortion—your policies aren't working. What can you do? How successful are you going to be if you never let her leave the house? What is more important to you: to try to prevent any other premarital sexual experience or to try to prevent another unwanted pregnancy? You can tell her you have not changed your own beliefs but that you believe she needs to be responsible and use effective contraception if she does have sex.

Setting limits. Practically speaking, parents are powerless to prevent sexual activity. The only hope we have of being influential is first to listen to our youngsters in order to understand their concerns and then to set reasonable limits according to their age and situation.

Parents have (as we have been saying) a right and an obligation to define for their children what's proper and improper, what's healthy and unhealthy, what will be allowed and what won't. This may well translate into rules such as "You will not go on a date with a boy alone, because you're too young," or "You may not have girls over when we're not home," or "You may spend time together downstairs and we won't intrude, but the doors stay open."

When in doubt, the wise course of action is the conservative one. There will always be another day for a date, even though your teen assures you otherwise. If you are not certain that all the girls are going to spend the night at the Smiths', you can call the Smiths and confirm it.

The Too Precious Adolescent may become overly reckless or overly careful.

Adolescents must make a choice: to move forward and take risks, to move backward and risk mental illness, or to refuse to move at all and risk school failure and peer rejection. If they choose to move forward, their parents can minimize the dangers by setting appropriate limits.

Too Precious Teenagers may react to what they see as excessive limits by excessive behavior. They may behave in defiant and reckless ways or they may give up the battle and retreat into a depressed, reclusive state. Overprotective parents may have trouble letting their teenager take necessary risks unless they come to realize that their heroic efforts to keep their youngster always safe and secure actually pose a risk to further growth. Overindulgent fathers and mothers may find it difficult to say no to behavior that needs some parental control.

Many parents communicate their helplessness in such ways as allowing their youngster to smoke at home ("I can't stop her") or to skip chores ("How can I make him do them? He's bigger than I am") or to stay out of school ("She's got a mind of her own").

Recklessness, a lack of concern for the possible or logical consequences of an action, is common in adolescence. Driving fast, skateboarding off the end of a pier, hotdog skiing, and having unprotected intercourse are all activities of the young that may seem unnecessarily dangerous. The parents' goal here is to set limits that will help promote safety—and survival.

For example, parents can clearly state that driving after having had a drink is not permitted, and privileges can be clearly linked to abstinence. In many parts of the country, parents are demonstrating their commitment to safety by offering to give rides to youngsters who have been drinking.

There are some situations in which a teenager's limited ability to make the best decision, and the social pressures to make a bad decision, combine to require parental intervention. For example, many high school athletes are capable of extraordinary risk-taking with little regard for the damage that injury or accident could do to life, limb, and future athletic plans. Unfortunately, high school coaches are not always knowledgeable enough or concerned enough to protect their players' health.

> *Chuck was a star quarterback, and with the deciding game for the state championship coming up the next day, he was determined to play, even though the doctor had warned him that if he did not stay off his recently injured knee, he risked even more serious damage. "Dad, the coach says I can play, and the team needs me," pleaded the agonized young quarterback. Chuck's parents were up late that night. They loved watching their son play; they dreaded seeing him injured; they dreaded even more denying him something he so desperately wanted to do. In the morning, they asked Chuck to call the doctor again; they all agreed they would abide by the doctor's recommendation.*

The Too Precious Child may have difficulty separating at the onset of adolescence and remain very bound and identified with the family.

> *When Seth was born, his two outgoing and independent older brothers were twelve and fourteen. A shy and introspective child, he often came home from school in tears because someone had beaten him up or was threatening to make mincemeat of him. Seth's parents felt he required extra love and protection, and they enjoyed having him need them now that the two older boys were never around. His older brothers had limited patience with this scheme, and when Seth was thirteen, they urged their parents to send their kid brother to the same camp*

*they'd enjoyed as youngsters. Everybody thought this was
a good idea, except Seth, but off he went to New Hampshire with a big suitcase and a sleeping bag. At six o'clock
the next evening, he called home. He hated camp. Everybody hated him; there wasn't anything to do; and the
counselors were mean. Seth's parents spent the three-hour
drive up to New Hampshire wondering what could have
happened to the good camp their two older boys had enjoyed so much. Not once did they pause to consider another possibility: that they hadn't prepared their son to
move out into the world beyond their home.*

Seth had been born after several miscarriages, and
with his big blue eyes and appealing shy smile, was very
special to his parents. All through his childhood they had
taken turns smoothing his path. Now Seth wasn't so sure
he wanted to grow up. His parents were always so nice
and considerate. They didn't tease him, or ignore him, or
threaten him the way his peers sometimes did. He didn't
want to be with a bunch of other teenagers, and he didn't
want to deal with the big questions of adolescence: "Who
am I?," "What am I?," and "What will I become?"

**The Too Precious Adolescent may develop a pattern of school
refusal.**

Sometimes overprotective parents are so successful
in convincing their child of the dangers of the outside
world that their youngster decides to stay home where it's
safe instead of going to school. Often, the family will
claim that chronic medical complaints make attendance
difficult or impossible.

Libby was absolutely adorable, and her parents and teachers loved her dearly. She'd had perfect attendance in grade school and was an exceptionally good student; so when junior high school rolled around and Libby didn't want to go, it didn't make any sense. She wouldn't get up in the morning. If she did, she'd return to bed complaining of severe cramps or a bellyache. Her parents took her to the family pediatrician, who evaluated her for ulcers and other causes of her pain, found nothing, gave her a clean bill of health and said there was no reason not to return to school. Libby insisted there was. On those mornings she did go to school, she developed pains and had to come home.

School refusal may appear during the grade school years and is sometimes mislabeled "school phobia." But the problem isn't really school. Even though "school refusers" may complain about mean teachers or insensitive fellow students or noisy lunchrooms, they are often very successful academically. Their root problem isn't going to school; it's the separation involved in leaving home.

Jesse, an intellectually gifted student, hated his first year of junior high school and managed to miss weeks at a time, always with a plausible reason. He seemed so susceptible to colds and sore throats that his parents made arrangements for him to be tutored at home. Their astute pediatrician asked the parents how they felt about this plan and found that they were actually pleased. Jesse, they felt, would now be safe from the dangers of drugs and sex and peer pressure. He was really better off at home. As the pediatrician explored some of the parents' concerns about their son and listened to Jesse's worries

*about growing up, she was able to introduce very gradu-
ally the idea that a therapist who knew a lot about adolescence might be very helpful to all of them.*

For many adolescents, the "world outside" represents a dangerous place, especially if they've been overprotected. Because Too Precious Adolescents have
inadequate preparation in dealing with the outside world,
the transition from the protection of elementary school to
the more demanding world of junior high school may
seem overwhelmingly scary; like Jesse, they may decide to
seek sanctuary at home.

**The parents of a Too Precious Adolescent may attempt to live
through their child.**

The great challenge of adolescence is to discover and
affirm an authentic separate self. Such a self cannot be
prescribed by parents, teachers, or peers. Seeking it requires decision, struggle, self-doubt, and accomplishment
—and the search must come from within. As teenagers
seek to define themselves, they and their parents engage
in an ongoing struggle for emancipation, a process that
continues for many years and is embodied in many small
battles, with victories declared on both sides.

But the Too Precious Teenager may come up against
a formidable obstacle: parents who would like to define
their child's self and impose their own agendas.

Sometimes the ambitions of the parent are unrealistic and fail to take into account the real nature and wishes
of the child. Such parents have never really believed that
their child is a separate a person.

Jim liked nothing better than to hang out with his friends, Alec, Willy, and Scott. Jim's parents couldn't stand to see their son waste his time doing nothing when he could be progressing in scholarship, music, and organized sports, areas of life in which Jim took a minimal interest. They actively discouraged his participation in the JAWS (Jim, Alec, Willy, and Scott) Club and disparaged his friends, while urging him to participate in the Latin Club, study the French horn, and play on the soccer team.

From his parents' point of view, either Jim would do what they wanted (which was good) or what he wanted (which was bad). Jim agreed halfheartedly to study the French horn, but could not be persuaded to practice. He did, to his parents' great annoyance, hang on to his friends. The self that Jim's parents envisioned may or may not have been a good idea—but that is beside the point. It was their idea, not Jim's.

Some parents extract their greatest satisfaction in life from the success of their child. When you ask them how they are, they answer with what their kids are doing. These are the stage moms and dads, waiting in the wings or the grandstands to glow in a reflected glory.

Elise was beautiful, lively, and talented, good at almost anything she tried—when she felt like trying. She was the child of superachievers. Her father was a partner in a major investment firm; her mother was an account executive at a leading ad agency. Both had graduated from Ivy League colleges, and they were determined to have children who produced. Their oldest daughter had performed satisfactorily and was now attending Harvard Business School. But promising Elise had, so far, done nothing to distinguish herself. While other people's kids won prizes, got all A's, or wrote computer programs, she read, daydreamed, and skimped on her homework. When she was thirteen, her parents stepped up the pressure. They told her that she was headed toward a life of failure and would only redeem herself by winning admission to the prestigious prep school they had chosen for her.

At some point, it becomes clear that the struggles between parent and child are not going to be solved by "fixing" the child. It's not really possible to turn a youngster whose only interests are in sports and fast cars into a first violinist in the school orchestra. Although her parents have high academic expectations, Elise may be better off in a less-rigorous school.

There is plenty of room in the stands for parents to be fans and to enjoy their children's school activities, and it's fine for them to have some feelings about which school they'd like to see their youngsters attend. But there should also be room somewhere for the youngsters to express their points of view on this and other subjects that are of such importance to them.

Too Precious Adolescents believe they are "better" than everyone else.

Tess was a delicately pretty blond, and she'd been the focus of admiration and envy since grade school. She'd always had her pick of friends to play with and now that she was in high school, she had her pick of boys to date. Her parents had always told her she was special, and she had taken their message to heart. She treated everyone with disdain. What a bunch of creeps they were!

> *She couldn't wait to leave her small Iowa town and move*
> *to Hollywood, where her true destiny lay.*

It's important that parents let their children know how special and talented and wonderful and fun they are. But the words of admiration need to be tempered with more mundane observations such as "Do your homework" and "Be thoughtful of others" and "Just because you're smart, doesn't mean you don't have to work hard." At some point, youngsters realize that the world of the family is different from the world outside and that the yearnings and ambitions that had such free rein in the imagination and at home have some realistic limits in that outside world.

The Too Precious Adolescent may have too much parental help.

Parents who at first glance seem like fierce advocates for their child may actually be attempting to deny the real problems their teen has in moving toward maturity and independence. Health professionals may encounter parents like these, who would prefer to attribute their child's physical symptoms to an undiagnosed disease rather than acknowledge that the problem has a developmental source.

> *Naomi was doing fairly well in school, but she was*
> *very unhappy socially. Tenth grade was a real drag. Her*
> *mother felt the other children were jealous of her daugh-*
> *ter because of her wardrobe. Naomi did have nice clothes,*
> *but they adorned a body that was significantly overweight*
> *and poorly groomed. "Fat runs in the family," said her*

less overweight mother, dismissively, to the family doctor to whom she had brought Naomi for treatment of her frequent headaches. When the doctor failed to find organic causes and suggested a psychiatrist might be helpful, the mother became indignant and demanded instead that her daughter have an elaborate series of X rays, an EEG, and maybe a spinal tap to "get to the bottom of this." She refused to allow her daughter to speak alone to the psychiatrist.

Naomi's mother appeared to be her daughter's true advocate and protective friend. But she was not interested in much beyond a medical diagnosis. She didn't seem interested in Naomi's emotional development, relations with peers, self-image, or attractiveness. In truth, she lacked empathy for her child's real developmental issues.

Phyllis was having a rough time at school. She was slow getting started in the morning. Each afternoon, she'd come home and dissolve into tears. Like Naomi's mother, Phyllis's parents would have nothing to do with the world of emotions. See a school counselor? Ridiculous. If Phyllis was unhappy, they felt the solution was clear. Take her out of the environment she disliked so much. They became interested in the home schooling movement, and were willing to fight all the way to the school board and beyond, if need be, so that their daughter could stay home.

Here, again, the parents appeared to be very devoted and concerned. But in their advocacy, they proposed to help the part of Phyllis that wanted to regress and give up and move back into the world of the child.

They didn't want to tackle any of her problems with separation and independence.

Sometimes, the solutions parental advocates come up with are so bizarre that they would be funny if they weren't so physically and emotionally dangerous.

> *Seventeen-year-old Perry had dropped out of high school and was spending his days watching television and, when his parents were at work, smoking pot. He didn't eat right and he didn't sleep right. His mother decided to take charge, marched him to the doctor and insisted that what he needed was a tonsillectomy. This, she had concluded, would be the cure for all his problems.*

Tonsillectomy has serious risks, and although there are certain clear reasons to have it performed, none of them bore any relationship to Perry's condition. He didn't have a documented history of strep throat. He was overindulged, lazy, poorly educated, and stoned, and he desperately needed help in order to begin to grow up and to value himself.

In our experience, most parents really are the best judges of what their children need, but in the stories we've just told, the normal parental radar was out of commission because these parents didn't want to explore and learn. They resisted any goal except the one they'd defined. Naomi needed encouragement to lose weight, to improve her relationships with other girls, and to express her interest in boys. Phyllis needed help in discovering why she was so unhappy at school. Perry needed help with his depression and his poor motivation.

These examples may seem atypical, but many loving and protective parents of Too Precious Adolescents find themselves rationalizing and defending their youngster's behavior rather than demanding accountability.

> *Jed was so bright, so talented, that his mother knew he was headed for Harvard or Yale. That's why she was having a hard time listening to what the high school teacher was saying. "He's gotten D's on all his tests this semester, Mrs. Miller, and he's been very sloppy about handing in his homework." She eyed the man coldly. "What a pedant," she thought. "He's not teaching concepts or theories; he's just filling them up with dates they're going to forget. No wonder Jed has tuned out of history class. He's smarter than his instructor."*

Jed's mother was angry at the teacher for his temerity in suggesting that her son might be less than perfect. In fact, she was sorry she hadn't sent Jed to a good prep school, where the teachers would be more intellectually challenging.

> *Larry was enthusiastic when he got his after-school job at the local hamburger stand. Two weeks after he was hired, he decided not to go in to work because he wanted to see a football game. He received a warning and after repeating the offense two weeks later, he was fired. His father called the manager and berated him for his unfairness. For Larry he had only words of consolation and excuse: "You were too good for that place."*

Larry never got the real-world message that would have helped him learn and change. His father intervened and tried to console his son rather than allow him to learn early in life a lesson that might be far more painful to learn later on.

Juliette had wanted to be a cheerleader for as long as she could remember. She practiced all the cheers for weeks and weeks and did well at the tryouts, but then so did a lot of other tenth-grade hopefuls. When she was named as an alternate, she was crushed. Her father reached for the phone to call the school principal to complain. He knew Juliette was good, and he couldn't bear seeing her so miserable.

But he parted company with the overprotectors when, instead of condemning the unfairness and stupidity of the cheerleading coach, he urged his daughter to go to all the practices. The next month, one of the juniors dropped cheerleading, and Juliette, who had faithfully learned all the routines, was named to the squad.

When the great promise of childhood does not become manifest, the Too Precious Adolescent may become depressed.

Stuart at ten had the clearest, purest, truest boy soprano voice that, combined with a fine musical sense, made him the star of the church choir. So remarkable was his voice that a famous conductor had come to hear him sing and offered him the lead in Amahl and the Night Visitors. *Stuart at thirteen, however, was looking at a bleak and ordinary future. Gone was the ethereal angel's voice and in its place was a reedy and undependable tenor. It was all over. His parents, too, seemed less interested in him now that he was just average.*

There are a thousand versions of the failure of apparent promise: the prepubescent ballerina who develops large breasts, the elementary school whiz who can't get the hang of calculus, the best catcher in the neighborhood who can't make the high school baseball team, the high school valedictorian who reaches Stanford only to find she's become a small fish in a big pond. But the results of this failure are similar: depression, disillusionment, or despair when the youngster finds out that he's not "the handsomest" or she's not "the smartest."

The tendency is to attack or retreat. The retreat pattern is familiar: staying in the bedroom, avoiding friends and family, showing apathy and pessimism. The attack pattern is to become angry and to take out on the world the fury of failed promise.

The Too Precious Child who is ill-prepared for the tests of adolescence and adulthood may attempt suicide.

Vinny, age fifteen, was so afraid of showing his father his poor report card that he hanged himself in the tree his father years before had helped him plant. His father had said he loved his son, but he had been severely critical and openly hostile to Vinny, reminding the boy endlessly of what a failure he was, even though his parents had "done everything" for him.

There is a true epidemic of adolescent and young adult suicides, a trend that has been on the rise since the 1960s and shows no sign of abating. In many ways, this is a silent epidemic, attested to only by a sense of failure and shame. Suicide is now the most common cause of death in the eighteen-to-twenty-four age group and a serious problem among younger teenagers. In fact, attempts by children in grade school are no longer uncommon.

Published figures show that four thousand to five thousand young people between the ages of fifteen and twenty-four commit suicide each year, and at least fifty thousand attempt it in such a way as to require treatment. The number of suicides is underreported, and some deaths that are intentional are labeled accidental—there is little doubt that many motor vehicle "accidents" are actually suicides. Those who work with adolescents do not find these figures surprising. Add to these the growing numbers of young people involved in clearly self-destructive behavior—anorectics and heavy drug and alcohol users—and it becomes apparent that we are witnessing a disturbing and nearly overwhelming public health issue.[6]

Not all suicides are the product of Too Preciousness, but many are. How does the overinvolved parent create conditions in which depression looms and suicide is a dangerous possibility?

Claire, age sixteen, was Too Precious from the start. Her mother had lost three babies, and Claire's birth was considered a "miracle." All through her childhood, she was pampered and adored, but she didn't seem much the worse for all the attention. She even turned out to be the perfect teenager! She and her mother were "best friends" and went shopping together and never fought. Imagine everyone's shock when Claire attempted suicide. Her reason? "I never thought I could get free." She went on to explain that she felt she would never be able to grow up and leave home, that if she left, her mother would die. Rather than kill her mother, she chose to kill herself.

Adolescents whose overinvolved parents impose heavy expectations are in a double bind: they risk failing their parents if they don't measure up and betraying themselves if they abandon their own identity in order to satisfy external demands. Claire couldn't be the wonderful, perfect child that would always stay with her mother and be her best friend, and at the same time be herself.

Overindulgent parents who allow their youngsters to grow up believing that they don't need to do anything to have whatever they want are creating conditions for disappointment, depression, and a deep sense of loss. How would you feel, after all, if you were told you were superlative and beautiful and brilliant, only to discover that in the real world, you weren't all that special.

You'd probably experience what these youngsters do. You'd feel tricked and betrayed. You weren't warned, you weren't prepared, you weren't told the truth about:

- how important the high opinions of other kids would be to you

- what an awful feeling it is to have pimples

- how difficult it would be to find a girlfriend or boyfriend

- how disappointed you'd be to have less-than-perfect grades

- what you would need to know to compete in a healthy way

- how to maintain a sense of self-confidence even when things aren't going your way

- how to handle missing first-string football or losing a class election

- what to do when your best friend gets some special recognition and you don't

What can parents do if their children seem depressed? Here are some suggestions for responses that parents may give that might prove helpful.

Youngsters suffering from depression are in great pain. (See previous chapter for a list of symptoms of serious depression.) They are isolated and seem unable to share their fears and worries. If your child is sad and withdrawn, it is important to let him or her know that you can see that something is going on.

- You can make observations such as "You look unhappy," or "You seem really down and I wonder if you might be sad or worried."

- You can indicate your availability to talk or be company or to help problem-solve.

- You can observe that you are available, but you can also give lots of space if that's what is needed. Sometimes, kids don't want to talk because they don't know how to talk. They may just want to know they've got your support.

- You can state your continued expectation that your youngster will go to school, come to meals, and do chores and homework.

If a depression lingers, if a youngster expresses suicidal wishes or makes any attempt—however minimal it appears to be—the best thing you can do is to reach for professional help. By taking things seriously at an early stage, parents may be able to prevent tragedies and start their children back on the road to positive emotional growth.

If the perils of adolescence seem overwhelming to you, the reader, consider how it must feel to be the teenager—untempered by adult perspective and experience—who must endure them. How many of us would elect to go back to our adolescent selves and once again navigate those turbulent waters? It's a wonder so many of us emerged with our identity and self-esteem reasonably intact, and with a sense of how we fit in and how we would cope with the world.

In her *Woman's Day* column, Eda LeShan answered the besieged mother of a young teenager with the following consoling words: "Moving from childhood to adulthood is impossible without struggle and rebellion. It takes enormous courage to be so hateful! Try not to feel rejected and wounded. It will be easier to live through this period if you can be proud of a child who feels secure enough to try to grow up."[7]

We know the parental task is never easy, and we know how hard it is to learn new ways to talk and negotiate and interact with children as they change into teenagers, whether they're pushing the limits or hiding out in their rooms with the door slammed shut—or some of both.

CHAPTER NINE
The Too Precious Child Grows Up

Parents are willing to spend significant time and energy, endure behavior that would tax the patience of Job, forgo all manner of present pleasures, pay out thousands of dollars—all to ensure their child a happy and successful adult life. While each parent's definition of "happy and successful" might well depend on the special abilities and needs of his or her child, most of us would probably agree that the good life requires attaining some degree of independence (financial and residential), finding responsible and rewarding work, and forming close relationships.

What is the adult destiny of Too Precious Children? Our thesis is that excess produces excess: excessive involvement may lead to a surplus of guilt; excessive adoration may result in the extreme self-absorption of narcissism. And this thesis is borne out empirically every day in psychiatrists' offices around the country, where victims of too intense parenting attempt to examine their insatiable need for achievement, their unreasoning feelings of failure, or their difficulties in sustaining relationships.

Is there any chance for a Too Precious Child to

escape this fate? Are guilt and narcissicism the only possible outcomes? Let's look at a range of possibilities from best to worst. We'll begin with the most wonderful outcome (and one that is rare) by telling the tale of an adult who was able to take the love and attention lavished on him during his childhood and share it generously with the world. The following is a true story.

> *Robert Ollendorff, a noted British psychiatrist, spent the last part of his life in the United States as a visiting professor of psychiatry. He touched many lives and many hearts through his intelligence, his humor, his generosity of spirit. Growing up as a young boy in a Jewish family in Germany, he had been totally adored. In his words, "My farts were trumpets from heaven." When he grew up, he became the adorer instead of the adored, making friends of students and faculty alike, sharing the abundance of love he had been given with others and encouraging those who surrounded him to become all that they could be.*

Ollendorff was a rare human being, but he does remind us that "preciousness" can have a happy resolution. There are adults—protected and indulged as children—who manage to grow up sane and sound, with a strong sense of self-worth *and* a great respect, and appreciation, for the rights and needs of others. At some time during adolescence or young adulthood, these fortunate few make their bids for individuation and emancipation. They resist the temptation to remain close to home, safe in the bosom of the family, and choose instead the excitement and adventure of the greater world. The adventure might be pursuing the study of counterpoint and harmony instead of the parentally approved course in engineering; it might be the exploration of a personal or spiritual path—or it might even be the taking on of a monumental physical challenge such as climbing Mount Everest.

If Too Preciousness could reliably produce this sort of human being, we'd quickly endorse it; but it rarely does. Alas, the results we're going to discuss now are far more typical. Our examples include the overprotected child who fulfills the parental dream at great personal cost, the cosseted young couple whose parents can only see separation as failure, the childhood superstars who can never live up to their childhood promise, the disturbed and psychopathic son of a criminally overinvolved mother, and a bevy of self-absorbed narcissists. As we explore some of the possible destinations on the path of overpreciousness, we'll look at the ways these outcomes might have been avoided earlier on.

FULFILLING THE PARENTAL DREAM

Right from the start, Ira was a special boy to his parents. They'd been in their late thirties when he was born, a good ten years after his older sister. He had been somewhat asthmatic as a child, but, thank God, nothing too serious, and he was a good eater. He was such an easygoing boy, so good-natured. He loved spending time with his parents. No wonder they dreamed he would come into the family clothing business after he finished college. When he did just that, his parents were thrilled. They were also delighted that he and his wife lived nearby so they could come over for dinner two or three times a week. Mother and daughter-in-law went shopping together; father and son worked side by side.

As far as mother and father were concerned, Ira was a wonderful son, the fulfillment of all their dreams. What they didn't know was that he worried constantly about their death and what would become of him after his parents were gone. They completely overlooked the fact that their dutiful son felt chronically anxious and inadequate and dissatisfied with life.

By his parents' standards, Ira was the perfect product of their perfect upbringing: married, employed, settled. But as a husband and father, he lacked stature and conviction. Inside, he was still a child, still being defined by his parents, still worrying like a child about what his destiny would be should his parents ever die. He was a successful member of a family but not a very successful individual.

Living close to parents and/or working in a family business can be deeply rewarding, but children who choose this path may have to struggle even more to achieve adulthood than do those who achieve separation by moving away.

THE RIP-ROARING MIDLIFE SEPARATION CRISIS

Imagine Ira, the once-exemplary son, at forty. His hairline is receding, his son is taller than he is, his wife doesn't appreciate him. Now we have the story of Ira the perfectly rotten husband who runs off with the cocktail waitress half his age (who knew he even drank?) or Ira the aging adolescent who can only find himself by abandoning his family just as his two children approach the college years, or maybe Ira, who couldn't do anything to hurt his family, committing suicide.

When the Iras of the world experience the violent separation-individuation crises they weren't allowed to have in their teens, they disappoint a lot of people who had counted on them to remain "good" forever. Children end up the innocent victims when an unemancipated parent decides to search for the freedom he or she might have more efficiently sought at a more appropriate stage —in adolescence, say, or in early adulthood.

WHERE DID WE GO WRONG?

When high school teachers Derek and Jan decided to marry, both sets of parents (who referred to the newlyweds as "the kids") were delighted. The young couple went to church with her parents and swam and played tennis at the club with his. One summer, Derek and Jan surprised their folks by deciding to skip going to the lake (where their parents summered) and elected instead to expand their horizons by traveling to the Orient. What an awful shock when a short telegram arrived from "the kids" stating that they were now living in an ashram in India and had found true happiness "for the first time in our lives" with a charismatic guru. What a blow! Here were parents who had given their children everything: piano lessons, summer camp, new fall wardrobes, expensive college educations, not to mention help and attention and love and worrying. Where had they gone wrong? Why did their lives feel so empty?

Derek and Jan were "good kids" until they decided to stop being kids and began to try to grow up. Too bad that they had to react to parental authority by running off to yet another parent. Perhaps they will experience a further crisis that will enable them to leave the commune and become autonomous. Perhaps there will be a time when they can sustain themselves without needing the fawning attentions of their parents or the constant incantation of the guru's motto: "Worship yourself."

Derek and Jan joined up with their guru because they needed to find some striking way to dramatize their separation from their parents without having to go it alone. If their parents had been prepared to suffer small amounts of pain as they allowed (or even encouraged) their children to leave the nest, perhaps they might have avoided the devastating rejection and sense of failure they felt when they opened that telegram from the Indian ashram.

THE GREAT BETRAYAL

Dale had, from an early age, shown unusual musical ability. Her parents were thrilled when she asked to study the flute, and they went to great effort and expense to provide her with the best: top teachers, an expensive instrument, music camps in summer. They were so proud of their talented daughter. Maybe she would be a famous concert flutist. All through high school and college, Dale studied. But then something happened. After graduation, Dale stopped playing, moved back into her room at her parents' house and took a clerk/typist job at the city Welfare Department. Her parents' disappointment was excruciating.

What had gone wrong? Had Dale lost her talent?

All through her childhood, Dale had been coddled and protected, excused from gym (she might hurt her fingers), excused from housework (she had more important things to do), excused from anything that might interfere with her parents' vision of Dale the Flutist. This vision grew more elaborate as Dale got older. In grade school, she played for family and friends and school assemblies, and was lavishly praised. During high school, she played with the local symphony orchestra, and there was a story about her in the newspaper. Dale was a star.

The came college. She chose Oberlin, with its famous Conservatory, filled with talented and aspiring young musicians, some even more accomplished than Dale. Her teacher taught only gifted musicians and didn't spend much time on praise. Dale was no longer unique, no longer a musical prodigy. She was a talented musician surrounded by other talented musicians—cellists, pianists, violinists, organists, and composers. And her sense of her own worth, built on the praise of others, collapsed. She thought that because she was no longer the star, she was nothing.

Children who are adored and indulged throughout childhood—hometown superstars—may find their self-esteem shattered when they enter a larger and more indifferent arena.

Kirk's parents believed he was destined to become a leader; after all, everything had always been so easy for him. He was so handsome, so athletic, so quick to learn, so popular with the other kids. He had the lead in the drama club play each year and easily won the presidency of his high school student council. It seemed only natural to his proud parents for him to be accepted by Dartmouth. But once in college, special Kirk was shocked to discover so many other special and talented people. There were a hundred Kirks, some even brighter, even more athletic, even more popular than he. He couldn't find a niche for himself, dropped out of Dartmouth, and went back to his hometown community college, where he sporadically attended classes when he wasn't drinking heavily. His parents, who still thought of their son as the superstar, had his high school trophies and framed awards on display on the mantelpiece in the living room.

Angry and bitter, these young adults may embark on a program of failure as striking as their former childhood success. Nothing that the adult world has to offer can match the brightness and color of their childhood. They wait for the applause, the appreciation, the adulation, lacking any notion of how to continue to strive and to endure.

Both Dale and Kirk had unusual ability, but neither had had a chance, surrounded as they were by uncritical admiration, to develop a real sense of self-worth. Their parents seemed to adore their ability, not them. When these two young people felt that they were no longer all that special, their fragile, almost nonexistent, sense of self collapsed like a house of cards.

Sometimes, the young superstar wants to find a way out of the bind that admiration, talent, and expectations have created, and parents can help by listening closely.

Monique's doll-like exterior belied her tremendous drive. When she was four, she began doing her "circus tricks." For hours each day she practiced doing handstands and cartwheels. Her parents signed her up for gymnastics, and it soon became clear that Monique had unusual grace and balance. Her parents were enchanted by the things their young daughter could do, and, of course, they were her biggest fans. They encouraged Monique to practice, moved the whole family so that she could work with a famous coach, and invested time, money, and energy on her training. She was clearly Olympic material. What a shock, then, to hear twelve-year-old Monique announce that she didn't want to do gymnastics anymore. Her parents were appalled: "How can you drop out after everything we've done to help you make the Olympic team?" Monique was equally upset. "All you care about is that I can do tricks. I want to spent time with friends and learn how to ride a horse, and go to movies. I want to be a regular kid."

Monique's parents were deeply disappointed by this decision, but as they thought about it, they began to understand her point of view. Unless she went on to become a gymnastics coach, her career in the sport would be over at a young age. If she gave up the normal pleasures and activities of adolescence, she ought to do so for her own reasons, not because they wanted to be parents of an Olympic star.

How then can parents help their talented or academically gifted children achieve balance and a realistic sense of self-worth? First, they need to offer some unconditional "just because you're you" kind of love. Often, children with special abilities suspect that their parents value them only for what they can do. Second, although these children do need encouragement to use their unique talents, they also benefit from structure and limit-setting and normal expectations. The young computer genius may be expected to put programming aside and spend Thanksgiving at Grandma's house with the family. Ballerinas can help with the dishes, and mathematical prodigies can vacuum the rugs. Brilliance and talent don't excuse rudeness or refusal to perform the daily tasks of life. By emphasizing that gifted children are still part of a normal world, parents can help them to a more balanced, less precious way of life.

THE NIGHTMARE

The most extreme, and fortunately the rarest, outcome of inappropriate and excessive involvement is the creation of a criminal. We're all familiar with that classic scene in which the young man who has been accused of some terrible crime is taken off to jail while his mother (always)—and often his father as well—insists that he was a wonderful son who would *never* have done such a thing.

Just such a scene was dramatized in the "The Burning Bed," a television movie about wife abuse. Despite evidences of bruises and injury and the obvious desperation of the battered wife, the husband's mother adamantly denies that her son would ever become violent and instead places all the blame on her daughter-in-law.

One of the most extreme and pathological examples of parental overinvolvement is chronicled in the book *"Son": A Psychopath and His Victims,* by Jack Olsen. The son in question is Kevin Coe, scion of a well-known family in Spokane, Washington. Coe was convicted in 1982 of several brutal rapes, and was retried and reconvicted in 1985. Throughout both trials, as overwhelming evidence of his guilt accumulated, Coe's father and mother steadfastly maintained their son's innocence and provided him with alibi after alibi. Their rigid postures of denial went so far beyond the parental role of supporting and continuing to love their son that, after the first trial, Coe's mother tried to hire a "hit man" to kill the judge and the prosecutor. She was convicted of her crime and went to prison, a deeply disturbed woman who played out a drama of excessive parental involvement.[1]

In contrast stands the family of John Hinckley, the young man who shot President Reagan and who was found not guilty by reason of insanity. His parents stood by him, declared their love, yet accepted the reality of what he had done. They have since become activists in the mental-health movement, helping other parents and families deal with the tragedy of mental illness. The Hinckleys did not stop caring, but they cared in the context of reality.

Obviously, these are extreme examples, but those of us who work with and care about youngsters—health professionals, teachers, friends, and neighbors—may see a family process of overinvolvement that looks ominous. Is there anything one can do to intercede? What if a friend's child seems to have taken the first few steps on the pathway to crime and the parents' adoring eyes are blind to what is happening? What if you feel that your own mother's indulgence is interfering with your child's character development; i.e., your daughter never has to face the consequences of her acts because she can run to Grandma, who will tell her she's adorable and always right. While there are no easy answers, we do have some recommendations.

Start by asking yourself some questions about what you are seeing and feeling. Are you concerned for the child or do you have some other agenda? Underlying your feelings about Grandma's indulgence may be thoughts such as "She never had time for me, so how come she gives so much time to my child?" Or, in a similar vein, "My friend thinks he's so smart and so knowledge-able about child-raising, but I think his son is obnoxious —and I can't wait to tell him."

After screening your reactions for hidden agendas and finding none, your next step should be to avoid the appearance of trying to break up a beautiful relationship. You may have more success in getting people to listen to the content of what you are saying if you refrain from putting them on the defensive. You can share your thoughts in a personal and responsible way. Instead of making statements like "Mother, you are ruining Lesley's moral development" or "Pete, your boy is beginning his descent into a life of crime," you can take ownership for your concern by using sentences with the word *I*. Examples: "I worry that..." or "I get concerned when I see..." These statements are much less threatening than the finger-pointing accusation of sentences that begin "You did..." or "You never..."

Finally, we recommend that you try not to be too at-tached to the acceptance of your opinion. It isn't likely that Grandma or your friend with the out-of-control child is going to listen to your suggestions, thank you, and change immediately. Most likely they will be received with annoyance or defensiveness, so be prepared to offer your thoughts knowing the risks and then drop the subject, hoping that it may be brought up again later in a differ-ent context or by someone else, with better results.

THE GRAND UNHAPPY NARCISSISTS

Most indulgent parents do not produce criminals. What they do typically produce are children who as adults are unable to cede the spotlight.

> *Walking back from the hot dog stand at the Astrodome, he heard a loud, booming cry: "Hey Steve!" He stopped, looked around, saw no one familiar and moved on up the stadium steps. There it was again, a great booming shout: "Hey, Steve!!" Once more he paused to scan the stands, shrugged, then moved on. As he neared the top of the steps, there it was one more time, the attention-getting yell: "Hey, Steve!!!!!" He'd had it. He put down the hot dogs and beer he was carrying, cupped his hands around his mouth and shouted back, "My name's not Steve!"*

This is the amusing side of the extreme self-absorption we call narcissism—after Narcissus, who fell in love with his own reflection. Adult narcissists, however, aren't always amusing. They were the children who were adored and indulged, whose clothes were monogrammed and who now continue to expect monogramming throughout life, who cling in adulthood to the childhood belief that they are the apple of the world's eye.

People with low self-esteem are often drawn to them, enraptured by their confidence and by what appears to be a strongly centered and decisive personality, only to discover how tight the center is, how exclusive the focus.

> *Robert, a recent law school graduate, and Heidi, newly employed in publishing, had been casual friends in*

college. Now that they were both working in the same city, they started dating and began to spend a lot of time together. Heidi was so caught up in Robert's excitement over his new job that months went by before she noticed that whenever she tried to talk about her job or her interests, Robert either turned on the television, announced he had an errand to run, or changed the subject to something that concerned him. *She tended to overlook and ignore a lot with Robert because she admired his self-confidence. Maybe she was just being childish, she thought, in wanting him to take time to listen to* her.

Heidi didn't have enough of the self-assurance that Robert possessed in overabundance, and so she remained his willing listener, waiting for the questions that never came, like "How was *your* day?" or "What do you want to do with *your* life?" Fortunately, she grew tired of his boundless self-absorption and moved on to a more reciprocal relationship. People like Robert, she realized, don't understand reciprocity or how to take the other person's point of view.

They also don't know how to give and take, how to nurture, how to postpone, how to share. They were always given to, yielded to, fed, solicited, protected; and they carry with them into adulthood an attitude of entitlement.

Norman grew up poor, with a mother who had to work hard to make ends meet after his father abandoned the family. Life in his modest childhood home was far from luxurious. Where then, puzzled his new wife, had he acquired the princely assumption that total service was his due. When she arrived home from work carrying heavy bags of groceries (real men didn't shop), climbed the three flights of stairs to their flat, and sat down to rest, he would complain that dinner wasn't ready. If his randomly scattered socks were not picked up and laundered, he became sullen. One day, his mother shed some light on the mystery of Norman. "Even though we didn't have a lot of money in those days," she said proudly, "if I served leftovers for supper, my son would never eat them. I always had to cook steak for him."

Norman's unrealistic childhood expectations, fueled by steak on demand, were a source of great bitterness in his adult years. He had difficulties with work relationships and difficulties with family life. Obsessed by a vision of instant riches, he was unable to commit himself to building a rewarding career and instead went from job to job, looking for the quick payoff.

What are the missing ingredients in Robert's and Norman's personalities? What is the problem here?

When we looked at infant behavior previously, we could see that a newborn's first focus is self: self-survival, self-satisfaction, self-soothing. At the same time, we noticed how naturally infants are programmed for reciprocity, how from the first moments of life, their looks and behavior seem designed to elicit caring responses from adults. As time goes on, infants begin to realize that the source of relief (from hunger, pain, wet diapers, or "I-don't-know-what's-wrong-but-I'm miserable") lies outside of themselves, and they begin to invest their love in the people who take care of them. Self-concern never completely disappears; instead, a healthy balance is struck, creating a dynamic tension between the inner and the outer worlds, between the self and the other, between the *me* and the *thee*.

Too little esteem, a balance tipped too far toward the needs of others, may result in feelings of inferiority and depression; our ability to take delight in involvement with others depends to some degree on the internal pleasure that that experience gives us. Certainly, we want to help our children develop a strong feeling of self-worth.

And just as certainly, we ought to avoid the creation of that extreme disturbance called "narcissistic personality disorder," where only the self seems real. While we are not contending that too much adoration in childhood will inevitably lead to this result, the histories of many narcissists are rooted in the Too Precious Syndrome.

PORTRAIT OF AN ADULT NARCISSIST

In the last chapter, we explained how self-centered behavior during adolescence is appropriate to the tasks of that phase: to separate from parents and define an adult self. In the normal course of events, this state of self-absorption is replaced by new abilities to feel empathy with others and to function well in both the social foreground and background.

Adult narcissists have no such skills. They are preoccupied with a grandiose sense of their own importance and driven by a need for constant attention and admiration. If their self-esteem is threatened, they react with rage or withdraw into cold indifference. They don't feel empathy. Instead, they exploit others and feel entitled to take while being under no obligation to give. Narcissists may adore you one day and hate or ignore you the next.

They are able to attract people—at first, anyway—with their sure self-confidence and positive energy. But at work or at home, any long-term relationship is apt to be an unhappy one. Narcissists lack the ability to recognize what others need and feel.

> *Carole, a fast-rising M.B.A., went to work for a management firm in the Midwest. When she first took over her department, her largely female staff greeted her with enthusiasm. They admired her drive and determination and hoped that a woman boss would be much more sensitive to their employment issues than their previous male supervisor had been. Were they in for a surprise! When Carole's personal secretary, Jodi, who had worked long, uncompensated hours to help launch one of Carole's pet projects, asked to take time off to be with her hospitalized daughter, Carole reacted with indifference to Jodi's concerns and anger at her temerity! "No special favors in my department," announced an outraged Carole. "I won't have you bringing personal issues into the workplace."*

Carole was glad she'd put her foot down. She knew her career was about to skyrocket, and she wasn't going to get a reputation as a weak manager. But in the months that followed, life in her department grew more and more difficult for her. Things never seemed to go out when they should anymore. She couldn't get anyone to work overtime. Carole's superiors wondered what had happened to the whiz kid they hired. She couldn't seem to produce.

The fate of the narcissist is a lonely one. When abilities are overinflated, failure is more devastating. The highs of self-importance may be paid for with the lows of a sense of special unworthiness. Unrealistic goals may lead to a life spent largely in fantasy or to a driven ambition that can find no pleasure in achievement. What appears to be solid self-confidence may be a fragile balloon needing constant compliments to remain inflated and aloft.

Surely we would never wish this fate on our own adored children, yet sometimes it's hard for us to know where to draw the line between love and indulgence. We don't want to create takers, but we don't want martyrs or masochists, either. How can we help produce an adult with a real sense of self-worth, one who feels secure and confident and appreciated? At the same time, how do we recognize and affirm our children's altruistic tendencies and teach them to value reciprocity?

HOW TO RAISE A VERY PRECIOUS CHILD

Throughout the book, we've pointed out the dangers of Too Preciousness and suggested ways to avoid it. We've begun by pointing out that we can't expect infants and toddlers to be concerned about others; it is not emotionally or socially necessary nor cognitively possible. But we may begin to expect reciprocity from young children. Even self-involved adolescents can have an appreciation for the workings of the family and the world. We can help our children find a healthy balance between interest in self and concern for others—

- By mixing unconditional love with conditional praise

- By making clear our expectations and rules

- By asking from an early age (three or so) for the child to help and contribute and by appreciating that help

- By avoiding constant comparisons and competitions with others

- By being authentic about our feelings with our children

- By working hard at our own identities, so we don't demand ego gratification from our children's accomplishments

These are goals we can strive for—bearing in mind that no one does everything "right" all the time. Fortunately, children are flexible and resilient and forgiving. Parents who want to make changes can use these guidelines to move toward more balance in their family life. They can turn down the wattage in the spotlight of adoration. They can take off the pressure for perfection. They can remember that their ultimate goal as parents is to enable their children to live *without* them. Little by little, if parents persist, children will become less demanding of self and others, and will learn to cooperate as well as compete. They will become Very Precious Children, productive, creative, responsive—very special human beings.

References and Recommended Readings

Note: By referring to the books and articles mentioned in the reference notes as well as the titles under "Recommended Readings," the reader will find a full spectrum of general and technical readings.

REFERENCES

CHAPTER ONE

1. Linda Wolfe, "Mommy's 39, Daddy's 57—And Baby Was Just Born," *New York*, 5 April 1982, 31.
2. Benjamin Spock, M.D., and Michael B. Rothenberg, M.D., *Dr. Spock's Baby and Child Care* (New York: Pocket Books, 1985), 23.
3. Grace Baruch, Rosalind Barnett, and Caryl Rivers, *Lifeprints* (New York: Signet, 1985), 114–15.
4. Viviana A. Zelzer, *Pricing the Priceless Child* (New York: Basic Books, 1985), 8.
5. Zelzer, *Pricing the Priceless Child*, 3.
6. Lloyd deMause, "The Evolution of Childhood," in

The History of Childhood, ed. Lloyd deMause (New York: The Psychohistory Press, 1974), 6.

7. Mairead Corrigan Maguire, "A Mother Pleads for Peace," *Parade Magazine*, 29 Dec. 1985, 14.

8. Eda J. LeShan, *The Conspiracy Against Childhood* (New York: Atheneum, 1967), 278.

9. Linda Wolfe, "The New York Mother," *New York*, 10 Sept. 1984, 35.

10. Susan Reed, "Gourmet Children," *People*, 26 Nov. 1984, 44.

11. Susan Reed, "Gourmet Children," 43–47, *passim*.

12. James Traub, "Good-by, Dr. Spock," *Harper's* magazine, Mar. 1986, 61.

13. Glenn Collins, "Children: Teaching Too Much, Too Soon?," *New York Times*, 4 Nov. 1985.

14. Glenn Collins, "Teaching of Infants: Does It Have Merit?," *New York Times*, 1 Feb. 1984, sec. N.

CHAPTER TWO

1. Linda Wolfe, "Mommy's 39, Daddy's 57—And Baby Was Just Born," *New York*, 5 April 1982, 33.

2. Linda Wolfe, "The New York Mother," *New York*, 10 Sept. 1984, 35.

3. G. Timothy Johnson, M.D., and Stephen E. Goldfinger, M.D., *The Harvard Medical School Health Letter Book* (Cambridge: Harvard University Press, 1981), 200.

4. Barbara Eck Menning, *Infertility* (New Jersey: Prentice-Hall Co., 1977), 140.

5. S. Fraiberg, E. Adelson, and V. Shapiro, "Ghosts in the Nursery: A Psychoanalytic Approach to the

Problems of Impaired Infant-Mother Relationships," in *Clinical Studies in Infant Mental Health*, ed. Selma Fraiberg (New York: Basic Books, 1980).

6. Marshall Klaus and John Kennell, *Maternal-Infant Bonding*, (St. Louis: C. V. Mosby, 1976), 14.

7. D. M. Kaplan and E. A. Mason, "Maternal Reactions to Premature Birth Viewed as an Acute Emotional Disorder," *American Journal of Orthopsychiatry* 30 (1960): 539–52.

8. Klaus and Kennell, *Maternal-Infant Bonding*, 14

9. Morris Green, M.D., and Albert J. Solnit, M.D., "Reactions to the Threatened Loss of a Child," *Pediatrics* 34 (July 1964): 58–66.

10. Elisabeth Kübler-Ross, *On Death and Dying* (New York: Macmillan, 1969).

11. Glenn Collins, "Perils and Pain of Growing Up Too Fast," *New York Times*, 24 Sept. 1984.

12. Gary Smith, "On Guard and Quite in Control," *Sports Illustrated*, 28 April 1986, 75–88.

13. Dr. Carl Whitaker, conversation with author, January 1987.

14. David Elkind, *The Hurried Child* (Reading, Mass: Addison-Wesley, 1981), 23–45.

15. Kate Douglas Wiggin, *Children's Rights: A Book of Nursery Logic* (Boston: Houghton, Mifflin, 1899), 11.

CHAPTER THREE

1. Joseph Chilton Pearce, *Magical Child: Rediscovering Nature's Plan for Our Children* (New York: E. P. Dutton, 1977).

2. Glenn Collins, "Children: Teaching Too Much, Too Soon?" *New York Times*, 4 Nov. 1985.

3. T. Berry Brazelton, M.D., "Do You Really Want a Superbaby?," *Family Circle*, 3 Dec. 1985, 74–76.

4. Pearce, *Magical Child*, 19.

CHAPTER FOUR

1. Benjamin Spock, M.D., and Michael B. Rothenberg, M.D., *Dr. Spock's Baby and Child Care* (New York: Pocket Books, 1985), 93.

2. Catherine Bateson, *With a Daughter's Eye* (New York: Pocket Books, 1984), 22–23.

3. W. S. Condon and L. W. Sander, "Neonate Movement Is Synchronized with Adult Speech: Interactional Participation and Language Acquisition," *Science* 183 (1974): 99–101, and also W. S. Condon, "Speech Makes Babies Move," *New Scientist*, 6 June 1974, 624–27.

4. P. H. Wolff, "The Natural History of Crying and Other Vocalizations in Early Infancy," in *Determinants of Infant Behavior*, vol. 4, ed. B. M. Foss, (London: Methuen & Co., 1969).

5. Betsy Lozoff, M.D., et al., "The Mother-Newborn Relationship: Limits of Adaptibility," *Journal of Pediatrics*, (July 1977): 1–12.

6. Anneliese Korner, "The Effect of the Infant's State, Level of Arousal, Sex and Ontogenic Stage on the Caregiver," in *The Effect of the Infant on Its Caregiver*, ed. M. Lewis and L. A. Rosenblum (New York: Wiley, 1974), 105–19.

7. Stephen Jay Gould, "Mickey Mouse Meets Konrad Lorenz," *Natural History Magazine*, May 1979, 30–36.

8. Roberta Israeloff, *Coming to Terms* (New York: Penguin Books, 1985), 107.

9. R. A. Spitz, "Hospitalism: An Inquiry into the Genesis of Psychiatric Conditions in Early Childhood," in *The Psychoanalytic Study of the Child*, vol. 1, eds. A. Freud et al. (New York: International Universities Press, 1945).

10. A. Freud and D. Burlingham, "War and Children," in *The World of the Child*, ed. Toby Talbot (New York: Jason Aronson, 1974), 329–38.

11. Bruno Bettelheim, *The Children of the Dream: Communal Childrearing and American Education* (Toronto: Macmillan, 1969).

12. John Rothchild and Susan Berns Wolf, *Children of the Counterculture* (New York: Doubleday, 1976).

13. Mary Ainsworth, M.D., "The Development of Infant-Mother Attachment," in *Review of Child Development Research*, vol. 3, ed. B. M. Caldwell and H. N. Ricciuti (Chicago: University of Chicago Press, 1973).

14. Angus McBryde, "Compulsory Rooming-In in the Ward and Private Newborn Service at Duke Hospital," *Journal of the American Medical Association* 45 (1951): 625–28.

15. N. M. Ringler et al., "Mother to Child Speech at Two Years—Effects of Early Postnatal Contact," *Journal of Pediatrics* 86 (1975): 141–44, and also N. M. Ringler et al., "Mother's Speech to Her Two-Year-Old, Its Effect on Speech and Language Comprehension at 5 Years," *Pediatric Research* 10 (1976): 307.

16. M. H. Klaus et al., "Maternal Attachment: Importance of the First Post-Partum Days," *New England Journal of Medicine* 286 (1972): 460–63.

17. R. Parke, "Father-Infant Interaction," in *Maternal Attachment and Mothering Disorders: A Round Table*, eds.

M. H. Klaus, T. Leger, and M. A. Trause (Sausalito, Calif.: Johnson & Johnson, 1974.)

18. M. Greenberg and N. Morris, "Engrossment: The Newborn's Impact Upon the Father," *American Journal of Orthopsychiatry* 44 (1974): 520–31.

19. Roberta Israeloff, *Coming to Terms* (New York: Penguin Books, 1985), 108.

20. Israeloff, *Coming to Terms*, 115.

21. Spock and Rothenberg, *Dr. Spock's Baby and Child Care*, 407.

22. T. Berry Brazelton, M. D., *Infants and Mothers: Differences in Development*, rev. ed., (New York: Dell, 1983), 106–7.

23. Stella Chess, M.D., Alexander Thomas, M.D., and Herbert G. Birch, M.D., Ph.D., *Your Child Is a Person: A Psychological Approach to Parenthood Without Guilt* (New York: Viking Press, 1965).

24. Stella Chess, M.D., and Alexander Thomas, M.D. *Origins and Evolution of Behavior Disorders from Infancy to Early Adult Life* (New York: Brunner/Mazel, 1984).

25. Anna Freud, "The Concept of Developmental Lines," *The Psychoanalytic Study of the Child* 18 (1963): 245–46.

26. Margaret Mahler, *The Psychological Birth of the Human Infant: Symbiosis and Individuation* (New York: Basic Books, 1975).

27. Mahler, *The Psychological Birth of the Human Infant*, 4.

CHAPTER FIVE

1. T. Berry Brazelton, M.D., *Toddlers and Parents: A Declaration of Independence* (New York: Dell, 1974), xi.

2. Eda LeShan, *When Your Child Drives You Crazy* (New York: St. Martin's, 1985), 202.

3. Bill Cosby, *Fatherhood* (New York: Doubleday & Company, 1986), 41.

4. Bruno Bettelheim, "The Importance of Play," *Atlantic Monthly* (March 1987), 37.

5. Vivianna A. Zelzer, *Pricing the Priceless Child* (New York: Basic Books, 1985), 3.

CHAPTER SIX

1. Dr. James Dobson, *The Strong-Willed Child* (Wheaton, Illinois: Tyndale House, 1985).

2. Benjamin Spock, M.D., and Michael B. Rothenberg, M.D., *Dr. Spock's Baby and Child Care* (New York: Pocket Books, 1985), 407.

3. Larry Freeman, M.D., conversation with author, Dec. 1986.

CHAPTER EIGHT

1. Anna Freud, "The Concept of Developmental Lines," *The Psychoanalytic Study of the Child* 18 (1963): 245–64.

2. G. F. Huon, and L. B. Brown, "Attitude Correlates of Weight Control among Secondary School Boys and Girls," *Journal of Adolescent Health Care* 7 (1986): 178–82.

3. K. A. Halmi, J. R. Falk, and E. Schwartz, "Binge-Eating and Vomiting: A Survey of a College Population," *Psychological Medicine* 11 (1981): 697–706.

4. Eda LeShan, *The Conspiracy Against Childhood* (New York: Atheneum, 1967), 137–39.

5. Carl Baum, "A Portrait of Bob Dylan as a Young Man" (senior honors thesis, Harvard College, 1969).

6. L. Eisenberg, "Adolescent Suicide: On Taking Arms Against a Sea of Troubles," *Pediatrics* 66 (1980): 315–20.

7. Eda LeShan, "Talking It Over," *Woman's Day*, 21 Jan. 1986, 10.

CHAPTER NINE

1. Jack Olsen, *"Son": A Psychopath and His Victims* (New York: Atheneum, 1983).

RECOMMENDED READINGS

The following sampler is geared primarily to the general reader who would like to explore the subject of child development. We also have mentioned a few books that may be useful for special areas of concern. In addition, we have included material intended for a professional audience. In some instances, these books are written in fairly technical language, but they contain valuable information that may not otherwise be available.

General Commentaries on Child and Parent Development

Brazelton, T. Berry, M.D.

Infants and Mothers: Differences in Development. Rev. ed. (New York: Dell, 1983).

Toddlers and Parents: A Declaration of Independence. (New York: Delacorte, 1974).

Dr. Brazelton's books are practical and supportive guides, which help to illuminate the complexities of infant and child behavior. Excellent for parents both new and experienced.

Bruner, Jerome, Michael Cole, and Barbara Lloyd, eds. *The Developing Child Series.* Cambridge: Harvard University Press.

This valuable series presently includes some sixteen or seventeen titles. We draw your attention to three that help to promote a deeper appreciation of the wonders of attachment and of the need for separation.

Dunn, Judy. *Distress and Comfort,* 1977.

Macfarlane, Aidan. *The Psychology of Childbirth,* 1977.

Schaffer, Rudolph. *Mothering,* 1977.

Chess, Stella, M.D., Alexander Thomas, M.D., and Herbert G. Birch, M.D., Ph.D. *Your Child Is a Person: A Psychological Approach to Parenthood without Guilt.* New York: Viking, 1965.

A readable account of the interaction between inborn temperament and the child's environment, this important book helps parents to adapt child-rearing advice to the needs of a particular child.

Cosby, Bill. *Fatherhood.* New York: Doubleday & Company, 1986.

Bill Cosby's humorous exploration of the parental condition is as funny and human as his TV series. The combination of his educational background (a doctorate in education), his personal experience (father of five), and his sense of humor makes this book a good antidote to Too Preciousness.

Erikson, Erik. *Childhood and Society.* New York: W. W. Norton, 1974.

This is a clear statement of the developmental tasks of each "Age of Childhood." By understanding the issues children struggle with at each stage, we may be able to promote more successful resolutions.

Fraiberg, Selma. *The Magic Years.* New York: Charles Scribner's Sons, 1959.

Here is an inspiring exploration of the formative first five years of life and their powerful influence on later development.

Greenspan, Stanley, M.D., and Nancy Thorndike Greenspan. *First Feelings.* New York: Penguin, 1985.

This useful book incorporates the fascinating research on emotional development of the infant and young child into a readable and very practical guide. There are suggestions on how to observe the changes children go through and how to create a supportive environment. Adds an exciting intellectual dimension to child-rearing.

Janov, Arthur. *The Feeling Child.* New York: Simon & Schuster, 1973.

A powerful and controversial book that speaks up for the needs of children and their parents to be authentic feeling beings.

Kaplan, Louise J., Ph.D. *Oneness and Separateness: From Infant to Individual.* New York: Simon & Schuster, 1978.

Illuminates the important theories of Margaret Mahler, who studied the issue of separation and individuation in infants and young children.

LeShan, Eda. *The Conspiracy Against Childhood.* New York: Atheneum, 1967.

A compelling plea to let children be children. Very readable, entertaining, and helpful.

————. *When Your Child Drives You Crazy.* New York: St. Martin's, 1985.

Very funny, very human, and very helpful advice to parents of children from toddlerhood through early adolescence.

Pearce, Joseph Chilton. *Magical Child.* New York: E. P. Dutton, 1977.

A controversial book that looks deeply and sometimes provocatively at the disturbing effects some of our child-rearing practices have on our children.

Spock, Benjamin, M.D., and Michael B. Rothenberg, M.D. *Dr. Spock's Baby and Child Care.* Fortieth anniversary edition. New York: Pocket Books, 1985.

With every edition, this book becomes more valuable. In the first section of the book, "The Parents' Part," there is good advice, simply and clearly presented, on emotional issues of parenting.

Sensitive and Difficult Children

Miller, Alice. *The Drama of the Gifted Child*. New York: Basic Books, 1981.

Alice Miller's work is revolutionary. This fascinating book, more aptly titled *Prisoners of Childhood* when it first appeared, looks at the special vulnerability of sensitive children, who may submerge their "true self" to the narcissistic needs of their parents.

————. *For Your Own Good: Hidden Cruelty in Child-rearing and the Roots of Violence*. New York: Farrar, Straus & Giroux, 1983.

————. *Thou Shalt Not Be Aware: Society's Betrayal of the Child*. New York: Farrar, Straus & Giroux, 1984.

Some of the material deals with the extremes of abusiveness, but the underlying issues—the power of parental agendas over children, the destruction of true self, and the transmission of pain from generation to generation are universal and make these books fascinating and moving reading.

Turecki, Stanley and Leslie Tonner. *The Difficult Child: A Guide for Parents*. New York: Bantam, 1984.

An interesting book by a child psychiatrist who found himself having to deal with his own "difficult" child. One word of caution: we hope parents would avoid too quickly labeling a child "difficult" and assigning all problems to his or her temperament. Most problems occur and must be solved in the context of parent-child interactions.

Adolescent Development and
Special Problems of Adolescence

Bruch, Hilde. *The Golden Cage*: *The Enigma of Anorexia Nervosa*. Cambridge: Harvard University Press, 1978.

Written by the "grandmother" of the field of eating disorders, this book deals with the difficult issues involved in the origins and treatment of these serious and life-threatening problems.

Elkind, David. *All Grown Up and No Place to Go*: *Teenagers in Crisis*. Reading, Mass: Addison-Wesley, 1984.

In this book, psychologist David Elkind explores the stresses and excessive demands our society places on its teenaged members. His last chapter contains advice to parents and schools on how to help young people cope.

Kaplan, Louise J., Ph.D. *Adolescence*: *The Farewell to Childhood*. New York: Simon & Schuster, 1984.

This book focuses on the world of the adolescent, with particular attention to the problems caused by the pursuit of perfection. It is a somewhat complex book, yet is still accessible to the general reader.

O'Neill, Cherry Boone. *Starving for Attention*. New York: Continuum Books, 1982.

A poignant first-person account by the daughter of singer Pat Boone, in which the author discusses how being too special and too visible contributed to her disease.

Divorce

Francke, Linda Bird. *Growing Up Divorced*. New York: Simon & Schuster, 1983.

A practical informative guide to the effects of parental divorce at different developmental stages.

Gardner, Richard A. *The Boys' and Girls' Book About Divorce*. New York: Bantam, 1971.

Intended for children, the book is useful reading for parents. Dr. Gardner discusses some of the fears and dangers children face when parents split up.

Wallerstein, Judith S. and Joan B. Kelly. *Surviving the Breakup: How Parents and Children Cope with Divorce*. New York: Basic Books, 1980.

Written by a psychologist who has spent many years studying and following up children of divorce.

Death

Bank, Stephen P. and Michael D. Kahn. *The Sibling Bond*. New York: Basic Books, 1982.

Chapter 10 of this wonderful exploration of the complexities of the sibling relationship has helpful information on coping with the death of a parent and with the death of a sibling.

Lynne H. Williams, M.D., first trained to become a pediatrician at Albert Einstein College of Medicine, and then went on to study adult and child psychiatry at the University of Miami School of Medicine. She now specializes in behavioral problems of children and adolescents. She has worked in both hospital and out-patient settings in New York City; Asheville, North Carolina; Miami; and most recently in Spokane, Washington. In addition to her private practice, she has served as speaker at numerous parenting workshops and is an adviser to hospitals and community health groups.

Dr. Williams is board-certified in pediatrics. She belongs to a number of professional organizations, and is included in *Who's Who of American Women* and *Who's Who in the West*.

Henry S. Berman, M.D., is board-certified in pediatrics, and specializes in adolescent medicine and behavioral problems in school-age children. He has served as assistant director of adolescent services at The Mount Sinai Hospital in New York City, as director of the University Health Service at SUNY at Stonybrook, and is currently president and chief executive officer of Group Health Northwest, a subsidiary of Group Health Cooperative of Puget Sound. He is a fellow of the American Academy of Pediatrics and a fellow of the Society for Adolescent Medicine. He is also the co-author of *The Complete Health*

Care Advisor, a book for consumers on how to get excellent medical care.

Louisa Rose is a professional health writer. She is editor of *The Menopause Book*, co-author of *The Complete Health Care Advisor* (which received an honorable mention in 1984 from the American Medical Writers' Association), and has published articles on health topics in national magazines such as *Glamour, Redbook, Self, Cosmopolitan*, and *New Woman*.

All three authors are parents of very precious children.